Love and Marriage

Love and Marriage

By

Ellen Key

With a Critical and Biographical Introduction by

Havelock Ellis

Source Book Press

All rights reserved. No part of this book may be reproduced
in any form without permission from the publisher.
Library of Congress Catalogue Card No. 72-134000
ISBN 0-87681-086-5
SOURCE BOOK PRESS, a Division of Collectors Editions Ltd.,
185 Madison Avenue, New York, N.Y. 10016
Unabridged republication of the 1911 New York edition: First printing 1970
Manufactured in the United States of America

Love and Marriage

By

Ellen Key

Author of "The Century of the Child," etc.

Translated from the Swedish by

Arthur G. Chater

With a Critical and Biographical Introduction by

Havelock Ellis

G. P. Putnam's Sons

New York and London

The Knickerbocker Press

1911

The Knickerbocker Press, New York

PUBLISHERS' NOTE

In this treatise, the veteran Swedish reformer attacks problems the most vital to the welfare of the human race, problems which have throughout the centuries engaged the attention of leaders of thought.

The writers who have given attention to the complex subject of the relations of the sexes, of the obligations of the state in the control of these relations, and of the organisation of the family as the foundation of society, include such authors as Plato, Goethe, Richter, Rousseau, Mary Wollstonecraft, Fourier, Comte, Mrs. Browning, Mill, Ibsen, Westermarck, Charlotte Gilman, Havelock Ellis, and many others.

These problems are complex, and the difficulties presented by them most serious. No writer has ever yet presented solutions that could be accepted as finally satisfactory. Ellen Key writes with a profound antagonism to the philistinism and hypocrisy which have characterised much of the consideration given by the community to the subjects. She points out (as has, of course, been emphasised by many earlier writers) that the ignoring of an evil does not dispose of it, and that

iii

so far from preserving society from its influence, the burying of an evil merely tends to increase its corrupting and demoralising results.

Whether or not the reader be prepared to accept the conclusions and recommendations of the Swedish thinker, he must recognise that these conclusions represent the result of painstaking and scholarly thought and investigation. Daring and iconoclastic as they may be, the views of Ellen Key are presented with a calmness and philosophy of method that is absolutely free from any trace of sensationalism. The book, which is being distributed in half a dozen languages to a world's public, must be accepted as a most important contribution to philosophic thought.

The introduction by Havelock Ellis, himself an authority on social problems, will help to make clear its purpose and character.

New York, January, 1911.

CONTENTS

INTRODUCTION

ELLEN KEY, whose most important book is here for the first time presented in English, is no stranger in the English-speaking world. Her *Century of the Child* has already found many appreciative readers in America as well as in England. Ellen Key is descended from a Scotch Highlander, Colonel M'Key (probably of the famous MacKay clan) who fought under Gustavus Adolphus, and she attaches no little significance to this ancestry. She has always interested herself in English matters, and is well acquainted with the life and literature of Great Britain; but she belongs first and foremost to Scandinavia.

She was born in 1849 in the Swedish province of Smaland, on a country estate of her father. He had played a distinguished part in the Swedish parliament as an avowed radical, but his wife was a representative of an old and noble family. Ellen, their eldest child, was marked from an early age by her love of nature and of natural things. This devotion to nature may be considered hereditary, for her great-grandfather was an ardent disciple of Rousseau, and a special admirer of Rousseau's famous treatise on Education. He

gave to his son the name of Émile, which was
handed down to Ellen Key's father. It was
perhaps owing to the Rousseau tradition that the
young girl was initiated from childhood in swim-
ming, rowing, riding, and other exercises then
usually reserved for boys. At the same time, she
loved music and devoured books including Scott's
novels and Shakespeare's plays. An early enthusiasm was for Goethe's *Hermann and Dorothea;*
it may be said, indeed, that the ideal of natural,
beautiful, and harmonious living for which that
book stands has never left Ellen Key. She was
educated for the most part at home by German,
French, and Swedish teachers, but it may easily
be believed that a girl of so much individuality of
character, so impetuous and so independent,
proved a difficult child to manage and was often
misunderstood. One may divine as much from
the sympathetic attitude towards children and
the reverence for their healthy instincts, which
are revealed in *The Century of the Child.* Fortunately young Ellen had a wise and discerning
mother, to whom she owed much; with a fine
intuition, this mother overlooked her daughter's
indifference to domestic vocations and left her free
to follow her own instincts, at the same time exercising a judicious influence over her development.
While still a young girl, the future author, inspired
by Björnson and other Scandinavian writers, conceived the idea of devoting herself to the study of
the condition of the people and wrote several

novels on peasant life. A remark of her mother's
—that her daughter surely could not be meant
to write novels, because the main questions for
her were "the questions of her own soul"—
opened her eyes to the truth that fiction could
not be her vocation. But she was very far from
knowing what her life's work was to be, and her
dreams were of love and motherhood, not of a
career.

With Björnson she was throughout in friendly
relationship. He had recognised her fine abilities
before she even began to write, and she on her
side was full of admiration for his genius, strength,
and goodness. The other world-famous writer of
Scandinavia Ellen Key learned to know through
his work at the age of eighteen, when her mother
presented to her *Love's Comedy*, *Brand*, and *Peer
Gynt;* this also was an influential event in her life.
Among writers to whom she was later attracted
were Elizabeth B. Browning, George Eliot, John
Stuart Mill, Herbert Spencer, and John Ruskin.

At the age of twenty-three, Ellen Key began
those constant excursions to all the great centres
of Europe, which may be said never since to have
ceased, at first in the company of her father,
whose secretary, confidant, and almost co-worker
she had become, and she was thus gradually led
to writing for journals. A love of art seems to
have been a primary inspiration of these early
journeys, for at this time Ellen Key was fascinated
by the art of painting as she has always been by

the greater art of living, and her wide knowledge of pictures has often happily illuminated her later writings. After 1880, however, when her father, as the result of an agricultural crisis, lost his property, she was compelled, at the age of thirty, to choose a career and for a time became a teacher in a girls' school. She had always been attracted to teaching and many years earlier, at the instigation of Björnson, had studied the school system of Denmark. At a later period she gave courses of lectures in literature, history, and æsthetics. For twenty years she occupied the Chair of History of Civilisation in Sweden at the Popular University of Stockholm.

The early years of her career as a teacher seem to have been a period in Ellen Key's life of much struggle, hardship, and mental depression due to personal sorrows. Amongst these were the deaths in rapid succession of several distinguished women with whom she was closely associated, Sophie Kowalevsky, Anna Charlotte Leffler, and (by suicide) Ernst Ahlgren. She had not yet reached full development nor found her true place in the world. Although her abilities, when she was still a girl of twenty, had been discerned by a distinguished Swedish woman's rights advocate, Sophie Adlersparre, who encouraged her to write for her journal, she has always been shy and diffident, with none of the self-confident qualities, which an outsider might be tempted to attribute to her, of an imposing Corinne. She published no book till she had reached middle-age—most of her best books belong to the present century—and though she had so far overcome her timidity as to discuss literary and æsthetic questions before a public audience, she had yet scarcely touched openly on those dangerous and difficult questions which arouse fierce antagonisms. It required some assault on her most cherished convictions to arouse her latent courage. This occurred when an old Swedish law against heresy was revived in order to send to prison some young men who had freely argued the consequences, as they conceived them, of the Darwinian doctrine in religion and sexual morals. There is nothing so sacred to Ellen Key as the right to personal opinion and personal development; the sight of any injustice or oppression has always moved her profoundly, and on this occasion she sprang forward into the fray like a lioness in defence of her cubs. She is, in the opinion of Georg Brandes, "a born orator," and she publicly brought her eloquence to the service of the cause she had at heart. Her discussion of the question was marked by moderation, skill, and learning, but her attitude on this occasion served to define publicly her real position. Thenceforward the conventionally respectable elements of Swedish society felt justified, according to the usual rule, in dealing out reckless and random abuse to the daring pioneer. She, on her side, retained her serenity, remaining a true woman, with much of the mother in her and something of the child, but before long her literary activities developed along her own native lines, and in full maturity she frankly approached the essential questions of life and the soul. A considerable series of volumes began rapidly to appear, often rather informal in method and personal in style, but freely following the author's thought and feeling, full, not only of ardent enthusiasm but of fine intuition and mellow wisdom. In 1903 was begun the publication of her most extensive work, *Lifslinjer* (Lines of Life), of which work the first two volumes constitute the book here presented to the English reader. A few years later appeared *The Century of the Child* and in 1909 *The Woman's Movement*, by many regarded as the best statement which has been made of that movement in its widest bearings. Ellen Key has also published a long series of essays on literary personalities— C. J. L. Almquist, the Brownings, Anna Charlotte Leffler, Ernst Ahlgren, etc.—who have appealed to her as illustrating some aspect of her own ideals. The latest of these is a lengthy study of Rahel Varnhagen.[1]

Ellen Key is a Scandinavian and may perhaps even be said to be a typical figure of the country whose foremost woman she is. Moreover, she

[1] Many of the facts in the foregoing pages are taken from a detailed biographical pamphlet on Ellen Key by J. F. D. Mossel in the series of *Mannen en Vrouwen von Beteekenis in Onze Dagen*. The reader may be referred to an interesting account of Ellen Key, from personal knowledge, by Miss Helen Zimmern, in *Putnam's Magazine*, Jan., 1908.

loves her own land and is resolved to spend the rest of her life in a house she proposes to build in a beautiful part of the country, Alvastra, near Lake Wetter, close to the ruins of the first Swedish monastery, a spot already sacred through its associations with the great Swedish saint, Brigitta. But the prophet is a prophet everywhere except in his own country. It is easy to find estimable Swedes who are far from anxious to claim the honour which Ellen Key reflects on their land. It is in Germany that her fame has been made. To-day the Germans, and not least the German women, awaking from a long period of quiescence, are inaugurating a new phase of the woman movement. The first phase of that movement dates from the eighteenth century, and its ideals were chiefly moulded by a succession of distinguished English women who claimed for their sex the same human rights as for men: the same right to be educated, the same right to adopt the occupation they were fitted for, the same political rights. In the course of a century these claims, although not yet completely realised, have gradually been more and more generally conceded as reasonable.

At the same time, however, it began to be seen that these demands, important as they are, by no means cover the whole ground, while, taken separately, they were liable to lead in a false direction; they tended to masculinise women and they ignored the claims of the race. In their ardour for emancipation, women sometimes seemed anxious to be emancipated from their sex. Thus it was not enough to claim woman's place as a human being—especially in an age when man was regarded as the human being *par excellence*—but it also became necessary to claim woman's place in the world as a woman. That was not, as it might at first seem, a narrower but a wider claim. For on the merely human basis women were reduced to the level of competitive struggle with men, were allowed to bring no contribution of their own to the solution of common problems, and, worst of all, their supreme position in the world as mothers of the race was altogether ignored. So that the assertion of the essential rights of women as women meant at the same time the assertion of the rights of society and the race to the best that women have to give. It was certainly by no accident that the Germans, who once before led the evolution of Europe by their triumphant assertion of the fundamental human impulses and have since been pioneers in social organisation, should take the leading part in the inauguration of this new phase of the woman movement.

The publication of Ellen Key's books corresponded in date with the recent tendency of the Germans to bring to bear on the questions of sex their characteristic Teutonic thoroughness and practicality. It is not surprising, therefore, that this Swedish woman, with her many-sided vision of the world, her daring yet serene statement of the secrets of human hearts, should be greeted as the natural leader of the movement on its most womanly side. Love, as Ellen Key regards it, is at the core of the woman question, and these opening volumes of *Lifslinger* are, above all, a contribution to the woman question, a modern and more mature version of that *Vindication of the Rights of Woman* which Mary Wollstonecraft had set forth a century earlier.

In England, and the same may be said of America, we are yet but at the beginning of this new phase of the woman movement. We have been mainly concerned with the rights of women to be like men; we are only now beginning to understand the rights of women to be unlike men, rights which, as Ellen Key understands them, include, although they go beyond, the rights embodied in the earlier claims. The dogmatic fanatics of every party, it is true, cannot endure Ellen Key; they cannot understand her, though she understands them, and even regards them with a certain sympathetic tolerance, as we should expect from a disciple of Montaigne and Shakespeare and Goethe. She is many-sided and is quite able to see and to accept both halves of a truth. In one of her earliest essays she showed how individualism and socialism, which some people suppose to be incompatible, are really woven together, and in the same way she now shows that eugenics and love—the social claims of the race and the individual claims of the heart

—are not opposed but identical. Similarly, she declares that to build up, to help, to console is the greatest of women's rights; but, she adds, they cannot adequately exercise that right unless they also possess the right of citizenship—so disconcerting the narrow partisan on each side. In matters of detail we may at many points reserve our opinion. Ellen Key is, above all,—like Olive Schreiner, to whom she is, in some respects, akin—the prophet of a movement which transcends merely isolated measures of reform. Her writings are the candid expression of her intimate self. In this book, especially, we feel that we are in the inspiring presence of a woman whose personality is one of the chief moral forces of our time.

Havelock Ellis.

LONDON, September, 1910.

Love and Marriage

CHAPTER I

THE COURSE OF DEVELOPMENT OF SEXUAL MORALITY

ALL thoughtful persons perceive that the ideas of the morality of sexual relations upheld by the religions and laws of the Western nations are in our time undergoing a radical transformation.

Like all other such changes, this one is opposed by the distrust of the guardians of society, a distrust which is based upon the view that human beings lack the power of themselves directing their development on an upward course. According to these critics, this direction is the concern of transcendental reason, which expresses itself in the real and thus causes the real to become rational. Marriage as it exists is a historically produced reality, and therefore also rational. Historical continuity—as well as religious and ethical needs—must entail the permanence of the actual

I

institution of marriage as an indispensable condition of the existence of society.

The reformers leave transcendental reason on
one side. But they too acknowledge the connection between the real and the rational to
this extent, that what has been real, has also been
rational—so long as in certain given sociological
and psychological conditions it has answered best
the needs of humanity in some particular direction. They acknowledge the necessity of fixed
laws and customs, since these alone intensify the
feelings into sources of impulse, strong enough
to be translated into action. They perceive that
the conservative, tenacious emotions have the
same importance for the soul as the skeleton
for the body.

But the historical necessity, on the other hand,
according to which it is alleged that mankind
awaits and surrenders itself to a fate over which it
has no control, is to these reformers an absurdity.
The "historical necessity" in every age is the
realised will of the strongest men, either in number or character, realised in the degree in which
nature and history favour their exercise of power.
The reformers know that the Western institution
of marriage has arisen partly from the permanent,
physico-psychological causes of the maintenance
of the race, partly from historical causes which
were transitory, although their effects in this
domain, as in many others, still continue. They
know that of all the fabrics of society marriage

is the most complicated, the most delicate, and
the most significant; they understand, therefore,
that the majority must be seized with terror when
the shrine of so many generations is threatened.

But they know also that all life is subject to
transformation; that each transformation involves
the death of once active realities, and the formation of new ones. They know that this dying-off
and replacing never takes place uniformly; that
laws and customs, which have become a drag
upon the lives of those in a better position, are
still of advantage to the majority, and therefore ought to continue in existence as long as
they remain so. But they know at the same time
that it is through the few in a better position—
those whose needs and powers are most ennobled
—that a higher standard of existence will finally
become the portion also of the majority. The
condition of all development is, not to be content
with the present, but to have the courage to ask
how everything can be made better and the good
fortune to find a right answer to this question
in thought or in action.

It is thus the dissatisfaction of the most cultured
class with the existing contradictions between its
sexual needs and the form of their legitimate
gratification which is now giving rise to attacks
on that institution of marriage which was still
sufficient for their own grandparents, just as it
is even now for a countless number of their contemporaries. These people know well enough

that their dissatisfaction will not destroy marriage, so long as the psychological and social conditions which now maintain it continue to exist. But they know at the same time that their will is destined gradually to transform these psychological and social conditions. And they already see on the hemisphere of the soul signs and wonders which portend that the fulness of time is at hand.

The reformers do not believe that the inconsistencies and contradictions which are indissolubly connected with the natural conditions of the maintenance of the race can be got rid of by any legislation. And since they understand that complete freedom is an idea which only corresponds with perfected development, they are also aware that new forms frequently entail hitherto unknown limitations, as well as extensions, of liberty.

What they desire is such forms as, whether they limit or extend liberty of action, will promote a life-enhancing use of the sexual powers both for the individual and for the race. They have no hope that the new form will arrive in a state of perfection, any more than they expect that all mankind will be prepared for it. But they hope to foster the higher needs, to awaken the richer powers, which are destined finally to render the new form necessary also to the majority. This hope kindles their calculated efforts, which are directed by the certainty that personal love is life's highest value, as well directly for the individual himself as indirectly for the new lives his love creates.   And this certainty is spreading from day to day all over the world.

Unless one believes in a superhuman reason which directs evolution, one is bound to believe in a reason inherent in humanity, a motive power transcending that of each separate people, just as the power of the organism transcends that of the organ.   This reason increases in proportion as the unity of mankind becomes established.   Less and less are the individual nations able to preserve their own peculiarities from the influence of their neighbours.   And this is now becoming especially plain with regard to sexual questions.   While Scandinavian and Anglo-Saxon ideas on sexual morality appear here and there in the literature of the Latin races, the Latin view of love has helped to shape the ideas which in Scandinavia go by the name of "the new immorality."

Thus from one country to another fly the shuttles of gold and shuttles of steel, drawing the fine and many-coloured woof of contemporary consciousness through thread after thread of the strong warp, made up of the laws and customs of various nations.   What follows is in part a drawing of the new pattern this weaving is fashioning, in part an insertion into this pattern of certain new motives.

.   .   .   .

Those who regard monogamy as the only stand-

ard of sexual morality and the only legitimate
form of personal love, do not mean the ostensible
monogamy now established by law but circumvented by custom. They mean real monogamy:
one man for one woman during that man's lifetime; one woman for one man during that woman's
lifetime, and beyond that complete abstinence.
In the way of development, they acknowledge
only one gradual realisation of this ideal; in the
tendency of the present day to adopt several lines
of development they see nothing but decadence.

Again, those who profess the faith of Life regard the ideals of mankind as an expression of
man's higher needs. Ideals which were once
incentives to development thus become a drag
upon it, whenever life's needs demand new forms
that are not recognised by the prevailing idealism.
Only he who believes in supersensuous, God-
inspired ideals will consider these fixed for all natures and all times. Evolution, on the other hand,
shows us that the same ideals never have been and
never can be accepted by all the beings we include
in the single expression, the human race, but which
in reality belong to almost as many separate
races as the animal world. Evolutionists indeed
rejoice that humanity cannot be equated under a
single faith, a single code of custom, a single ideal,
since in the diversity of life they see a great part
of its worth. They think that this in itself is a
sufficient reason for gradually granting to individuals of the same time and country that liberty

which, from a historical point of view, is allowed
to the same nation at different periods, and, from
an ethnographical point of view, to different nations at the same period: namely, the liberty, within certain limits, of choosing its own form of sexual
life.   And they would be the more ready to do so,
since the geographical, climatic, historical, and
economic differences between individuals are just
as great as those between nations and periods, and
thus what is adequate to the needs and development of one cannot answer to those of the
rest.

Few propositions are so lacking in proof as that
monogamy is the form of sexual life which is
indispensable to the vitality and culture of nations.   Neither history nor ethnography need be
appealed to against an assertion which is sufficiently refuted by the fact that *monogamy*, according to our strict definition above, *has never yet
been a reality even among the Christian nations*,
except for a minority of individuals; that all the
progress that is ascribed to Christian civilisation
has taken place while monogamy was indeed the
law but polygamy the custom.   During the period
which is rhetorically alluded to as that of "virtue
and manliness," the days of heathenism in the
North, those laws and customs prevailed which
now—after a thousand years' further refinement
of the emotional life under Christianity—are
regarded as involving the dissolution of society!
Our excellent forefathers, whose morals seem so

greatly to have outshone our own, were all born in civil matrimony and brought up in homes where not infrequently the concubine lived by the same hearth as the wife, and where the latter was liable to be repudiated for reasons as trivial as those for which she might herself obtain divorce. Indeed, these ancestors were sometimes the offspring of a "free love" which found a home in the wilderness when the guardian had forbidden the lawful union of a loving couple. The introduction by the Catholic Church of an indissoluble marriage tie did not prevent the people from narrowly escaping ruin in the Middle Ages. No one, again, will give to eighteenth-century France the credit for monogamous morality. Nevertheless, France retained vitality enough to determine the history of Europe by her economical, intellectual, and military power. And, in spite of its erotic "immorality," the heart of the French nation still possesses a great reserve of health and tenacity, together with excellent civic virtues and powers of work.

Those who are so fond of asserting that monogamy and indissoluble marriage determine the existence of nations, are either ignorant of the past history and present condition of the nations, or conceal their knowledge behind the prejudiced view that the white humanity of Europe is to be taken as the criterion for the morality as well as for the faith of the whole race.

On the other hand, what can be proved is this:

that the vitality of a people depends first and fore-most on the capacity and willingness of its women to bear and foster children fit to live, and on their husbands' capacity and willingness to protect the national existence. In the next place, it depends on the whole people's fondness for work and ability in the achievement of prosperity for itself and of value for mankind at large, and finally on the will of the individual to sacrifice his own ends when the common weal demands it. What can further be proved is that, if a people wastes its strength in sexual dissipation, this will often prevent its fulfilling the conditions we have mentioned as necessary to its progress, and will thus bring about its ruin.

But this does not involve any proof that a nation will be ruined if it alters the forms of sexual life according to a newly-acquired knowledge of the most reasonable sexual morality!

Monogamy was victorious from many causes, above all from experience of its advantages. It minimised the struggle of the men for the women and thus economised forces for other ends; it provided an incentive to work for offspring; it developed modesty and tenderness within the sexual relationship and thus raised the position of the woman and with it her importance in the bringing-up of the children; it provided them and her with a protection against the arbitrary will of the husband; through home life it fostered self-command and co-operation; the need of the two for each other led to mutual kindness. The authority of the husband was ennobled by the sense of responsibility and the joy of protection; the dependence of the wife by devotion and fidelity. This last was strengthened by fear of the husband's proprietary jealousy, by his craving for the certainty that his property would be inherited by his own children; by religions, according to which the admixture of foreign blood in the race was a sin; by the hope of Christianity for a life together beyond the grave; and by their common children, the feeling of tenderness for whom grew deeper as development proceeded. And monogamy still continues to exercise this cultivating influence on the morals and on the soul. It might, therefore, seem that this admission of the value of even an imperfect monogamy rendered all further proof unnecessary for those who assert that the true development of sexual morality can only be secured through a gradually perfected monogamy. But they forget that monogamy, which was a custom long before the introduction of Christianity, *became injurious as well as beneficial to true sexual morality, from the moment the Church prescribed it as the only form of this morality.*

Then, by a common trick of thought, the conclusion was drawn that the mighty development of culture which had taken place under monogamy would have been impossible if this had not been the sole legitimate form of sexual relationship.

And thus it was established as the indispensable condition of all higher culture!

The import of the moral controversies which now arise with increasing frequency is *the examination of the relatively higher value for real sexual morality of marriage or love*.

So long as man believed that he had been created perfect, had then fallen and continued in everlasting strife between the spirit and the flesh, no doubt could arise of the absolute value of the Christian ideal of morality. Even those who strove hardest to attain this ideal, even those vanquished in the strife, confessed themselves sinners in so far as the flesh triumphed over the spirit. It was evolutionism that first gave man courage to wonder whether he may not also be "sinning" when the spirit triumphs over the flesh; to ask himself whether perchance marriage did not exist for mankind, and not mankind for marriage; to assert the right of the present time to more universal experience with regard to the sexual customs most favourable to the development of the race. For "the idea of marriage" is to them nothing else than to further this development. But universal experience cannot be won so long as religion and law prescribe a single custom as certainly the right custom and all others are thus condemned and obstructed—as soon as they show themselves with serious frankness—while secret trespass against the monogamous ideal is countenanced. It cannot be denied that the sanctioning of this

ideal has incited many to try to realise it; indeed, hypocrisy itself is an indirect tribute to its
worth.   But its fixity has now become a danger to
continued evolution.

.   .   .   .

On the question of marriage, as in all other
respects, Lutheranism is a compromise, a bridge
between two logical views of the universe: the
Catholic-Christian and the Individualistic Monist.
And bridges are made to go over, not to stand
upon.

None of our "immoral" authors has insisted
more strongly than Luther and Olaus Petri on the
power of the sexual life.   Both regard modesty
without marriage as unthinkable.   Both see in
marriage the means given by God to satisfy
desire, just as food is the means given by God to
satisfy hunger.   But man has as little right to
satisfy the former by unchastity as he has to still
the latter by theft.   There would be nothing to
object to in this if unchastity had not been made
synonymous with every form of sexual relation
outside matrimony, while chastity became equivalent to every form of marriage.

Luther showed some knowledge of nature when
he taught that, though it may be possible for
human beings to repress their actions outside wedlock, they cannot repress their feelings and
desires.   On the other hand he knew nothing of

that creation of culture, love, and therefore he
failed to see that exactly the same sentence which
he used to confute celibacy may also be employed
to confute marriage, for the vow of fidelity no
more entails real faithfulness than the vow of
chastity is the cause of true purity. Real fidelity
can only arise when love and marriage become
equivalent terms. The substance of Luther's
controversy on marriage was not a higher conception of matrimony than that of the Catholic
Church, it was merely the restoration of marriage
to churchmen and monastic communities. We
have to thank Luther for the Lutheran parsonage
and with it for a great contribution to the poetry
of country life, to popular culture, to the production of many great minds, and—indirectly—to the
moulding of many passionate freethinkers. The
Lutheran doctrine of marriage, on the other hand,
deserves no thanks, since—like Protestantism as
a whole—it stopped short in an insoluble contradiction. Instead of upholding, in the spirit of the
Catholic Church and of Christ, the indissolu-
bility of marriage and demanding the suppression
of sensuality when the peace of the soul required
it, Luther, by his insistence on the strength of
natural inclinations, was forced into concessions,
which—quite in accordance with the teachings of
the Bible—went so far as to approve of bigamy.
To the gross apprehension of the Reformation
period the choice of a personal love meant nothing.
With marriage possible from a natural point of

view alone, it might be contracted with any one; indeed, to the genuinely pious it seemed a higher thing to enter into matrimony without any earthly love, which interfered with the love of God. The Lutheran doctrine of marriage made God "indulgent" towards all the impurity that the sexual life shut up within the whited sepulchre of lawful wedlock. He has shut his eyes to all the wifemurders that the command of fecundity involved; to all the worthless children produced by illmatched and impure marriages. He has "blessed" all unions entered into, even though from the lowest motives, under the most unnatural circumstances: between a sick person and a healthy one, an old and a young, a willing and an unwilling or two unwilling ones, coupled together by their families. To-day, countless women are still being sacrificed to this doctrine of marriage, or to its unconscious effects; their exhausted wombs are a poor soil for the new generation; their crushed souls a broken support for the growth of new wills. For one woman who defends herself with the resolution lent by horror, there are thousands who have conceived and still conceive children in loathing. For one wife who is met with the modest prayer of love, there are thousands who with a feeling of humiliation concede to their proprietors the right inculcated by the Lutheran doctrine of matrimony. But the signs of the times are visible even within the Lutheran Church. There are to be found younger men who maintain that love—not merely the formula about love in the marriage-service—must be present if the marriage is to be regarded as a moral one. And probably these neo-Lutheran prophets of love use their influence to prevent a number of repulsive marriages. But it does not occur either to them or to their congregation to treat with contempt a couple who have been married for the most despicable reasons. On the other hand, if two young and healthy people, united only by their love, should live together and fulfil the command of fruitfulness, then indeed this couple would be made to feel, through shameful treatment—if not by the young clergyman himself, then by his flock —that a sexual connection sanctioned by law is the only one that is respected, and that, therefore, it is not the seriousness of personal love in itself, but primarily society's official stamp that makes it pass as a moral ground for the cohabitation of two human beings. And if a person who is unhappy in a loveless marriage frees himself and establishes a new home on "personal love, the moral ground of marriage," then the churchmen hasten to substitute for "the moral ground of marriage" that of duty.

The doctrine that love is the moral ground of sexual relations is thus as yet only an unendorsed sequence of words. The attempt to realise it was for a long time a punishable crime in Lutheran countries, and will probably be still treated about the year 2000 as a culpable error.

Thus the marriage doctrine of Lutheranism—like that of Christianity in general—has ended, according to the moral ideas of the religion of Life, in immorality, since it no more protects the right of the race to the best conditions of life than it admits the right of the individual to realise his love according to the needs of his personal morality. The object of the Lutheran marriage was to unite man and woman, with or without love, as a means to securing their mutual morality, to make them breeders of children for society, and in addition to retain the husband as breadwinner. By relentlessly pursuing this object, the church has succeeded in damming up but not in purifying sensuality, in developing the sense of responsibility but not of love. It has thus merely rough-planed the material for a higher morality. This rough-planed material may still be the most suitable for general use, but more and more people will now require finer instruments.

The new conception of morality grows out of the hope of the gradual ascent of the race towards greater perfection. Those forms of sexual life which best serve this progress must therefore become the standards of the new morality. But as the nature of a relation can only be determined by its results, those who hold the faith of Life will *apply a conditional judgment also in the case of sexual affairs*. Only cohabitation can decide the morality of a particular case—in other words, its power to enhance the life of the individuals who are living together and that of the race. *Thus sanction can never be granted in advance* nor—with certain exceptions relating to children—*can it be denied to any matrimonial relationship. Each fresh couple*, whatever form they may choose for their cohabitation, *must themselves prove its moral claim.*

This is the new morality, which is now called immoral by the same type of souls as condemned Luther on his appearance as immoral,—a judgment which is repeated in the Catholic world, where to-day the same abuse is heaped upon "the unchaste monk" as is poured upon the adherents of "free love" within the Lutheran communities. The question for Luther's present-day "liberal" followers, both in this matter and in that of faith, is whether they shall turn back or go forward; back to the firm ground of absolute authority, or over the bridge of free experiment into the untrodden country of an entirely personal faith; back to indissoluble marriage or over the bridge of coercion to the rights of love. The right course of a consistent thought admits of no third possibility.

The neo-Protestant doctrine of marriage is already much less logical than Luther's. They agree with him in admitting the right of the sensual side of love, and with their contemporaries in granting to love its share in human life. But when they proceed to draw limits for both, they bring themselves into an untenable position.

2

They bring themselves into an untenable position not because they insist upon self-control within as well as outside of matrimony (all preparation for a final enhancement of life involves temporary checks upon life) but because the self-control they demand is so comprehensive that it will be in a high degree obstructive to life without the compensation of a final enhancement, for they limit the sexual part of love to the task of continuing the species, and the part of love in human life to a single relationship.   Those couples who are unable or unwilling to take upon themselves the responsibility for a new life are thus condemned to celibacy in marriage.   Those couples who have once founded their marriage on love must maintain the relationship even without love.

These demands are more ruthless to human nature than those opposed by Luther.   Complete celibacy is easier than married celibacy. The needs of the soul are stronger than those of the senses.   This ought not, however, to prevent the setting up of the strict demands if these were really conducive to a higher existence from the sexual point of view.   But only one who disregards life's reality (and the Christian is often such a one) can at the same time set up personal love as the ground of sexual morality and limit its rights within certain bounds of morality.

Personal love, as now developed by civilisation, has become so complicated, comprehensive, and involved that *not only does it constitute in*

itself (independently of its mission to the race)
*a great asset in life, but it also raises or lowers the
value of all else.* It has acquired a new significance
besides its original one: that of bearing the flame
of life from generation to generation. No one
calls him immoral who—disappointed in his love—
abstains from continuing the race in his marriage;
nor would the couple be called immoral who continue in a marriage made happy by love, although
it has shown itself to be childless. But in both
these cases, the parties concerned *follow their
subjective feelings at the cost of the race and treat
their love as an end in itself.* The right already
granted to the individuals in these cases at the
cost of the race will in future be extended more and
more in proportion as the significance of love
grows. On the other hand, the new morality will
demand of love an ever greater *voluntary limitation
of its rights, during the times that a new life claims
it*, as well as *voluntary or compulsory renunciation
of the right to produce new lives, under conditions
which would render them of less value.*

The marriage doctrine of neo-Protestantism,
like that of Tolstoy, rests finally on the ascetic
distrust of the sexual life. Neither doctrine sup-
poses that the sensual side can be ennobled otherwise than by being placed exclusively at the
service of the race. It is this point of view which
is finally decisive in all Christian conceptions of
morality. Christianity is sustained by the knowledge that the object of man's life on earth is his

development as an eternal being.   Therefore none of his expressions of life can be an end in itself, but must serve a higher purpose than the earthly life and happiness of the individual—or even than that of the race.

When the foundation of sexual morality was laid in an existence beyond this world, it lost its connection with the continuation of the race and thus was brought into contradiction with itself.   This is the reason why Christianity, while it has indirectly done much for the spiritualisation of love, has yet never succeeded in combining the needs of the individual with those of the race, the cravings of the soul with those of the senses. That moral standard will alone be all-embracing which is determined by the belief that the meaning of life is its development through individuals towards higher and higher forms of life for the whole race.   This standard will not regard any asceticism as moral which contemplates the freeing of the soul from the bonds of sensuality, as is the great aspiration of Eastern asceticism.   It only recognises the claim of such self-discipline as brings about an ever-increasing unity between the soul and the will of the body.   Such a self-discipline, indeed, renounces the nearer and lesser good for the more distant and greater.   But it finds this good, in the domain of love as in everything else, *in an increasingly soulful sensuousness, or in an increasingly sensuous soulfulness*, not in the spirituality of asceticism, more and more freed from the senses. To the chapel of this spirituality a mountain path leads, which—however arduous every step may be—yet goes straight to the goal. The soulful-sensual existence again is a cell to which a labyrinth leads. Here each step is less difficult, but the whole journey involves infinitely greater dangers and excitement. It may be for this reason that as yet it only attracts the strongest —those who never renounce pleasure, since they find pleasure even in renunciation. For him who seeks the latter goal a single standard of morality will appear inapplicable—simply because human nature is manifold. Sexual abstinence in youth, for instance, may strengthen nine out of ten young men. The tenth it may change into a man of bestial impulses, who, although before marriage he has been chaste, may show, when married, a coarseness or depravity which drags down the wife to his level or opens an abyss between them. Purely sensual unions may in nine cases out of ten deteriorate both the man and the woman. In the tenth case such a connection may deepen into a feeling that determines the course of two lives, and the resulting marriage offers better prospects of happiness than that of many a young couple who have entered upon married life according to the rule which is regarded as the only one to give security of happiness. Thus it is possible in one case out of ten that the love for which a young man has kept himself pure until marriage really is personal love. In the other nine cases it is not

so, but on the contrary the most impersonal of all
love. Thus in nine cases out of ten, it is possible
that such disappointments can be borne through a
sense of duty, so that personality grows beneath
them. In the tenth, again, persistence in the mistake will be the ruin of personality.

Those who make—and rightly—complete purity
before marriage and personal love in the married
state the standard of morality, ought, on account
of innumerable similar experiences, to make up
their minds to let every one decide for himself
how this purity can best be attained, before as
well as after marriage, and what personal love
shall be held to imply. Either it must mean nothing for or against the sanctity of marriage; or, if it
is to mean sanctity at the outset of married life,
then it must also mean the same during its continuance. But only the individual himself knows
how long his marriage remains sanctified by personal love or when it ceased to be so. No one can
be burdened with the duty of remaining in an un-
hallowed relation, and neo-Protestantism must
therefore either declare personal love to be the
moral ground of marriage or unconditional fidelity
to be the expression of moral personality.

The monist in these questions does not ask
whether a sexual relationship is the first and
only one, before he acknowledges its morality.
He only wishes to know whether it was such
that it did not exclude the personalities of
the lovers; whether it was *a union in which*

"neither the soul betrayed the senses nor the senses the soul."

In these words George Sand gave the idea of the new chastity.

.   .   .   .

The claims of the new sexual morality show curious similarities and dissimilarities to those to which the age of chivalry gave rise in the same sphere. Thus the Courts of Love held the principle that marriage and love are mutually exclusive. On the other hand, the conception of personality has given rise to a desire for unity which makes it repulsive to many people to live in matrimony unless there is a longing of the soul and of the senses for one's partner in marriage. The age of chivalry in its idea of love ignored the new generation whereas the hope of the present day is through love to perfect the race just as much as the lovers themselves.

Nor does the new morality deny to the many, who have not even been capable of dreaming of personal love, the right to contract a marriage, which will at least contribute to their poor existence the interest of home and the joy of parentage. But it will be severe with those who, having had experience or intuition of love, have entered without it into a marriage which will certainly impoverish and perhaps ruin more lives than their own. Prudence may counsel leniency of judgment in the individual case, since the majority of human beings learn to know their hearts late in life, if at all. Once more, *as a guiding principle of morality, the unity of marriage and love must be maintained*. By his power of creating ideals, and the ever-increasing demand for happiness which results, man has deepened his instinct of spiritual needs, and the same power of idealisation is now ruthlessly withdrawing the outward supports of sexual morality and replacing them by the idea of unity. That the halt and the lame are thereby deprived of their crutches will be no stumbling-block to him who looks beyond the halt and the lame to the finer and healthier men of the future.

It is true that the idea of unity involves the right of every person to shape his sexual life in accordance with his individual needs, but only on condition that he does not prejudice unity or the rights of the beings to whom his love gives life. *Love thus becomes more and more a private affair of the individual, while children are more and more the business of society*, and from this it follows that the two lowest expressions of sexual division (dualism) sanctioned by society, namely, *coercive marriage and prostitution, will by degrees become impossible, since after the triumph of the idea of unity they will no longer answer to the needs of humanity*.

By coercive marriage is meant that under which not only are the morality of cohabitation and the rights of the children dependent on the form of cohabitation, but the possibility of divorce for one of the parties is also dependent on the other's will. By prostitution is meant all trading with one's sex, whether this traffic is carried on by women or by men, who from necessity or inclination sell themselves with or without marriage. Both these things occur under grosser and under milder forms. There is a scale of degrees for loveless marriage, as there is for loveless—"love." The distance is great between, for instance, "La Dame aux Camélias" or Raskolnikoff's "Sonja" on the one hand, and a prowler of the gutter on the other. So it is between a woman who contracts a marriage from the longing for motherhood and one who does it from love of luxury; between a man who seeks a partner in his work and one who only wants a wife to console his creditors. But whether one, with part of one's person, buys one's self free from hunger or from debts, loneliness or desire; however great in itself the value one gains may be, still the transaction remains, for buyer as well as for seller, a humiliation from the point of view of the sexual morality which sees things as a whole.

The development of the consciousness of erotic personality is at present hindered in an equal degree by the "morality" settled by society, and by the "immorality" regulated by society. Whether it is a question of maintaining the former or of excusing the latter, we are told that idealism must make way for "the needs of real life." The same men who with reason are afraid of the dissolution of society if the right of the hungry to steal were preached in the name of "the needs of real life," consider themselves wise when, in a far more important sphere than that of property, they proclaim the necessity of stealing, in the form of prostitution.

Real life has certainly its claims: in the one case, that all who are hungry for food should have work, at such a rate of pay that they can eat; in the other, that all who are of marriageable age should have the possibility of contracting marriage at the right time. But the changes that must take place before this can come to pass will fail to appear so long as society—under the assumption that prostitution is a necessary evil—superintends its results and thus gives itself the illusion that its dangers can be provided against. For thus society escapes the search for expedients which would better provide for the two fundamental needs—love and hunger—for the satisfaction of which prostitution at present provides the only means for many men and women.

But these changes will also fail to appear so long as society—under the assumption that marriage is a necessary good—retains this as the sole mark of morality in sexual relations.

For this state of things, those preachers of morality are to blame who persuade themselves that the only cure for the evil is a still stricter maintenance of the claims of monogamy. They are afraid of any mention of the wealth of varied experience, of the longing for happiness, or the joy of life. They proclaim nothing but the sense of duty, responsibility for one's individual soul, and obligations to society. But this has been constantly preached from the dawn of Christianity, and yet the standard of sexual morality as a whole is no higher than it was. This gives food for reflection. The more so when this dread of love is carried as far as Tolstoy's—or rather, the Oriental world's—detestation of the senses; when marriage is regarded solely as a palliative for a hereditary disease, which ought rather to be stamped out so as to render the remedy unnecessary.

.   .   .   .

When psychical phenomena have been as much investigated as physical, love will also receive its cumatology—that is, its science of waves. We shall follow the curves of the emotions through the ages, their movement of rise and fall, the oppositions and side-influences by which they have been determined. Such a rising wave in our time is the growing detestation of young men for socially protected immorality, their longing for singleness in love. An opposing influence, again, is the disinclination of many young women for love. They are not content, like the neo-Pro-

testant clergymen, with demanding that carnality
shall be sanctified by marriage: they want to kill
it. They do not merely hate—and with reason—
desire apart from love: they depreciate love itself,
even when it appears as the unity of soul and
senses. According to them, marriage ought to
be merely the highest form of sympathetic friendship, in conjunction with a sense of duty directed
to the procreation and rearing of children. When
marriage is freed from feelings of carnal pleasure
as well as from claims of personal happiness, when
it is the union of two friends in the duty and joy of
living entirely for their children—then alone will
it become "moral"!

On the other hand, love, treated as a synthesis
of spiritual sympathy and the life of the race, as
the vital force through which a human being's
existence is enhanced and beautified, is to them
worthless; and the idea of a distinction between
the nature of woman and of man is to them meaningless. They demand of both complete abstinence
outside marriage, and within it they permit only
certain few exceptions, which nature's yet imperfect arrangements render necessary for the
continuance of the race. With the advance of
science, they hope that chemistry and biology will
set humanity free from its degradation in love, just
as Werner von Heidenstam expects his "food-
powder" to bring freedom from degradation by
hunger. Possibly they will both be right. But
with these possibilities the people of the twentieth

century have nothing to do. What we rather require at present is more love—and more food—not less.

It is therefore not likely that the line we have just touched upon will be that followed by the development of sexual morality, for even now an increasing proportion of mankind shows itself too exacting in erotic questions to allow of the realisation of the above-mentioned ideal of purity. No thought of the end will to their minds sanctify a means which when deprived of love appears to them ugly.

The children begotten under a sense of duty would moreover be deprived of a number of essential conditions of life; among others that of finding in their parents beings full of life and radiating happiness, which constitutes the chief spiritual nourishment of children—and it may be added that parents who "live entirely for their children" are seldom good company for them.

The programme of morality here alluded to is explicable from a justified hatred of socially protected immorality and a—partly—justified resentment against the love which leaves the child out of account. But its solution of love's deepest conflict—that between the claims of the individual and those of the race—is prejudicial to the will of nature as well as to the conditions of civilisation. Independently of both factors, these zealots believe they can attain that white world of purity which attracts their minds, afflicted as they are by the impurity and misery with which sexual relations still load existence. They forget that above the snow-line only the poorest forms of life can flourish. But human development tends towards the production of an ever richer and stronger series of forms. Any attempt to separate morality from sensuousness will not accelerate development but only retard it, since the transplantation of sexual emotion to a soil other than that of the senses is an impossibility in our present earthly conditions.

The demand for purity which aims at non-sensuousness—or supersensuousness—may perhaps provide protection from minor dangers. In great ones it will be as futile as a hedge against a forest fire. No obstructing of appetites, but only their release in other directions, can really purify them. Passions can be curbed only by means of stronger passions. In the same appetite and the same passion in which the danger lies, in the instinct of love itself, we have the true starting-point for its ennobling. He to whom the destruction of this instinct is a passionate desire possesses in this passion itself a prospect of attaining his unnatural end. He, again, who does not wish to kill, but only to control the sexual instinct, will become, in his struggle against this desire—still immeasurably stimulated through heredity and social custom—a strong and proud conqueror only when he imagines and finally experiences unity in love. Assuredly also secondary expedients are to

be found. Before all, that of acquiring the instinct
of chastity from parents; of being strengthened and protected from childhood against the
dangers of callousness as well as those of soft-
ness; of being instructed in a refined and gentle
way of the great purpose and great dangers of
sexual destiny; of receiving impressions through
public opinion of the possibility of self-control and
its importance to the happiness of the individual
himself and of the race; of avoiding the abuse
of means of enjoyment, especially of intoxicating
liquors, which both directly and indirectly weaken
the will-power in the case of sexual, as of all other
kinds of, temptation. It is beyond question that
noble sport, dancing, and games—and they are
only noble when practised finely and worthily,
with the mind as well as the body—are a means
of replacing and controlling the sexual instinct.
Equally certain is it that bodily and mental labour, whether undertaken independently or as a
participation in some form of social endeavour, is
important as occupying and consuming the sexual
powers in a substituted form. All genuine artistic
enjoyment is in the highest degree important for
the ennobling of sexual life. But all this self-discipline, all these aids from the world of beauty and
labour, all this cultivation of the body to strength
and beauty, will be as lines without a centre so
long as they do not all lead in the direction of love
—love, which certain preachers of morality would
leave altogether outside the question, as though

even it were a danger and a temptation. No one would venture to deny that healthy habits of life and strict self-control may be elevating for the individual, even if love means nothing in his life. But life in its entirety gains nothing by the production of hardened or harassed ascetic types, which by exhausting bodily exercise, by reading that leaves the imagination arid, and by art that smothers nudity, have succeeded in lulling to sleep the sensuousness which, nevertheless, will perhaps some day awake. Life has as little joy of these harsh guardians of their "higher" nature as they themselves have of life. We have not gained much if we are to have a youth which attains sexual abstinence at the cost of other excellent qualities equally necessary to the race. A youth, with large blinkers, shunning the delights of the senses, the varied joy of life, the mobility of the fancy; a youth devoid of all spiritual adventure—such, with all its "purity," would be a dead asset in life.

Those on the other hand who preserve but control the wealth of suggestion of the sexual life will be—even though their control has not always been complete—of infinitely greater service to existence.

The prejudice originally fostered by Christianity, that sexual purity is in itself so great an asset in life that it outweighs the sacrifice of all others—this prejudice must be overcome. A person is estimable for sexual purity only to the extent to which it fits him to fulfil the purpose of life for himself and for the race: that of leading an ever higher life. His purity is too dearly won if it costs him, and through him the race, irreparable losses of vital joy, courage, and power.

And for the present—until many generations of marriage and bringing-up have arrived at a transformation of present-day human, and especially men's, nature—the demand for purity will not admit of realisation without such losses; that is, if this demand takes the shape of the neo-Protestant formula, or, even more, that of Tolstoy.

.   .   .   .

Those ascetics who recommend only self-control as a remedy for the mastery of the sexual instinct, even when such control becomes merely obstructive to life, are like the physician who tried only to drive the fever out of his patient: it was nothing to him that the sick man died of the cure.

But these ascetics may have arrived at their fanaticism by two different paths. One group—which includes most of the female ascetics—hates Cupid because he has never shown to them any favour. The other group—embracing the majority of male ascetics—curse him because he never leaves them in peace. Meanwhile, those who put a tremendous emphasis on purity and those who rave about pleasure, meet on the common ground of distrust of love's possibilities of development.

3

Love to them means desire and nothing else; if the soul enters into it, it becomes friendship and that alone.   They have never experienced a love which is creative in the fullest sense of the word.   Sterility—of the soul or the body or both—is the mark of the only love these two groups are acquainted with.   The slaves of eroticism are admirably characterised by Lord Chesterfield's confession that he had made violent love to at least twenty women, all of whom personally were entirely indifferent to him.   They know nothing of the soul's desire for one single person, from among an unlimited selection; a desire which—when it is deeply rooted—is met by the desire of the other. They do not know that the elective affinity of sympathy causes the one to gather from the other's eyes an all-mastering, liberating force.   For they themselves experience in the violence of desire only prostration and humiliation of their higher being.   An otherwise sensitive man may feel unnerved by eroticism to such a degree that now he will wish all women dead, to be thus freed from his thraldom; now he will desire, as Caligula did of the Romans, that they had but a single neck—but not to sever it.   The hatred of these men for eroticism is that of the savage for the hideous gods on whom he believes himself dependent, and whom he knows to be making sport of his destiny.   And nothing is more certain than that love, thus conceived, makes men degraded and ridiculous.   Even he who in his innermost soul

loves tragedy and hates farce, is made, under the
attraction of this love, to halt between the two
and to turn his life into a tragi-comedy; for in
order to attain to the true tragic greatness a man
must be prepared to surrender himself unconditionally to, and to suffer through what is greatest
in, his nature, his innermost ego.   But the tragic
destiny is apt to pass a man by against his innermost will, and then arises the impure form of the
tragic that we have just mentioned.   Thus men
and women, who have only sought fresh stimulants
in eroticism, at last come across a person who does
not understand love in that way, and who ends
the game for ever.   Or perchance they themselves
are gripped by a great emotion, but their past
destroys the hope of its now being granted to them
to worship in any holy grove the divinity to whom
hitherto they have only burned paper lanterns in
the turmoil of a fair.   In most cases the tragi-
comedy takes the same form as with the drunkard:
satisfaction becomes more and more impossible; the insatiable one is continually forced to
fly to grosser means in order to quench his
desire in some degree, to indulge with increasing frequency, but with diminishing festival
gladness.   He who has sunk to this kind of intoxication becomes by degrees as weak-willed,
as heartless, as devoid of character and conscience
as the dipsomaniac, and equally incapable of
selection and appreciation within the sphere of his
appetites.   The most sublime woman's love will

at last leave him as insusceptible as is the drunkard to the liquid topaz of Rhenish wine, its bouquet and dewy freshness. "Love's freedom" will finally mean to him nothing but freedom from responsibility, from consideration, from danger, and from expense. In comparison with this kind of "free love," prostitution is doubtless more dangerous to health, but far less injurious to personality. Prostitution detracts from personality by a cleaving which excludes the soul; but it does not consume the personality in the same way as the "love" with which a man buys women who are not venal. If they expect him to redeem his bonds in true coin, they will be disappointed. Love may possess, according to his belief, no sterling value: he regards it as always a forged note with which nature obtains the co-operation of human beings —especially of women—to her ends.

This love knows no atmosphere but that of the alcoves where it has pursued its bought or stolen pleasure. It has never breathed the air of the wilds, the air which quivers with sunshine and shakes with storms; the air through which murmurs all life's] longing for renewal, all the wistful intuition of eternity born of a hunger for happiness, which raises generation above generation towards unknown goals; an air which immeasurably enhances and eternally absorbs vitality; the air of the wide expanses, where ferocity and madness are not yet extinct, where man and woman fight their eternal battles and suffer their eternal pains; pains whose source even Lucretius knew to be dualism.

But that only unity is capable of sealing up this source—that was known to none before our own time.

In literature it is sometimes from the alcoves, sometimes from these wilds that the complaint arises of the mastery of the sexual instinct.

In the works of not a few of the writers on morality one fails to find even a suspicion of these wildernesses of human life. These teachers betray their ignorance in a boundless narrow-mindedness, a narrow-mindedness which includes the most far-reaching questions of humanity among—gymnastic and bath apparatus! To their shortsighted view, immorality has revealed itself not only as venal but in the shape of "free love." They do not suspect that free love as well as marriage includes many degrees of morality and immorality, rising above or sinking below the ethical zero, at which both the free love and the marriage of the majority are to be found.

Between the free or lawful love which becomes ugly, revengeful, or murderous and the love which may perhaps take its own life but never that of the loved one, the distance is therefore great. From the point of view of enhancement of life there will be nevertheless a great difference between the free—or lawful—love which is devoted, courageous, self-sacrificing, faithful, and that which leaves all the best human qualities unemployed.

In the same way, the distance is great between the sterile erotic "adventures" of a paltry vanity, a sordid hunger for sensation, and the passion through which a human being attains to new creative power. The concession to the storm of passion is in one case the pennant, in the other the sail.

The artistic temperament often expresses itself in the demand for erotic renewal. But while some thus increase their strength and health, others grow ever poorer and uglier. Goethe was one of the former sort, George Sand likewise. Natures of this type contain a wonderful power of renewal. They can love several times without becoming erotically depreciated. Their souls, like the volcanic soils of the South, can bear three crops without being exhausted. But this is not the spiritual soil or climate of humanity at large. And even such Olympian gods and goddesses suspect that love may have some secret kept from them. Goethe, who prayed of fate that he might only be required to love once in another existence, may have known less of love than Dante, to whom was vouchsafed the marvellous vision described in the wonderful words

Vede il cuor tuo . . .

George Sand, who implored of the gods the flame of a great love, was never so thoroughly fired thereby as her sister poet, Elizabeth Barrett

Browning, who gave witness of her sympathy for her in the perfect lines which begin,

Thou large-brained woman and large-hearted man . . .

But great love, like great genius, can never be a duty: both are life's gracious gifts to its elect. *There can be no other standard of morality for him who loves more than once than for him who loves once only: that of the enhancement of life.* He who in a new love hears the singing of dried-up springs, feels the sap rising in dead boughs, the renewal of life's creative forces; he who is prompted anew to magnanimity and truth, to gentleness and generosity, he who finds strength as well as intoxication in his new love, nourishment as well as a feast —that man has a right to the experience. Those on the other hand—and they are the majority— whom every new love makes poorer in the qualities common to humanity and in personal sense of power, weaker in will, less efficient in work, have, from the point of view of the religion of Life, no right to such self-deterioration. By its fruits love is known. Nothing is truer than that " there is no such thing as local demoralisation." A person who in all his other doings is healthy and genuine; who continues strong and sound in his work, is in most cases moral also in sexual matters according to his conscience—even if this does not harmonise with the doctrine of monogamy. He, on the other hand, who shows himself a cheat or a wretch in his other dealings will probably be the same in the affairs of love, whether his morals are those of monogamy or polygamy; and it is therefore more unreasonable to judge of a man's morality in other matters from his sexual code than it is to judge of his sexual morality from his ethical standpoint in other questions. Nor does the latter afford an infallible criterion, for these are people who reach the summit of their natures in a great love, but remain below it in the rest of their affairs. Others again never succeed in raising their erotic dealings to the level of the rest of their personality. But in regard to the accuracy of the result the latter standard is nevertheless as superior to the former as a chemist's scales are to an old-fashioned steelyard. It may often be the case that a person's other manifestations are in a certain sense greater or less than himself, but his love, on the other hand, will in a thousand cases to one be his inmost self. Great or mean, rich or poor, pure or impure as he is in that, so will one also find him in the other important relations of life. Of all summary characteristics of a person, therefore, none is more sure than this that, as a man has loved, so he is.

     .   .   .   .

Although in this way a follower of the religion of Life regards the Tolstoy code of sexual morality as profoundly immoral, he recognises that it has a purer as well as a less pure origin.

The former is the case with those who have suffered deeply from the passions which they now advise others to uproot for the sake of their peace; also with those who are in the early spring of their age, when life is still asleep and nature appears to wear the hues of autumn.

The latter is the case with those for whom life has been all autumn, since they were born withered; women and men who have been seized with a hatred of the conditions of procreation because they have been the victims of those vices and sufferings which still make of erotics the *Divina Commedia* of earthly life; but not as in that of Dante an architectonic arrangement of hell, heaven, and purgatory, giving them a definite sequence in space and time, but a drama wherein the three states break in upon one another like waves on the shore. But whether the haters of sexual life belong to the exhausted or to the excluded, to the sterile or to the immature, the withered or the poisoned, they may doubtless be entitled individually to more or less leniency; their doctrine of morality, however, must for the reasons we have given, be rejected as entirely worthless.

The same holds good of those who solve the sexual problem as though it were one with the claim of individual liberty, irrespective of any consideration for the race.

These latter are in the habit of comparing the right to satisfy sexual desire with the right to satisfy hunger. The former, on the other hand, reject this comparison as untenable, since, of course, a person can live healthily in lifelong sexual abstinence. Instead of it they compare the erotic passion with other passions, such as gambling and drunkenness, in which popular opinion recommends self-control and the will is capable of it.

Both regard the question in an equally superficial way. To compare the fundamental conditions of natural life, the motive forces of civilised life, love and hunger, with any other passion than each other, falsifies the whole statement of the problem. The instinct of love, as that of hunger, may to a certain extent be suppressed; in both cases an increase of strength in a certain direction may incidentally be gained. But both needs must be satisfied in the right way if the individual being and the human race are to live and fulfil the intention of life in a higher development. Fasting men in the question of love are of as little value to the enhancement of life as they are in other fields.

Christianity has so accustomed us to treat sexual purity as a question of the individual that, whether we regard it from the point of view of the enthusiast for chastity or from that of the enthusiast for liberty, we do not perceive that, while one satisfies hunger to prolong one's own life, one produces children to prolong that of the race. This renders the ascetic talk about the innocuousness of abstinence as superficial as the alleged right to satisfy sexual desire with the same freedom as hunger.

If the individual remains without food, he himself loses his life; *but if he remains without the right of procreation, the race loses the life he might have given to it.* Again, if the individual dies of overeating, he is the only one who suffers; *if the sexual instinct is abused through excess, it is the race that suffers.*

The existing immorality involves an uninterrupted blood-poisoning of the organism of humanity. The existing order of society and morality starves this organism. It is not only with the melancholy their own inevitable fate inspires in them, but also with indignation against unnecessary suffering, that innumerable excellent men and women know that they are condemned to die without having given their blood, their souls, as an inheritance to a new generation of beings.

It is beyond all question that the instinct of the individual to continue his existence in the race must be controlled, if it is to be an enhancement, and not an obstruction, to life. *But this, in the most literal sense, is the vital question for the individual and for the race:* HOW *and* WHY *and* TO WHAT EXTENT *this control is to be exercised.*

Thus both the life of the individual and that of the race are enhanced when young people live in abstinence till they have reached full maturity. The development of the race gains when the lives less worthy to survive are not reproduced in offspring; but the life of the individual and of the race suffers when young people, mature and in every way fit, are not in a position to produce and rear offspring.

At a low stage of development, hunger as well as celibacy has been an ennobling force. Man has gradually learned to limit the quantity of his food while improving its quality and regulating the supply. He now knows that the value of food depends to a large extent on the enjoyment it provides and the gratification with which it is associated; that what is unappetising does not fulfil its purpose. He knows too that the organism cannot be nourished by a diet accurately calculated for every age or for every class of work, but that only a certain superfluity really gives the necessary satisfaction. Experience has shown that too great economy is as injurious as excess and that personal needs must within certain limits be the deciding criterion in a full and life-enhancing system of diet. Our understanding of this subject is now far in advance of the ability of the bulk of mankind to follow it. In the question of the racial instinct, on the other hand, we are still a long way from knowledge of the conditions of equilibrium, and we have much farther still to go before we actually arrive at that equilibrium between the starvation and excess in the satisfaction of this need which are at present characteristic of our Western communities.

It was natural that Luther should put an end to fasting as well as celibacy.   Both were expressions of the Oriental longing to attain the ideal condition of freedom from desire; both had been necessary factors in the education of the Germanic peoples. But at the same time it was unfortunately inevitable that Luther's work of liberation should be inconclusive; that he was incapable of adopting the belief of the ancients in the divinity of humanity, the rights of nature; that he continually sought the sanctification of human nature by means exterior to itself.   Some one has said that the courage of Luther the monk in marrying a nun was worth more than all his doctrine.   That is a true saying.   Filippo Lippi certainly did the same.   The world gained thereby some magnificent madonnas and—Filippino Lippi.   But neither Fra Filippo nor any other vow-breaking monk brought about a revolution: that was the achievement of Luther alone, who asserted his divine and natural right to his action.

The problem of the present day is to follow up the consequences of this declaration of natural rights.

But nature is no more infallible than she is perfect, no more reasonable than unreasonable, no more consistent than contrary in her purposes; since she is all these.   She may be transformed— ennobled or debased—by culture, and therefore a natural declaration of rights implies only *the right of man consciously to cultivate nature*, so that in a certain direction she may fulfil her own purpose with a gradual approach to perfection; or, in other words, that the needs created by nature in and with human beings may by them be satisfied in a more beautiful and healthy way. But this culture of the erotic nature cannot find its moral criterion in any divine command or transcendental idea. *It can only find it in the same mysterious longing for perfection, which in the course of evolution has raised instinct into passion, passion into love, and which is now striving to raise love itself to an even greater love.*

There are some who think that love should therefore advance a claim to a glory of its own, which is incompatible with its "natural" mission, namely the perpetuation of the race.

Every one knows, however, that evolution brings about a more complicated, heterogeneous state than the original one; and in this respect love is the most conspicuous example. Love—as we have already shown—has now become a great spiritual power, a form of genius comparable with any other creative force in the domain of culture, and its production in that region is just as important as in the so-called natural field. Just as we now recognise the right of the artist to shape his work, or of the scientific man to carry out his investigations as it seems good to him, so must we allow to love the right to employ its creative force in its own way provided only that in one way or another it finally conduces to the general good.

From this point of view, then, we cannot extend the proposition that love is an end in itself so far as to say that *it may remain unfruitful.* It must give life; if not new living beings then new values; it must enrich the lovers themselves and through them mankind. Here as everywhere the truth which gives faith in life and creates morality is to be found included in the experience which creates happiness; and the most serious charge against certain forms of "free love" is that it is unhappy love; for there is no unhappy love but the unfruitful.

The capacity of mankind for forgetting is more wonderful than its capacity for learning. If this were not so, there would be no necessity to recall again and again that every band of apostles includes a Judas; nay, that the truth can only be accepted by disciples in the hands of its enemies. One is reminded by this that every reformation has its visionaries who arrest the blow when the reformers have put their axe to the root of the tree; and one is not surprised that with every spring flood not only the ice but the earth itself is washed away.

Mankind seems determined not to remember. They must therefore be reminded once more that the new morality's band of combatants, ever more closely united and more rapidly increasing, are distinguished from their scattered followers and from their light advance-guard by the knowledge that *love is subject to the same law as every other creative force; the law of dependence on the whole for its own enhancement to its highest possible value.* Love, indeed, whose origin is the very instinct of the race, must be more deeply bound up with the race than any other emotion. And experience shows too that it cannot preserve and promote its vital force if it lacks any connection with, and does not stand in some relation, either of giving or receiving, to the race. It is therefore an indisputable necessity that every love entirely detached from the rest of humanity must die for want of nourishment.

But the band which attaches it to humanity may be woven of several materials; the gift to the race may express itself in various ways. In one case a great emotion may bring about a tragic fate, which opens the eyes of humanity to the red abysses it contains within itself. Another time it may create a great happiness, which sheds a radiance around the happy ones, illuminating all who come near them. In many cases love translates itself into intellectual achievements, or useful social work; in most it results in two more perfect human beings, and new creatures, still more perfect than themselves.

Those couples, on the other hand, who have shed no radiance either in their life or in their death; who have not taken one step on the golden ladder to a higher humanity, and who have only found in each other the lust of the beasts—without their readiness to sacrifice themselves for offspring

—these are immoral, since their love has not served the ascending development of life.   Whether this lifeless love has taken the form of a light and irregular or of a lifelong and lawful connection, it has in no respect enriched the life of the couple, much less therefore that of the race.

With the enhancement of life as love's standard of morality, it is thus impossible, as we maintained at the beginning, to decide in advance whether either a free or a married love, an interrupted or a continued marriage, voluntary childlessness or parentage, is moral or immoral; for the result depends in each individual case on the will, the choice, which lies behind it, and *only the development of events can decide the nature of this will and this choice.*

It is true enough that human beings are often weaker in execution than in resolve.   But then they must content themselves with enlarging old ideas of morality, for such as they are not called to make new morals.   And it is true that life occasionally lends an unexpected hand in the correction of a mistake; but as a rule the consequences are as the cause.   A woman who for purely selfish reasons shuns motherhood will thus usually show herself to be a mistress without affection; a wife who breaks loose from a marriage before she has tried to extract from it its possibilities of happiness will probably throw away her chances in the same way in a new one.   No relation can be better than the persons who compose it.   This law is so inflexible that the administration of moral justice

4

might confidently be left to time.　This does not imply that love, more than any other expression of life, can be withdrawn from human arbitration, but it implies that *such arbitration will be faulty when it is decided by the forms of a union instead of by its results.*　Here we are on the watershed between the old and the new morality.　The course of the former is determined by doubts of, and that of the latter by belief in, the resources of the power in human nature.　The doubts of the former lead to the obligation of the individual to submit himself to the claims of society; the belief of the latter leads to the liberty of the individual to choose his own duty to society.　On account of the weakness of human nature, and of consequent care for the well-being of society, the conservatives claim that the individual must convince society in advance of his willingness to serve its ends in his love, by renouncing a part of his easily misused liberty.　On account of the richness of human nature and the claims of development, the reformers demand for the individual the right of *serving the community with his love according to his own choice, and of using the freedom of his love under his own responsibility.*

He who does not allow his eye to be caught by the light straws that float and are lost upon the stream of time will soon become aware that the new morality is growing deeper and deeper with fresh tributaries.

.　　.　　.　　.　　.　　.　　.

Christian morality starts from the conception of human nature as complete in its constitution though not in its culture, and of a human being divided into body and soul. The soul is of divine origin, but fallen, and must be raised again by a process of culture determined by religion, the object of which is that mankind may attain the ideal provided by religion, that is, Christ.

There is another morality which rests—or which rested—upon the belief in the inborn divinity of human nature and the equality of all men; this belief ended in the efforts of the eighteenth century towards universal welfare, and in the expectation that liberty, equality, and fraternity could be realised even with the existing human material.

The new morality, on the other hand, adopts humanism in the form of evolutionism. It is determined by a monistic belief in the soul and body as two forms of the same existence; by the belief of evolutionism that man's psycho-physical being is neither fallen nor perfect, but capable of perfection; *that it is susceptible of modification for the very reason that it is not constitutively completed.* Both utilitarian and Christian humanism saw "culture," "progress," and "development" in man's improvement of material and non-material resources within and without himself. But evolutionism knows that all this has only been the preparation for a development which is to *improve and ennoble the very material of mankind, hitherto, so to speak, only experimentally produced.*

Our present "nature" means only what, at this stage of development, is psychologically and physiologically necessary that we may exist as people of a certain time, a certain race, a certain nation. Hairiness was once "nature," as nakedness is now. Marriage by capture was once "natural," as courtship is now. What new transformations the race is destined to undergo; what losses and gains, at present unsuspected, of organs and senses, faculties and properties of the soul, await it — this is the secret of the future. But the more mankind is convinced of its power of intervening in its own development, the more necessary does a conscious purpose become. We must understand what obstructions we will root out, what roads we will block up, and what sacrifices we will impose upon ourselves.

The new morality is in the stage of enquiry on many questions—such as labour, crime, and education—but above all on the sexual life. Even on this question it no longer accepts commandments from the mountains of Sinai or Galilee; here as everywhere else evolutionism can only regard *continuous experience as revelation*. Evolutionism does not reject the results of historical experience, nor the fruits of Christian-human civilisation—even if it were possible to "reject" what has become soul and blood in humanity. But it regards the course of historical civilisation that lies behind us as a battlefield of mutually conflicting ideas and purposes, with no more conscious plan than the warfare of savages.   Not until humanity chooses its ends and its means— and makes its more immediate end the enhancement of all that is at present characteristic of humanity—not until it begins to measure all its other gains and losses by the degree in which they further or retard that enhancement, will it also adopt the right attitude towards its inheritance from former ages.   Then it will reject what hinders and select what assists *its struggle for the strengthening of its position as humanity and its elevation to super-humanity.*

We stand on the verge of a stage of culture which will be that of the depths, not, as hitherto, of the surface alone; a stage which will not be merely a culture *through* mankind, but culture *of* mankind.   For the first time, the great fashioners of culture will be able to work in marble, instead of, as hitherto, being forced to work in snow. The true relation between the rights of the individual and those of the race will become in the field of love as important as the relation between the rights of the individual and those of society in the field of labour.   The conditions of labour raise or lower the value of the present as well as of the future generation.   The same holds good— and in an even higher degree—of the conditions of love.

How the boundary will finally be defined—in the one case as in the other—we cannot know at present.   It is true that there is here and there a glimmer of light which already shows the way; but until these gleams become more frequent, mankind can only grope and stumble along the path by which perhaps it will one day march in full daylight.

Many who regard sexual morality from the point of view of evolutionism have never enquired whether monogamy—and an increasingly perfect monogamy—is really the best means of human development. These evolutionists unite with the champions of Christian idealism in condemnation of "the immorality of the present day," which declares itself in sexual matters in the form of free connections outside matrimony; of an increase of divorce among those married; of disinclination for parentage and of the claim of unmarried women to the right of motherhood. Other evolutionists think that all this is the earliest announcement of the awakening which will assign to love its full importance, not only for the perpetuation, but for the progress of the race. With the will of active, effective life they attack the current standard of morality and the rights of the family. The object of the conflict is not itself new; what is new is only the boldness, fostered, consciously or unconsciously, by the evolutionary idea, of thus asserting the rights of love against those of society, the code of the future against that of the past.

The new morality knows that in a wide sense civilisation will only attain lasting power over nature when it combines higher emotions of

happiness with the ends in the pursuit of which
harsh means may be demanded. That creed of
life which makes the mission of the race co-
operate with personal happiness in love, will also
demand of the latter the sacrifices which the former
renders necessary. But it must not augment
these requirements by ascetic demands for purity
which are meaningless for the racial mission. The
followers of this creed will take love as the criterion
of the individual's sexual emotions and actions,
above all because they believe that *the happiness
of the individual is the most important condition
also for the enhancement of the race.*

They desire to fill the earth with hungerers for
happiness, since they know that only thus will
earthly life attain its inmost purpose, that of
forming—in an altogether new sense—creatures
of eternity.

The word, which through Eros became flesh and
dwells among us, is the profoundest of all: *Joy
is perfection.*

If we accept this dictum of Spinoza as the highest revelation of life's meaning, our eyes are at
the same time opened to the harmony of existence. We perceive that the more perfect race
will be in the fullest sense of the word *created by
love.* But this will not take place until love has become a religion, the highest expression of the fear
of life—not the fear of God;—when faith in life
has scattered the superstition and unbelief which
still disfigure love. When the eldest of the gods

has no other god before him, then will the monsters who now fill the murky deeps over which the spirit of the god moves perish in the light of the new day of creation.

.　　.　　.　　.　　.　　.　　.

For the sake of clearness, it has been necessary to sum up here the main ideas of the following exposition. In some measure it will therefore be also necessary to return to them during the following treatment of the movements which have the deepest influence on sexual morality: *the evolution of love*, its *freedom* and its *selection;* the claims of a *right to* and an *exemption from motherhood;* of *collective motherhood*, of *free divorce*, and of *a new marriage law.*

CHAPTER II

THE EVOLUTION OF LOVE

Just as the Swedes, in comparison with some other of the Germanic peoples, are behindhand in their view of *l'amour passion*, so are the Germanic races as a whole behindhand as compared with the foremost Latin peoples. The Gallic counterpart of the Lutheran doctrine of marriage is to be found in another monk, Luther's contemporary, Rabelais, with his joyous project of a new kind of convent, where every monk should have his nun, with the power of separating after a year of probation; a plan which perhaps would not have been a much more roundabout way of educating mankind to love than was the Lutheran doctrine of marriage. Nothing is farther from the truth than that the Reformation increased respect for love and woman. It raised the esteem for the married state as compared with the unmarried, but it enhanced neither the position of woman in matrimony nor the importance of love in regard to marriage. Even in the Middle Ages, the Latin nations render a homage to woman which to-day is still almost incomprehensible to the

57

man of a Germanic race. And if, on the one hand, this homage took the form of the cult of Venus, which is born in the Latin blood, on the other, it expressed through the cult of Mary its reverence for what is deepest in woman, motherhood. Even to-day, the Frenchwoman is esteemed not according to her age but according to her qualities. It is not only the mothers who worship their sons, but also the latter their mothers; and not only the mother, but besides her every admirable elderly woman receives attention in social life as in the family from men of all ages. The middle-class wife—though indeed at the cost of the children—co-operates in her husband's calling with a seriousness unknown in the Germanic middle-class. In France as in Italy, family life has a kind of warm intimacy which the German does not understand; since the Latin temperament lacks that geniality which sheds its light over the frequently rough lines and harsh colours of the landscape of the Germanic soul. It is rather the coldness of his disposition than the strength of his soul that makes the German so much less erotic than the Southerner; it is more indifference to woman than respect for her that expresses itself in the distinction between the erotic customs of North and South. But when all this has been admitted for the sake of justice, we may fairly lay stress upon the influence of the Germanic spirit in the struggle to put an end to that cleavage between love and marriage which has prevailed among the Southern nations ever since the days of the Courts of Love. For the peculiarity of the Gallic spirit is to discriminate. This gives it the power of following out an idea to its uttermost conclusions, but at the same time renders it liable in actual life to split itself up among superficialities. The strength of the German, on the other hand, is his desire of unity. This makes him inconsistent as a thinker, since he must include everything, but against this it makes him strive after consistency in life. The same deep sense of personality which created Protestantism has in the Germanic world sought to make love as well as faith the affair of the individual and to make marriage one with love. Among the educated classes in the North, marriages of convenience or those arranged by the family are now things of the past, while in the Latin world they are still the rule, though with increasingly frequent exceptions. But in most cases it is still in free connections, before and during marriage, that the Frenchman engages his erotic feelings ; and the French wife has abundantly shown the emptiness of the assertion that "a woman always loves the father of her child," the most dangerous of the false doctrines which have led women into marriage and thence into adultery. In Shakespeare, on the other hand, we already find the wife and the mistress united in the same person, and it is always in English literature that we meet with the highest expression of the Germanic feeling for unity in love. Since the mediæval minnesingers ceased to sing, the literature of Germany and Scandinavia, dominated by Lutheranism, bears witness chiefly of "the lust of the flesh." Women are esteemed according as they fulfil their destiny as bearers of children and housewives. The abolition of the cloister and celibacy has, however, brought about the good result of the transmission of spiritual forces which formerly died with the individual. And it may well have been through some of those who formerly took refuge with their idealism in a cloister, that the longing for a great love has been left as an inheritance to sons and daughters.

In Germany, the leading poet of the "age of enlightenment," Gottsched, asserts woman's right to culture; in America, during the War of Independence, the women gave evidence of their sense of citizenship; and it was during a more recent struggle for liberty, that against slavery, that the woman's question came to the front in that country.

In France, the eighteenth century, more than any other period of history, is "the century of woman." The salons are the focussing point of all ideas; the most eminent men write for women, who become electric batteries from which the ideas of the time send out kindling sparks in all directions. Thus the women of France help to prepare the French Revolution. During the Revolution, Olympe de Gouges writes her "declaration of the rights of woman," as a counterpart to that of the rights of man, and Condorcet speaks in support of woman's claims. The same spirit of a new age confronts us in Mary Wollstonecraft's *A Vindication of the Rights of Woman* (1792), as also in Hippel's *Ueber die bürgerliche Verbesserung der Weiber*, published the same year, and in the Swede Thorild's contemporary treatise *Om kvinnokönets naturliga höghet* ("On the Natural Greatness of Women"). Each in its way was a remarkable sign of the time which already included the whole "emancipation" programme of equality of position: the same rights for woman as for man as regards education, labour, a share in legislation, and an equality of position under the law and in marriage.

Isolated instances of emancipated women were nothing new. In Greece, the type was common enough to be employed in comedy; in Rome, self-supporting women were to be found; during the Middle Ages not only Bridget but many another woman—in the quality of abbess or regent—exercised a great and often beneficial activity. The days of antiquity, of the Middle Ages, and of the Renaissance all possessed female scholars, physicians, and artists. But it is not until the century of the great Revolution that we find among women themselves as well as among certain men a persistent and conscious striving to elevate the education and to secure the rights of women.

And wherever this striving has been profound, it has been united with the desire to reform the position of woman in love and in marriage.

.   .   .   .

It is a very common but erroneous opinion that monogamy has given rise to love. Love appears already among animals, and with them, as in the world of men, has shown itself independent of monogamy.

The origin of the latter in human society was the relation of proprietorship, religious ideas, considerations of collective utility, but not perception of the importance of love's selection. On the contrary, love has been in perpetual strife with monogamy, and it is therefore a profound mistake to suppose that the higher view of love has been formed solely through monogamy. The idea of love has been developed in as great a degree by attacks on marriage as in association with marriage itself.

While, in spite of the accumulation of evidence to the contrary, Christianity's share in the origin of human love is constantly exaggerated, sufficient stress has not been laid upon its indirect influence on the development of sexual love. It is true that all over the world—from Iceland to Japan—songs and legends are to be found which give glorious evidence of the power of love in the heart of man in all ages. But the sexual emotion, nevertheless, held a subordinate position in the life of the human soul until Christianity granted to woman also a soul to save—in other words, a personality to cultivate. Christianity, moreover commended the womanly rather than the manly virtues, and although Christ himself ignored woman, love, and the family life, his ethics became thus in an indirect form a glorification of woman. The importance attached by Christianity to the value of the individual as a soul—in contradistinction to the insistence by paganism on his value as a citizen—was likewise one of the unseen contributary causes which during the Middle Ages made love a life-power.

In antiquity, marriage was a duty to society; friendship, on the other hand, was the free expression of sympathy. Not until man's consciousness admitted a soul in woman, could personal love arise. But so mysterious are the influences through which the soul of mankind grows, that the youthful love of the ancients indirectly developed the need of sympathy also between grown men and women; and the suppression of the sexual instinct by Catholic asceticism indirectly furthered the introspective, soulful emotion of love which rises above sensuality.

The modern view of love as the most lofty state of the soul had already taken shape in the time of the Crusades sufficiently to bring into

existence at this period the Courts of Love in
the south of France. Woman, the knight, and
the singer together intensify and refine love, in
part by laying stress upon its incompatibility
with marriage!

Students have shown how the refined expression
of love in poetry corresponds with the forms of
the sexual life of the upper classes, since monogamy
became the law and a secret polygamy the custom.
This dual division of the erotic feelings has on the
one side brought about such fine and lofty, and
on the other such coarse and debased manifestations that neither one nor the other has any
counterpart among the nations—or classes within
a nation—where this division is unknown, since
there the freedom of sexual choice is undisputed.

And this is natural; for there the sexual life
preserves its innocence of "paradise," one of
simple animality perturbed by no higher consciousness. This innocence can only be .replaced
on a higher plane after a long period of development. The way thither is by the cleavage which
"the division of labour" involves even in regard
to the development of the feelings.

The Middle Ages were thus only capable of
dividing love from marriage. This is witnessed
by the greatest singers of love and by the greatest
love stories. Tristan and Isolde in the world of
poetry, Abelard and Heloïse in that of reality,
are the highest types of the new age, even then
dawning, which is finally to bring about the

declaration of rights of human emotion as of human thought. These lovers, united in life and death, are the highest testimony of the Middle Ages to that free love which makes its own laws and abolishes all others; to that great love which is the sense of eternity of great souls, in opposition to the ephemeral inclination of small ones.

Scholasticism, ever extending introspective psychology; mysticism, ever refining the life of the soul devoted to God, unconsciously pour oil upon the red flame of love as upon the white flame of faith. The *Vita Nuova* of love breaks out in the fire of poetry, whose most aspiring flame was Dante. It lived on in the souls of the elect among Latin peoples. The Platonism of the Renaissance refined the mediæval conception of love as the most excellent means of bringing to perfection the highest human qualities. And thus was established the right of lovers to independence of the customs of society.

It is significant that, at the mediæval Courts of Love as at the courts of the Renaissance and in the contests of wit of the seventeenth century, women are granted not only the same right of sentiment as men but also the same liberty of using their spiritual gifts; for every intensifying of love is connected, openly or otherwise, with the augmentation of woman's spiritual life and with man's thus enhanced estimation of the value of her personality. Instead of being to him "the sex," the means of enjoyment, woman

5

becomes the mistress, when love has come to mean an exclusive desire for one woman, who is only to be won by devoted service. Whenever woman has taken the lead in erotic matters, man's love has been ennobled. In Shakespeare, we find the whole of the preceding spiritual culture summed up. All his best women are chaste in the same degree as they are devoted, but they are also in the same degree spiritually rich and complete personalities. Therefore they are also leaders through their clear-sightedness and promptness in the moment of action. And although Shakespeare, like every other great poet, formed his women more of the material of dreams than of reality; although the foremost men of the Italian Renaissance probably had more often a Boccaccio's than a Petrarch's experience of love; although the age of baroque turned *le Pays du tendre* into a stiff garden surrounding decorative figures, nevertheless life itself, especially the life of the Latin peoples— as well as their best literature—can always show proud and beautiful examples of loving couples and sacrifices for love, even in that century whose male "philosophers" deprived woman of the lead, when love became "galanterie," gay and ugly by turns.

At the time when Rousseau appeared, love was equally degraded through Latin–Epicurean immorality and through Germanic–Lutheran "morality."

What he did for love was the same that he would have done for the lungs, if in one of the boudoirs of those days, stuffy with perfumes and wax candles, he had thrown open the windows to the summer night, with its scent of productive earth and blossoming plants, dark masses of foliage and the star-sown sky.

But Rousseau did not follow out the ideas that lay nearest to his own: that only love ought to constitute marriage; that only the development of the woman's personality deepens love. Even Goethe, who after Rousseau carried the gleaming trail farther, by showing love as the mysterious fateful power of elective affinity, saw the happiness of love rather in the directness of woman's nature than in its development. The French Revolution drew the consequences of Rousseau's propositions also in the questions of love and woman; it made marriage civil and divorce free, but it did not give to woman the franchise; indeed, it did not even preserve the form of it which she had previously possessed. All the spirits influenced by Rousseau and the Revolution have since, in literature and in life, followed out love's declaration of rights.

In the nineteenth century as in the Middle Ages, it was women, poets, and knights—the last under the name of social utopians—who took the lead in this. In Germany, it was first the romantic school, then "Young Germany," which went foremost; in England, Shelley, Byron, Browning, and a number of other thinkers; in Norway, Camilla Collet and some great poets among the men. In France,—in the midst of the reaction which reintroduced indissoluble marriage,— Madame de Staël attacks this in *Delphine*. In the country of literary salons, it is attempted to prevent woman's genius from acting as a social force—and through *Corinne* and Coppet, Mme. de Staël makes it a universal force. Her confidence that honour for a woman can signify only a means of winning love; her complaint that life denies to the woman of genius the fulfilment of her most beautiful dream, love in marriage, were the prologue to innumerable tragedies during woman's century. After her, came the followers of St. Simon and the rest of the social revolutionaries, and above all another of Rousseau's spiritual daughters, the woman in whose veins all the blood was mingled which the Revolution had poured out on the scaffold and on the battle-field: blood of the mob, blood of the bourgeois, noble blood, royal blood! The courage of her nation to follow truth to its utmost consequences, the fervent faith of her childhood, the wistfulness of her blood, her soul's longing for eternity, the volcanic ardour and ashes of her experiences— all this George Sand hurls forth in her indictment of the marriage upheld by Church and State, which to her was "lawful ravishing" and "prostitution under vows." Long before her time, the rights of love had been asserted in the case

of exceptional natures. George Sand's new courage was shown in demanding this right for all;
in branding it upon the conscience of her time
that, when two human beings wish to be together,
no bond is needed to hold them together; that,
when they do not wish it, to hold them together
by force is a violation of their human rights and
of their human dignity.

From this moment the battle was transferred
from Olympus to the earth. And since then all
"saviours of society" have sought to quench,
and all "enemies of society" have striven to
spread, its flames.

The love which a George Sand herself sought
in vain on paths from which she returned with
feet wounded, and sometimes soiled; the love a
Rahel Varnhagen suffered from and lived on, a
Camilla Collet implored, and an Elizabeth Browning realised—this is the love of which the woman
of the new age is also dreaming.

George Sand—like the followers of St. Simon,
and like the modern feminists—looked upon
freedom in love as the central point in the woman's question. Like George Sand, the feminism
of the present day asserts the right of free thought
against the creed of authority in every field;
the solidarity of mankind and the cause of peace
against the patriotism of militarism; social reform
against the existing relations of society. The
American–English–Scandinavian woman's question—whose supreme confession of faith is still

J. S. Mill's book, published in 1854, on *The Subjection of Women*—has, on the other hand, overlooked to a great extent erotic, religious, and social emancipation, and asserted only woman's rights as a citizen. Thus, especially in Scandinavia, the new gospel of love has had to encounter from the leaders of emancipation, now indifference, now resentment.

Ridicule and resentment from men have also fallen to the lot of the women's demand for a new love. With arguments, for which Schopenhauer and Hartmann once provided the philosophical formulæ, it has been shown that soulful love is an illusion of nature, and that the unity in love, which woman now claims of man, demands sacrifices which are opposed to his physiological and psychological nature.

Undisturbed by ridicule and resentment, however, the women of the new age have continued to preach the love of their dreams—which is also that of the dreams of poets.

For thousands of years, poetry has been picturing love as a mysterious and tragic power. But when anyone says the same thing in plain prose, and adds that life would be colourless and poor without the great passions, then this is called immorality! Century after century, poetry sets forth the loftiness of love. But if anyone in every-day prose ventures to say that love may become an ever loftier emotion, then this is called extravagance; for it does not occur to the people of the present day to regard poetry as prophetic.

The new love is still the natural attraction of man and woman to each other for the continuance of the race. It is still the desire of the active human being to relieve through comradeship the hardships of another and of himself at the same time. But above this eternal nature of love, beyond this primeval cause of marriage, another longing has grown with increasing strength. This is not directed towards the continuance of the race. It has sprung from man's sense of loneliness within his race, a loneliness which is ever greater in proportion as his soul is exceptional. It is the pining for that human soul which is to release our own from this torment of solitude; a torment which was formerly allayed by repose in God, but which now seeks its rest with an equal, with a soul that has itself lain wakeful with eyelids heated from the same longing; a soul empowered by love to the miracle of redeeming our soul—as itself by ours is redeemed —from the sense of being a stranger upon earth; a soul before whose warmth our own lets fall the covering that the world's coldness has imposed upon it and shows its secrets and its glories without shame. Richard Dehmel has summed this up in two immortal lines:

Liebe ist die Freiheit der Gestalt
Vom Wahn der Welt, vom Bann der eignen Seele.

The same feeling has possessed many a man before our time. One of them was Eugène Delacroix, who speaks in his journal of the pain of only being able to show to each of his friends the aspect of himself which that friend understood, and of thus being obliged to become another for each of them, without ever feeling himself completely understood; a suffering for which he only knew one remedy, *une épouse qui est de votre force.*

But what is new about it is that this sentiment has become diffused and has taken shape in the consciousness of the many; that it is beginning to set its stamp upon the whole spirit of the age.

Meanwhile, mankind continues to be guided by erotic impulses which lie deep below its conscious erotic needs. Man's senses are spurred by a desire which thrusts aside that of the soul. The culture of the idea of love is far in advance of the instincts of love. And thus our time is brimful of love-conflicts.

To this must be added that the increased sensibility of mod⁻ ⸲ man has rendered him more and more inclined to wear masks, protective disguises, artistically decorated armour. Protection is indispensable, since no one would be able to endure life if he were hourly seeing the ill-bound or still open wounds of others, or feeling his own touched by anyone. Existence would lose much of its excitement without secrets, suspected or unsuspected, in the destinies and souls of men. But at the same time this protection renders love's struggle to penetrate appearances more and more difficult. Therefore a certain form of "flirtation" serves as the attempt of awakening love to tear off the mask, to outwit the protective disguise, a game of fence which aims at the joints of the tight-fitting armour.

But the attempts are often unsuccessful and life is more and more crowded with destinies that have miscarried, while more and more people wring their hands in solitude over what might have been! Man feels more deeply than ever before that life gave him a poor portion, when his love has been nothing but sinking in an embrace. An ever greater number know that love is absorption into that spirit, in which one's own finds its foothold without losing its freedom; the nearness of that heart which stills the disquiet in our own; that attentive ear which catches what is unspoken and unspeakable; the clear sight of those eyes which see the realisation of our best possibilities; the touch of those hands which, dying, we would feel closed on our own.

When two souls have joys which the senses share, and when the senses have delights which the souls ennoble, then the result is neither desire nor friendship. Both have been absorbed in a new feeling, not to be compared with either taken by itself, just as the air is incomparable with its component elements. Nitrogen is not air, nor is oxygen; sensuousness is not love, nor is sympathy. In combination they are the air of life

and love. If either of the component elements
is in the wrong proportion to the other, then love—
like air—becomes too heavy or too rarefied. But
as the proportions between oxygen and nitrogen
may within a wide limit vary without disadvantage,
so also may the components of love. Affinity
of soul is doubtless the most enduring element in
love, but not therefore the only valuable one;
the love that fills life with intoxication is separated
from even the most lofty friendship by an ocean
as deep as that which divides the India of legend
from utilitarian America—a lifetime in which
will not equal a single day in the other!

Great love arises only when desire of a being
of the other sex coalesces with the longing for a
soul of one's own kind. It is like fire, the hotter
it is, the purer; and differs from the ardour of
desire as the white heat of a smelting-furnace
differs from the ruddy, smoking flames of a torch
carried along the streets.

.   .   .   .

The constantly increased importance of sympathy in the life of the soul finds expression,
however, at the present time within the feminine
world in an over-estimation of friendship, both
between one woman and another and in relation
to love. A passionate worship between persons
of the same age—or of an elder by a younger
member of the same sex—is among women as

among men the customary and beautiful morning glow of love, which always pales after sunrise. An entirely personal, great friendship is, on the other hand, as rare as a great love, and equally rare among women as among men. Those who expect to find the complement of their being in friendship have therefore no greater prospect of attaining the essential in this sphere, and moreover they run the risk of missing it in the sphere of love, through shutting themselves off from or impoverishing themselves of love's emotions. The women of older times also cultivated friendship. But they did not content themselves with it in the place of love. And if women were once seriously to do this, then winter would have come upon the world. The way of evolution is to demand of love all that friendship affords—and infinitely more! But the rich spiritual intercourse between female fellow-workers and fellow-students, as also between comrades of different sexes, is now preparing the third historical stage of development, that of individual sympathy. It is true that great love has been individually sympathetic in all ages. What is new is that an ever greater number of spirits are guided by the same need; that the possibility of great love has become apparent to many, not only to a chosen few. Just as we have been able to gauge the revival of love by the diminution of marriages of convenience, by the recognition of young people's liberty of choice, and by the popular condemna-

tion of marriages for money, so can we now measure the strength of the new revival by other,
equally significant phenomena; those, namely,
called "the new immorality." It has been said
with truth that love as it now is — the great
psychological reality with which one has to
reckon—in its present complicated, manifold,
and refined condition, is the result of all the
progress of human activity: of the victory of intelligence and sentiment over crude force, of the
transformation in the relations between man and
woman which new economic, religious, and ethical
ideas have brought about; of the growing desire
for inward and outward beauty, of the will to
ennoble the race, and other causes. But among
these we have not named the most important, that
in which many now see a sign of degeneration,
but which is really one of development, the cause
on which rests the hope of the final abolition of
erotic dualism: the conciliation of the excessive
opposition of sex.

So long as man and woman are so divided in
their erotic needs as is at present often the case,
love will be the "everlasting conflict" described
by those poets and thinkers who see only the
immediate present, without faith in the development of love or mankind's education in loving;
for in the midst of the age of evolutionism men
neither think nor feel according to its doctrines.
To him, however, who does so feel, nothing is
more certain than that "the everlasting con-

flict" will one day end in the conclusion of peace.

The sceptics just referred to smile ambiguously at the mention of friendship between women, as at that of the refinement and craving for sympathy in woman's love. It is not until a mistress or a wife, misunderstood in the depths of her being, leaves him, that such a man discovers that the being he believed himself to be making entirely happy, has not even had her senses satisfied—since the soul received nothing from the senses and gave them nothing.

Those men—for the rest often men of fine culture—of whom this is true, are generally verging on middle age. Among men comparatively young, on the other hand, the erotic longing is often as refined and craves as much for sympathy, as with women, although it is still rare for the man to possess that balance between soul and senses which his equal in the other sex has attained. That women now venture to acknowledge that they possess erotic senses, while men are beginning to discover erotically that they have souls; that woman demands feelings in a man and he ideas in her—this is the great and happy sign of the times. Sensitive young men of the present day suffer perhaps as much as their sisters when loved only for their sex, not personally and on account of their personality. They for their part love just that womanly individuality for which they provide freedom of movement, instead of—as their own fathers did—trying to assimilate it to their own.

On the highest plane—as on the lowest—the similarities between man's love and woman's are already greater than the dissimilarities; and there may be more danger to love in the growing likeness between the sexes than in continued unlikeness. Man becomes a human being—and woman likewise—at the cost of his secondary sexual characters. There are already some who think that the close of psychical development will present the same phenomenon as the beginning of physical development, namely, that the embryo at a certain stage is neither male nor female but includes both possibilities!

The romanticists, F. Schlegel in particular, lay stress upon the distinction that, while the ancients put greatness of heart, nobility of mind, and strength of soul above the purely sexual qualities, the moderns have made woman onesidedly feminine and man one-sidedly masculine, and assert that this extreme view on both sides must be got rid of in order to arrive at morality, beauty, and harmony in sexual relations; a view which was also that of Schleiermacher. And if we will see a deeper meaning in the tale of Aristophanes of the cloven human being, it will be the same that an apocryphal tradition ascribes to Jesus, in the saying that "the kingdom of God is at hand when the two again become one." That Plato already emphasises the sufferings imposed on both halves of the being by the "cleavage," is evidence of the commencement of development of love; for this development has progressed through the increasing opposition of the sexes, with the passion and the pain it has caused. Now at last the moment has arrived when the divided sections again converge towards a higher unity.

In reality, this desirable conciliation of sexual opposition is proceeding with such rapidity that there might be a fear of its becoming a danger to love in a near future, if the psychical opposition of sex were not always dependent finally on the physical, and if the modern man and woman were not becoming simultaneously more and more individualised.

And it is in this circumstance that the future possibilities of great love lie. Individualisation is already so powerful that a thoughtful person is ever more inclined to check himself when the abstract expressions "man" and "woman" escape his lips. For already men and women respectively differ among themselves almost as much as the two sexes from each other. And as a compensation for the enfeebling through conciliation of universal erotic attraction, we have the charm of individual contrasts. Love's spiritual longing —to be resolved together with another soul into a higher harmony—will not be enfeebled, but, on the contrary, will be enhanced in proportion as this contrast is more personal.

A. Rodin—who like every great Frenchman understands great love—has glorified it in his statue of a pair of lovers, who have through each other become more perfect beings than either could have been alone. Rodin makes the man thoroughly masculine, the woman thoroughly feminine, while each line in their two figures shows primitive force ennobled into spiritual power, and love as the consummation of the human man and the human woman.

When life from time to time shows us this proud and beautiful vision, then we are in the presence of a happiness which is overpoweringly great. For as an economical housewife shuts out the sunlight, so life often lets fall the curtain of death when happiness shines; or indeed men kill their own happiness through instincts surviving from a lower stage.

Chief of these is that instinct which makes the force of primitive animality still erotically attractive even to the spiritually sensitive. Men and women with this power of elementary passion, intoxicate because they are themselves intoxicated, because, without being checked by any consideration or held back by the soul, they give themselves up wholly and hotly to the moment. It is as superficial a psychology to say that Don Juan's reputation makes him irresistible as that conquest of Cleopatra is tempting because it is also conquest over Cæsar. No, the power of these natures lies in their undivided, unscrupulous will to use all the resources of their being to attain their end. And only that by which one's whole being is held at the moment has the power of holding others. Thus the question is answered

> *Comment fais-tu les grands amours,*
> *Petite ligne de la bouche?*

Soulful people, especially women, have hitherto only loved partially. But when sensuousness—in alliance with the mission of the race—regains its ancient dignity, then the power of giving erotic rapture will not be the monopoly of him who is inhuman in his love. The wise virgins' deadly sin against love is that they disdained to learn of the foolish ones the secret of fascination; that they would know none of the thousand things that bind a man's senses or lay hold on his soul; that they regarded the power to please as equivalent to the will to betray. When all women who can love are also able to make goodness fascinating and completeness of personality intoxicating, then Imogen will conquer Cleopatra.

As yet the charming ones are not always good, the good not always charming, and the majority neither good nor charming. During this transition between an old and a new womanliness it is natural that she should be strongest who unites in herself

> *Ève, Joconde, et Delila.*

From observation of love's realisation in marriage—as it is still realised in the majority

6

of cases—young women have been more and more possessed by a disinclination to wed. They wish for the love of their dreams or none at all. A lower claim, a poorer gift of love has for them no value which can be compared with their free personal life. To the man who only seeks her lips but does not listen to the words from them, who longs for her embrace but smiles or frowns when she reveals the nature of her soul, such a woman has nothing to give. Her love is now filled with the whole nourishing force of her human nature, replete with the whole sap of her woman's nature, and she desires that the sacrament she thus dispenses shall be received with devotion.

She will no longer be captured like a fortress or hunted like a quarry; nor will she like a placid lake await the stream that seeks its way to her embrace. A stream herself, she will go her own way to meet the other stream.

. . . .

We live in a period of spiritual reformation of immense importance in the history of the world. Every human being who himself has soul is being more and more penetrated by the sense of the mysterious effects of elective affinities; of sympathetic and antipathetic influences; of subconscious powers, above all in the erotic sphere. Sensations of the erotically dæmonic are not new. But they were formerly condemned to as great an extent as they are now recognised and indeed sometimes assisted. It is this exquisite sensitiveness, these vibrating nerves, these changing moods, this irritability of sensation that the woman—like the man—of the present day has acquired as her superiority, her gain through culture, her right of precedence before any other generation. But this new wealth involves innumerable new conflicts. The senses go their own way and are attracted where the soul is estranged, or repelled although the heart is filled with tenderness. Until the physiology and psychology of loathing are understood, we shall not have gone far towards the solution of the erotic problem. Every day—and night—these innumerable influences, conscious or unconscious, are at work transforming the feelings of married people and lovers. And although our time is becoming increasingly conscious of this, it does not yet understand either how to counteract the dangerous or encourage the favourable influence of the important trifles of married life.

Only the foremost of women with a genius for love have arrived at that degree of sensitiveness which makes it impossible for them to give or receive anything in love without the feeling which one of Charlotte Brontë's women expresses in the words: *You fit me into the finest fibre of my being*.

Every developed modern woman wishes to be

loved not *en mâle* but *en artiste*.   Only a man
whom she feels to possess an artist's joy in her,
and who shows this joy in discreet and delicate
contact with her soul as with her body, can retain
the love of the modern woman.   She will belong
only to a man who longs for her always, even
when he holds her in his arms.   And when such
a woman exclaims: "You desire me, but you
cannot caress, you cannot listen . . ." then that
man is doomed.

Modern woman's love differs from that of older
times by, amongst other things, the insatiability
of its demand for completeness and perfection
in itself, and for corresponding completeness and
perfection in the feeling of the man.

Our soul is doubtless often deeper, but occasionally also shallower, than our conscious
existence and will.   Therefore it may happen
that the new love in all its force exists in a woman
who is unconscious of her own erotic greatness,
while, on the other hand, another, who desires
it with all her will, perhaps may lack the depth
of feeling, the instinctive sureness of choice.

The women of the present day learn everything
and arrive at much, even at the finest ideas of
love.   But, full of insight as they are into the
ars amandi, have modern women indeed learned
how with all their soul, all their strength, and all
their mind to love?   Their mothers and grand-
mothers—on a much lower plane of conscious
erotic idealism—knew of only one object: that

of making their husbands happy. This then meant that the wife ought to submit to everything and ask for nothing; to serve her husband's ends untiringly, even when she did not understand them, and to receive with gratitude any crumbs of his personality that might fall to her from the table to which his friends were bidden to feast. But what watchful tenderness, what dignified desire to please, what fair gladness could not the finest of these spiritually ignored women develop!

The new man lives in a dream of the new woman, and she, in a dream of the new man. But when they actually find one another it frequently results that two highly developed brains together analyse love, or that two worn-out nervous systems fight out a disintegrating battle over love. The whole thing usually ends in each of them seeking peace with some surviving incarnation of the old Adam and the eternal Eve. But not with a clear conscience; for they are continually aware that they were intended for the new experience, although their powers of loving were small while their ideas of love were great.

Not until the spring rain of the new ideas has fallen sufficiently to penetrate the roots and rise as sap in the tree of life, will a greater happiness grow from the new love, which is not to be blamed because men have dreamed it greater than they themselves are at present.

Individualism has made love deeper and at the same time increased its difficulties. It has

called forth an enhanced consciousness of our
own nature, our own moods; it has created new
spiritual conditions and—as already pointed out
—set in vibration innumerable formerly latent
feelings of pleasure and aversion. But our personal irritable sensitiveness has not yet been
developed to the point of a corresponding delicacy
of feeling for the equally sensitive spiritual life
of others. The capacity for giving and sacrificing has not grown at an equal pace with that
of accepting and demanding. Of love's double
heart-beat—the finding one's self, and the forgetting one's self in another—the first is now
considerably more advanced than the second.
Not until those women who are absorbed in
self-analysis combine their own personal store
of life's riches, their individual diversity, their
unique spirituality with the sunny, healthy
peace, the self-sacrificing devotion of older times,
will their new development render them more
powerful than the women who preceded them.
It is a healthy sign that men and women exchange
experiences and ideas on these subjects with a
frankness that was never known before; that they
are much less affected before marriage, as women
indeed have ceased to be so after marriage. There
was a heroic kind of affectation, of which Mrs.
Carlyle was the typical example, but in itself
it was borrowed from man's ethical development.
Nevertheless one would often wish that the
young wives of the present day possessed more

of the old-fashioned gift of conceding the desires of the beloved with a happy smile, instead of insisting on their own. The modern woman will not feign anything for the sake of occasional peace or understanding. And she is right—when anything of real importance in the domain of ideas or will is at stake; she is doubly right in holding that all the lies and ruses which married "happiness" enforced on the wives of an older time were degrading to both parties; that what was thus gained was no real gain. Nothing is more true than that the souls which are parted by a lack of perfect frankness never belonged to one another; that complete mutual confidence is the true sign of union. Nothing could be wiser than the modern woman's desire to see life with her own eyes, not—as was the case with the women who went before her—only with those of a husband. But has she also retained the power of seeing everything with the thought of what the loved one's eyes will find in it?

.   .   .   .

Upon the answer to these questions of conscience will depend the success of the new woman in guiding the development of love in the direction of her will. For only by herself loving better will she gradually humanise man's passion and liberate it from the blind force of the blood, which makes of the capercailzie's play or the rivalry of stags a spectacle beautiful in its animality, but, on the other hand, renders man's love bestial. Those who think that the healthy strength of nature will be thereby enfeebled are as foolish as those who try to prove that the artistic instinct in the woodcock's note is healthier and stronger than that which created Beethoven's symphonies.

But it is not sufficient that woman should take the lead and appoint the goal. She must herself be developed for the task, and that not only in the direction just mentioned. Her soul is as yet no sure guide to her senses, nor her senses to her soul. So much the less can she then be a guide to man's soul or senses, which moreover she frequently fails to understand and therefore unhesitatingly condemns—for the sins to which she herself has not unfrequently seduced him!

The new woman demands purity of man. But has she any suspicion as to how her treatment, on the one hand, of the awkward and uncertain youth, on the other, of the experienced and confident "lady-killer" type, acts upon the former, who is perhaps striving after erotic purity in the hope of being rewarded by the happy smile of a woman, but who sees that woman treat him with haughty commiseration while, on the other hand, she regards the leopard's spots of his rival with admiration? One may ask whether all young women who now express their detestation of the impurity in man's sexual habits are themselves guided only by a soft and noble joy in giving pleasure. Do they never permit themselves the most despicable of hypocrisies, that of love?

So long as "pure" women take pleasure in the cruel sport of the cat; so long as with the facile changes of mood of the serpentine dancer they evade the responsibilities of their flirtations; so long as they delight in provoking jealousy as a homage to themselves, so long will they be helping to brew the hell-broth around which men will celebrate the witches' sabbath in the company of the bat-winged bevies of the night.

There are more men led astray by "pure" than by "impure" women.

And not even those women who are pure in the true sense of the word are free from blame in this. Woman—for whom love is a life-and-death matter in a much deeper sense than for man— experiences on the approach of love those tremblings that follow a sunrise for which one has lain awake and waited. Her physico-psychical timidity takes on by turns the expressions, incomprehensible to the man who loves, of dumb avoidance, of abrupt change, of empty girlish giggling, of sullen misunderstanding. And all that is contradictory—not that which is mysterious —in woman stirs the unrest in a man's blood.

.   .   .   .

The modern woman's great distress has been the discovery of the dissimilarity between her own erotic nature and that of man; or rather, she has refused and still refuses to make this discovery and thinks that only the custom of society—with its wholesome severity towards her, its reckless leniency towards him—has brought about the difference which exists and which she would abolish. But while one group proposes to do so by demanding feminine chastity of the man, the other would claim masculine freedom for the woman.

The book world is now full of works on purity, written by men as well as women, of literary tone and otherwise. Now it is the story of a woman who breaks with the man she loves when he confesses his past; now that of a woman who forces her lover to marry another because the latter has borne him a child; and so on to infinity. Finally there is one who takes her life from grief over her husband's past, which she thinks will ruin their future. Literature is the roll of the drum which announces the approach of the troop —that army of strong women who are to educate men to chastity by denying them their love.

But will it really be the Amazons who will play the leading part in the struggle against man's erotic dualism? Will not perhaps wisdom be found also in this case in the hope of being able to conquer the evil with the good, not the evil with the worse, by allowing a man awakened by love to the desire of unity to turn again to disunion?

Would not woman accomplish more in the renovation of morals if she stayed with the man she loves, so as with her whole being to let him learn how a woman can suffer and be made happy through a man? The means of salvation for men suffering under erotic dualism may well be an increase of tenderly chaste, delicately feeling, and kindly wise wives. Even such a mother, sister, or friend is a strength to a man. But only the wife who remains a mistress can be sure of victory.

It is true that she cannot efface her husband's past. But she can create together with him a new and stronger generation. The man who knows what his beloved has suffered through his past; who has seen the wings of her courage lose something of their power, her confidence something of its smile, her joy something of its playfulness—he will in time teach his sons that a man may certainly become once more strong and healthy through happiness in love, but that he cannot win so beautiful and sure a happiness as self-control can prepare; such queenly pride as his victory might have given the loved one, he will never see in her. But if woman is to help man's struggle for purity, she must for her share take another view of what has been degrading to man's nature and what has not.

A woman who marries a widower has to go through a pain which will be deep in proportion as her love is personal. She will then wish to be not only her husband's last, but also his first love; she suffers from all the memories they have not in common. She would fain have sat by his cradle and received his first smile; she longs to have played with him as a sister, to have shared as a friend his troubles and his joys. She envies all who have been able to see him at those stages of his life and in those spiritual conditions that she has not seen. Above all she envies the woman who first saw him made happy by the love she gave him.

But all these sufferings do not bring her to regard the beloved as morally sunken, because before her he has been the husband of another woman. And the same must hold good of earlier relations of love. The man may have developed, through a former marriage or free connection, his powers of giving a personal love, or he may, in the same way, have lost them. If no baseness is connected with these earlier experiences, if he has not degraded himself to voluntary division of his erotic nature—and bought love is always such a degradation—or to contemptible duplicity; if he has not treated any woman as a means, but received and given personality, then he does not enter "impure" into his marriage, even if he has not evidence of abstinence.

At present it is unfortunately often the case that men enter into marriage with deep stains from earlier connections, and it is this circumstance that gives the demand for purity its general applicability.

During each new phase of the development of love women, probably earlier and certainly more consciously than men, have connected the demand for unity with the idea of love. The sense of unity is quite another and a far later phenomenon than monogamy. The enforced fidelity in monogamy, the voluntary fidelity in love, gave rise in woman first to control of desire, then to the weakening of desire through control. Thus by degrees erotic unity became with many women an organic condition, or, as is significantly said, a physical necessity. Not with all, not even with the majority, but still sufficiently frequently to enable us to call the unity of soul and senses in love—as also a lifelong fidelity in a single love—the provision of nature for innumerable women, while with men both are still exceptions so rarely to be met with that they are often called unnatural. But he who concludes from this that one has only to demand the same of men for the effect to be the same, is attributing the same effect to two different causes. For the erotic conditions of man and woman are and will remain different causes. The purity which a man is capable of attaining must always, therefore, to a certain degree be different from a woman's, but not on that account of less worth. He will certainly remain more polygamous than she, but this does not involve a division of himself in the satisfaction of his erotic needs. Love possesses, nay, besets, dominates, and determines woman's whole being in an entirely different way from man's. He is more strongly possessed at rapidly passing moments, by the erotic emotion, but at the same time he liberates himself more quickly and completely. On the other hand, in the degree in which a woman is womanly, is she completely determined by love. This gives a unity, completeness, and equilibrium to her sensuousness which man lacks. When he is warm, he often believes woman is cool; when he sees her warm, he thinks that she is so in the same way as himself. Women are undoubtedly to be found, shifting, like men, between sudden ardour and abrupt chill, and these women are ever the most exciting erotically. With the majority of women, however, love is, for the reasons already given, a constant warmth, a never-quenched fervour. But this makes the woman suffer through the man, who in the intervals of his passion is so much more tranquil than she, so little capable of her unremitting tenderness. Therefore she seldom finds herself occupying his thoughts and feelings so completely as he occupies hers.

A woman has aptly said that "it is precisely woman's greater sensuousness that makes her less sensuous than man: on account of motherhood —and all that it implies—she is sensuous, so to speak, from head to foot and chronically, while man is so only acutely and locally." If one transfers one's thoughts from erotics to motherhood, the truth of this will at once be clear: the feeling of motherhood is the most thoroughly sensuous and therefore the most thoroughly soulful of emotions; the same transport of the senses in which the mother exclaims that she could "eat" her child, expresses itself in the affection which would prompt her to die for it. But the author just quoted goes on to consider that even with men the erotic emotions could be transposed or released in many ways besides the one which to most of them still represents the whole expression of "love." What Rousseau revealed to his unbelieving contemporaries will perhaps one day become true in a psycho-physical sense: that a look may fill a lover with voluptuousness; that the great emotions are the chief conditions of love's happiness; that the lightest touch of the loved one's hand gives greater bliss than the possession of the most beautiful women without love—feelings which all great lovers in all times have confirmed, and as to which even the most contrary natures give the same testimony. The peasant's love, which knows nothing of caresses, comes lower in the scale of happiness than that of the cultivated person, who finds in love all the refined delights of the senses; and this again is far below the happiness of those who even in the encounter of two ideas or two moods can experience all the transport of love.

The conviction that sensuousness can only be controlled through being spiritualised is what directs those women who are now hoping to convert men, not to the duty of monogamy, but to the joy of unity.

Before woman's will could thus become conscious, her long struggle for liberation had to take place. Marriage had to cease to be a trade among the upper classes, as prostitution still is among the hungry lower classes. Love must have become free at least in the sense that a woman had no choice but charity from her family or forced sale to her husband; her personality must have attained consideration, not only for her value as a woman and dignity as a human being, but also individually. Not until—by her own labour and activity—she no longer exclusively depended on a man's courtship for both her livelihood and her life's destiny, did woman's salvation come to be, not "that the man wills" (Nietzsche), but that she herself can exercise her will. Language already reflects the change of custom. We seldom hear it asked nowadays of a woman: *Why has she not married?* but it is all the more frequently enquired: What has her love-story been, *since she has never married?*

Here also the line of development is a zigzag. Women sometimes act as though their whole liberation was of no avail. But in spite of much that is contradictory, the evolution of love—above all through the new woman's claims of love— is to him who stands high enough to have a full view of the situation, the most certain of realities.

Evidence of this evolution can be found in life as well as in literature, where it now takes every kind of form, from experiences translated into genuine poetry down to the productions which tempt one to think that these people have only loved to get "copy" for a book. The feminine fiction of the present day reminds one of a relief on a sacrificial altar in the Roman Forum, where the ox, the sheep, and the pig proceed in file to meet the knife. Hecatombs of these animals—in the likeness of husbands or lovers—are now sacrificed to Eros by the new woman. It may not be very long before the vow of fidelity is exchanged for an oath of silence and the marriage contract contains a provision that in case of a rupture love-letters are not to be used as literature.

No doubt it will ever remain true that a living book on love is never written with other ink than blood. But such books are not those which resemble a trial in which the prosecutor, witness, judge, and executioner are united in one person.

But whether powerful or weak, discreet or audacious, noble or ignoble—the new woman's books are always instructive to those who seek to follow the course of love's evolution.

.   ￮   .   .   .   .   .

The great danger to this evolution is that women never take sufficient account of sensuousness, nor men of spirituality. And it is especially woman who now onesidedly applies her own erotic nature—with its warm penetration, its completeness that frees it from temptation—as the ethical and erotic standard for that of man with its sudden heat, its dangerous incompleteness.

It is without doubt a feminine exaggeration to say that a "pure" woman only feels the force of her sex's need when she loves. But the enormous difference between her and man is that she cannot obey this need without loving. It is doubtless true that besides her love a woman may have a calling in life. But the profound distinction between her and man is at present this: that he more often gives of his best as a creator than as a lover—while for her the reverse is nearly always the case. And while thus man is appraised by himself and others according to his work, woman in her heart values herself—and wishes to be valued—according to her love. Not until this is fully appreciated and working for happiness does she feel her own worth. It is no doubt true that woman also wishes to be made happy by man through her senses. But while this longing in her not unfrequently awakes long after she already loves a man so that she could give her life for him, with man the desire to possess a woman often awakes before he even loves her enough to give his little finger for her. That with women love usually proceeds from the soul to the senses and sometimes does not reach so far; that with man it usually proceeds from the senses to the soul and sometimes never completes the journey—this is for both the most painful of the existing distinctions between man and woman. It is quite certain that both man and woman are humbled by their great love, and that the knowledge of having awakened reciprocal love turns even the freethinker into a believer in miracles. But man often conceals his humility behind a security which wounds the woman; she, on the other hand, hides hers in an uncertainty which wounds the man. And from this difference of instinct arises a new kind of complication, when man also has begun to desire an unspoken understanding on the part of woman; when he becomes convinced of her love only when she has guessed this and loved his reticence itself. But against this conscious and refined will of the modern man stands his hereditary instinct of a conqueror. And no woman is more sure of all the older as well as all the newer sufferings of love than she who really acts according to the words of her lover: that he will accept love only from a woman who herself has the courage to declare it to him. For, on the other side, the primitive desire of being captured survives in woman. And therefore also her strongest instincts come into conflict with her newly acquired courage in action.

For all these reasons it is difficult for a person

of the present day to believe himself loved or
to know that he is loved.

And it is this which will preserve to love its
excitement, even when the animal habits—with
pursuit on one side and flight on the other—have
gradually ceased. Conflict and the intoxication
of victory will always form a part of the vital
stimulation and pleasurable emotion of love,—
but they will be removed to a higher plane.
Man's forward rush to win a woman who perhaps
would not otherwise have remarked him; woman's
turning aside to egg the man on, or else to defend
in some measure the independent decision of her
feelings, will be transformed by the desire of each
to wait until the other has chosen. The erotic
tension will then be released in the contest for
the most refined expressions of sympathy, the
most convincing assurances of comprehension,
the most rapidly vibrating sensitiveness to the
other's moods, the fullest communication of
confidence. Victory will mean a constantly deeper
penetration into the other's nature, an ever richer
fulness and joy in the communication of one's
own; a constantly growing faith as regards what
is mysterious, and a like gratitude for what is
revealed. The stimulation will be renewed daily
in moods the transitions of which are as im-
perceptible as those of the evening sky from the
reddest gold to the purest white; in the border
lines of sympathy and antipathy, now fine as a
straw, now broad as a river. It will be renewed

through the test of innumerable uniting and re-
pellent emotions, as rapidly and irrevocably
decisive as the fall of a star in space, or of a silver
piece in the river.

And this tension of married life will not be
relaxed as now by the puffed-up arrogance of
proprietorship on the part of the man or by dull
complaisance on that of the woman. Since all
sense of happiness is connected with the exertion
of force to attain an end and with the equilibrium
that results from its attainment, it has been the
misfortune of love that courtship has absorbed
all the tension, and married life the subsequent
equilibrium. Only the sense of impending loss—
through life or through death—has, as a rule,
evoked a new spiritual tension. This, for reasons
mentioned above, has especially concerned the
husband. Wives have often suffered long from
the self-satisfied comfort of the daily life of
marriage before they have resigned the peace of
consummation, the equilibrium without movement, which was their dream of happiness.

But now women will no longer resign, nor
allow themselves to be cheated of life. More
and more their demand for a new love becomes
one with the demand for a new marriage, the
chief value of which will not, as now, consist
in "security and calm."

Woman knows—and man still more—that it is
in periods of calm, when all vital stimulation is
wanting, that the temptation comes to seek it in

new relations. But at the same time they are beginning to see that when one and the same feeling affords an unceasing excitement—through the desire of constantly attaining higher conditions of that feeling—then such temptation becomes of necessity less and less dangerous, simply because the human soul can only with great difficulty transfer the spiritual wealth it has accumulated in one place. Love in its impersonal form is movable capital, easily realised. In its personal form, on the other hand, it is fixed property, which increases in value the more one sinks in it, and which, owing to its very nature, is difficult to disperse.

Whenever a woman has captivated a man with a lifelong fascination, the secret has been that he has never exhausted her; that she "has not been one, but a thousand" (G. Heiberg); not a more or less beautiful variation on the eternal theme of the female sex, but a music in which he has found the wealth of inexhaustibility, the enticement of impenetrability, while she has given him an incomparable happiness of the senses. The more the modern woman acquires courage for a love as rich in the senses as in the soul, the more complicated and self-inclosed her personality becomes, the more will she obtain that power which is now only the fortunate advantage of the exceptional.

Man tells woman that her new way of love is opposed not only to man's nature but to the welfare of the new generation.

She answers that great love doubtless betrays a childish lack of understanding in all departments of worldly wisdom, but that in its own sphere— with all its riddles and problems—it is godlike wisdom, the gift of divining, the power of working miracles; that the only thing needful in order that love may re-create the race is that it shall become an even greater vital force, through mankind investing it with more and more of its spiritual power.

.   .   .   .

Even at the present day couples are to be found who are inspired by great love.   They show an insatiable desire for all the riches of life, so as to have the means of being regally lavish towards each other.   Neither defrauds the other of so much as a dewdrop.   The fervour they give one another, the freedom they possess through one another, make the space that surrounds them warm and ample.   Love is constantly giving them new impulses, new powers and new employment for their powers, whether these are directed inwards to home life or outwards to that of society.   And thus the happiness, which for themselves is the source of life, becomes also a tributary stream by which the happiness of all is raised.   The power of great love to enhance a person's value for mankind can only be compared with the glow of religious faith or the creative joy of genius, but surpasses both in universal life-enhancing properties. Sorrow may sometimes make a person more tender towards the sufferings of others, more actively benevolent than happiness with its concentration upon self. But sorrow never led the soul to those heights and depths, to those inspirations and revelations of universal life, to that kneeling gratitude before the mystery of life, to which the piety of great love leads it.

Like faith, this piety sanctifies all things. It gives significance to attention bestowed on one's self, since

> . . . *If I am dear to some one else*
> *Then must I be to myself more dear.*

It combines the most trifling things of life into an intelligent whole. He who is loved and loves in this way bears the same stamp as the Christian mystic, who grows ever clearer and yet more rich in mystery; ever fuller of life and yet calmer; ever more introspective and yet more radiant.

There are some who think that this state is visionary and unnatural.

But the truth—for everyone who has beheld it—is that *le vrai amour est simple comme un bas relief antique*. Such a relief, which before all others corresponds to the image, is to be found in the Naples museum. It shows a man and a woman, standing still on either side of a tree. An artist of antiquity may have already foreseen all the significance that a son of our time interpreted, when he placed a youth and a maiden beneath the tree of life with a cloven apple in their hands: *they divided the apple of life and ate it together. . . .*

For a couple who share it thus, every-day life will scintillate with little delights as a wheatfield at midsummer with cornflowers; and the high days will be white with joy as a spring garden with fruit blossoms. A couple who live thus will be able to play so that beyond their sport will always be the calm of tenderness; to smile so that behind their smiles will always lie an easily-aroused seriousness. Unless death interrupts them they will thus build up their life together as the Gothic cathedrals were built: buttress upon buttress, arch above arch, ornament within ornament, until finally the gilding of the topmost spire catches the last rays of the sunset.

.   .   .   .

Thus great love already gives to two human beings what only completed development can give to mankind as a whole: unity between senses and soul, desire and duty, self-assertion and self-devotion, between the individual and the race, the present moment and the future.

This condition—in which every advantage gained becomes a gift and every gift a profit; in which are united a continual emotion and a calm peace—is even now that which dreamers await as that of the third kingdom.[1]

[1] In England, Tennyson, in *The Princess*, was the first to give to "the new woman" her name and to speak of her objects, and many others began in the middle of the last century indirectly to develop the idea of love, especially Elizabeth Barrett Browning, the sisters Brontë, and Miss Muloch among women writers. Robert Browning, George Meredith, and other great poets among the men have also furthered it indirectly. In later days, George Egerton in *Rosa Amorosa* and Edward Carpenter in *Love's Coming of Age* have, in their different ways, given a remarkable treatment of the evolution of love. *Woman Free* by Ellis Ethelmer, *A Noviciate for Marriage* by Edith M. Ellis, *The Woman Who Did* by Grant Allen, belong to the same group of writings.

CHAPTER III

LOVE'S FREEDOM

THE most delicate test of a person's sense of morality is his power of interpreting ambiguous signs of the times in the ethical sphere; for only the profoundly moral can discover the dividing line, sharp as the edge of a sword, between new morality and old immorality.

In our time ethical obtuseness betrays itself first and foremost by the condemnation of those young couples who freely unite their destinies. The majority does not perceive the advance in morality which this implies in comparison with the code of so many men, who without responsibility—and without apparent risk—purchase the repose of their senses.

Those young men who choose "free love" know that bought love may destroy their finest instruments of mental activity; that it may result in injury to the wife as well as in the danger either of degeneracy on the part of the children, or of childishness, and may finally bring about their own premature downfall.

But they also know that these results may not

occur and that, on the other hand, they may
suffer spiritually by curbing their personality
and ruining their possibilities of single-hearted
love. At the same time they despise their fathers'
less dangerous, but for that reason more unprin-
cipled, expedient for sexual satisfaction, the
seduction of women of the people, women with
whom they never had any thought of community
of life.

"Free love," on the other hand, gives them an
enhancement of life which they consider that
they gain without injuring anyone. It answers
to their idea of love's chastity, an idea which is
justly offended by the incompleteness of the
period of engagement with all its losses in the
freshness and frankness of emotion. When their
soul has found another soul, when the senses of
both have met in a common longing, then they
consider that they have a right to the full unity
of love, although compelled to secrecy, since the
conditions of society render early marriage impossible. They are thus freed from a wasteful
struggle, which would neither give them peace
nor inner purity and which would be doubly
hard for them, since they have attained the end—
love—for the sake of which self-control would
have been imposed.

.   .   .   .

When in this connection we speak of youth,
we can mean only the young men and girls of the

upper classes. For among the rest of society the free union of love has long been the custom. Our working classes—as those of many European countries—simply use the same freedom which the custom of society allows to many extra-European peoples. Ethnographical research shows that this is no new degraded habit, but, on the contrary, a relic of primitive customs. Among certain extra-European peoples—for example, one in north Burmah — this custom was accompanied by definite guarantees for the possible children. Young people may without hindrance unite freely, and separate if they do not find their feeling deep enough for continued life together. In the contrary case, they marry, and after marriage infidelity is as good as unknown. If the girl becomes a mother, without a marriage following, the man is obliged to secure the child through a sum paid to the girl's father, who is then answerable for it.

It is from similar sexual customs that the majority of our Swedish people derive theirs—that people which in royal and academic speeches has gained the character of being "the most law-abiding and loyal" in the world. Failing a deeper love or a sense of responsibility, these customs involve the abandonment of the woman, infanticide, and sometimes the prostitution of the woman, when she has passed from one man to another; finally the encumbrance of society with the children of different fathers to whom she has given life, besides the neglect of the children. And the custom leads—even in those cases where both love and responsibility are present, but where the lovers are too young—to the enfeebling of themselves and of the children, and to the great mortality of the latter. Not only hard labour and scanty food, but also a premature sexual life, contribute to hinder the full bodily development of the lower classes and to hasten their growing old.

But by the side of these evil effects there are good ones. In most cases, a young couple's prospect of parentage leads their relatives to make their marriage possible. When this cannot take place immediately, the daughter and her child stay with the parents of one of them, or she leaves the child with them, while she on her side, and the young man on his, work for the future. Even when the man has not always been disposed for marriage, their common life of work and the sense of parentage soon show a uniting force. Such couples who have come together in youth probably have better prospects for their life together than an upper-class couple, worn out by a long engagement, in which the bride has a full right to her orange-flowers—to say nothing of the health contributed by the man of the people in comparison with the majority of men of the upper class, who have bought their injurious substitute for marriage while waiting for the promotion which should make marriage possible. One thing at any rate is certain: that matrimonial fidelity among the people is as great as freedom before marriage is unlimited. That the free love of the peasant and working class ends, as a rule, in marriage, often depends on the fact that public opinion supports this as a point of morality. But—in those cases where love itself does not bring about community of life—the sense of parentage and the need of a helpmate are as decisive as public opinion; for even among the erotically undeveloped the need of cohabitation makes itself felt for other purposes than the instinct of the race. It is the desire for such community of life—with its sharing of pleasure and hardship, sorrow and attention—which makes it really uniting. Where no such desire exists, the relationship becomes immoral from the point of view of life-enhancement. If this standard of morality be not adhered to, free love among the upper class—as among the lower class—will, it is true, contribute to the abolition of prostitution, but not to the exaltation of mankind through a greater love, a higher morality.

For if, on the one hand, the sexual customs of the lower class allow more right than those of the upper class to the direct claims of nature, on the other hand, the customs of the latter still provide the same opportunities for the elevation into love of the instinct which, from an historical and ethnographical point of view, has everywhere

been provided by self-control. Among those
nations with which sexual connections begin
early, morals are, as a rule, loose, and where morals
are loose, the emotion of love has small importance.
The control of sensuality develops the deeper
feelings of love. We need not go to the nations of
the past, or to existing extra-European peoples,
but only to the town and country labourers of
our own and other European lands, to see how
the feelings become lax and feeble, the senses coarse
and greedy, when they have acquired the habit
of satisfying physical hunger before that of the
soul has awakened. The miserable conditions
of dwelling among the lower classes are enough
by themselves to rob sexual life of its discretion;
immature age or the tie of blood is frequently
no hindrance to unchastity, and its consequences
—coarseness and lack of responsibility towards
one another as well as towards the offspring—
at times take hideous forms. The first condition
therefore for love's freedom is that the freedom
shall concern love, the most universal sign of
which is the desire of continued community of
life. As this sign is, as a rule, to be found among
young people of the educated class who now claim
love's freedom, they are thus far within their
rights, as also are the young people of the lower
class when they use the same freedom and as
a result form many excellent connubial unions.
We could with every reason—and with more
reason—draw the same conclusions with regard

to the upper class, if it were not the case that among these love has become a so much more penetrating force. While the majority of the working class—for even there a minority with more refined erotic feelings is to be found,—in addition to the satisfaction of its instincts, contents itself with a capable and devoted comrade to bear its burden, the developed man or woman of the present day has deeper erotic needs. It is the satisfaction of these that is often missed by a youthful decision in life; for even when youthful love is soulful—and nearly all youthful love can so be described—it is nevertheless in most cases a longing for love rather than love, a craving for experience rather than the new life itself. And therefore the erotic feelings of early youth are founded upon the illusions which make a Romeo lament the harshness of Rosalind a moment before meeting Juliet, and a Titania to fondle Bottom's ass's ears. Never in after life has the world such a marvellous glamour as when the first dream of love has swathed all contours in its opalescent mists of sunrise, but—never do we so easily go astray. It may happen that the lifting of the mists will disclose the most beautiful landscape. But there are more chances that the course one has steered in the fog will end in one of many shipwrecks. Therefore the " 'teens" should be the age of the erotic prologue, not of the drama. For this reason also, that no one can decide to what degree the transient may injure the final relations of life; nor to what degree great love may be missed or spoiled, when accidental love has anticipated its rights, even though this happened in the full and frank belief that the accident was destiny.

No part of the art of living is more important for youth than developing in one's self the knowledge of a predestined fellowship which permits of waiting. People curse the hazards which separate lovers. But it is less the hazards which separate than those which unite at the wrong time, that ought to be cursed. First youth seldom loses in love anything but what is unimportant; the reality shows itself—when both are free— as what cannot be lost. Those who belong to each other come together in the end; those whom chance parts, never belonged to each other. A man may fail of happiness by finding out too late what is real in himself or others; not by abstaining from action before this discovery. Therefore youth should wait before making decisive plunges into its own and others' destinies, since great love may resemble the Japanese divinity, to pray to whom more than once is a crime, since it answers prayer only once.

．　．　．　．　．　．

But even when a young couple has the profoundest mutual sense of the permanence of their feeling, it does not follow that their love ought immediately to involve the rights and the accompanying reponsibilities of a later age. For young trees break or bend under too heavy a weight of fruit, nor does the fruit attain its full value on trees that are too young. Here nature herself is the opponent of youthful marriages. Let us leave on one side the possibility of people being unwillingly bound together through the consequences of an over-hasty union, and deal only with the certainty that the young people in a profound sense continue to belong to each other. They will nevertheless as surely suffer through the possible or probable consequence of their action, the child. Their consciousness of not being able to bear this consequence will doubtless make them try to avoid it. But this is an ugly beginning to a life of love. Many consider that it also involves dangers. For those who have already given to the race their tribute of new life, or who ought never thus to give, the choice must be free between the two dangers. But for the opening of a life in common this resource may be equally unsafe and unwholesome, since the racial instinct as a whole is left unaccomplished. And thus love is robbed of a part of its spiritual meaning, and sensuousness of its natural restraint. But even if these consequences do not follow, "failure" may yet be the most fortunate occurrence in these cases— and also the most usual. How then does it appear in reality?

In most cases young people have entered into their free union because they have seen no possibility of an open marriage. They are the less able to support a child, as they themselves are supported by others, in so far as they are not keeping themselves by running into debt or by badly-paid labour. In the latter case, the child means a further hindrance to life, the more so as it must involve for the woman a diminution, perhaps a total loss, of her powers of work. It is therefore the young people's relatives who have to help. And, when this is possible, the form it takes is that the lovers are obliged to marry and receive the help that the parents can afford. In the case of the poorer classes, this is comparatively slight, as the newly-married pair frequently stay with the parents of one of them. But in the upper classes, on the other hand, they prefer, with full reason, to form their own home, and then there ensue the inevitable cares of child and housekeeping, however simple the latter may be. But these will be a hindrance to their studies, their freedom of movement, and general development. They become cage-birds, at best fed by their parents; bound by duties during the years which should have been wholly devoted to their self-development.

Thus premature marriages, whether lawful or unlawful in form, may arrest in their growth countless excellent forces, and ruin the full possibilities of happiness in later years. It is true that the early union will have stilled a powerful longing in the young people's being. But they soon find out that it has at the same time rendered difficult, perhaps impossible, the satisfaction of their desire of knowledge, the taste for research, the creative power, and freedom of action in other, more or less important, directions; for example, in the love of travel which is felt by all young people of spirit, and in the love of pleasure in a wholesome sense. The young mother's beauty probably never attains the fulness designed by nature, and she is destined to grow old before her time. And even when her children are not weaklings—as is most frequently the case— they do not afford her the happiness they might have brought if they had been longed for; if she had not had to sacrifice to them her youthful joy, the fulness of her strength and beauty, but, on the contrary, had felt this enhanced through motherhood. Above all, the children do not receive the bringing-up which the mother might give them at a somewhat maturer age.

Even if a pair of lovers are themselves willing to be subject to the hindrances imposed in most cases by a premature union, this must be their own affair; but for the child there must be loss.

In order that the child may enjoy the full possibility of favourable conditions of life—in birth as well as in bringing-up—in northern Europe the age of the woman at marriage should be at least twenty, that of the man about twenty-five.

This is the period of full maturity, and until this age is reached youth itself gains by complete abstinence, in order by its marriage at the proper age, in the words of Tacitus, to "let the children witness to their parents' strength." In the opinion of most younger men of science it is less and less probable that acquired qualities are inherited. Others, again, who have defended or still hold this view, have maintained with more or less force—as a condition of the progress of the race—that procreation should not take place until the activity and surroundings of the parents have acquired a definite character. Acute psychologists who have given attention to woman's nature, consider that it does not attain its full spiritual maturity before about the age of thirty, while she then still possesses her youthfulness unimpaired; that until then her countenance does not acquire its true completeness of expression; that her individuality, intellectual powers, and passion are then for the first time fully awake; that only these properties can inspire deep love, and that thus woman gains everything by a later marriage, whereas the result of early marriages, where the husband has to "educate" his wife, is frequently, as a witty lady has remarked, that he is destined instead to educate a wife for someone else.

Nor is it only narrow-viewed preachers of morality, but men of science with the broadest outlook in these matters, who declare ever more positively that abstinence until the age of maturity is in a high degree favourable to the physico-psychical strength and elasticity of both sexes, and that such favourable effect may sometimes extend beyond this age.

To this direct gain must also be added the indirect one: that all self-control for a greater and gladdening end—and what end can be greater than this one?—gives to the will that force and to the personality that joy in its strength which will later be all-important in every other department of life.

Such an advancement of the age of marriage will probably not be opposed by many women. Young girls have learned by the experience of others, and now there is scarcely to be found a woman married before the age of twenty who has not discovered that it was premature before she reaches twenty-five. Moreover it is seldom the woman's desire that hurries on a secret union; for, in the absence of any admixture of Southern blood, it is a long time, many years indeed in some cases, before the senses of the Northern woman are consciously awakened.

But the young girl loves and wishes to satisfy the longing from which she sees her lover suffer, the more so when she comes to know that the demonstrations of affection which have satisfied her needs have increased his suffering. And therefore she silences her own innermost consciousness, which adjures her to wait.

This silencing of the inner voice not infrequently has for its result that the two souls are
never fully united, since the senses have stood
in their way; or in Nietzsche's words: *Die Sinn-
lichkeit übereilt oft das Wachsthum der Liebe so dass
die Wurzeln schwach bleiben und leicht auszureissen
sind.* In every pure feeling of morality, a young
woman who thus surrenders herself in love stands
immeasurably above the engaged girl of good
family who allows the man she says she loves to
toil alone during the best years of his young
manhood, so as at last to prepare for her the
position which her own ideas of life, or those of
her family, demand. But higher than either
stands the young woman who has known how
to preserve the freshness of love's springtime.
And when women's own claims of happiness have
become more refined, when their insight into
nature is more profound, when they thus become
fit to take the lead in erotic development—which
in Scandinavia during the last generation has
unfortunately been in man's hands,—then they
will also understand this. They must prolong
the happy time when love is unspoken, unfettered
by promises, full of expectation and intuition.
And they need not on this account give up the
comradeship in sport, in walks, and studies, which
is wholesome in itself, cheerful and preparatory
to happiness, but which now leads to premature
unions. Women will come to understand when
they ought to be on their guard, in order that the

sufferings of the period of waiting may be minimised. They will shorten the secret engagement,
and they will do away with the public engagement,
with the dangers both involve of attenuation of
the feelings, and with the latter's profanation
of love's privacy.

If the youth of the North does not feel its
soul in harmony with this mood, its life will have
lost its springtime—without receiving in exchange
a longer summer; for premature warmth has
its revenge in life as in nature. To experience
fully the peculiar beauty of each season of life
is the attribute of a profounder comprehension
of life's meaning—and this truth is not less true
because a Juliet was only fourteen. What
Shakespeare has revealed in her is not the force
of early love, incomparable with any other power;
rather does he show the love, instantaneous,
fatal, overcoming all obstacles, which—equally
powerful at every age—yet shows its force most
unmistakably when it drives two human beings
to death just at the time when the yet unlived
life they have before them makes the thought of
death most full of horror. Only such an exception can anticipate in springtime the flowering
of summer. It is therefore not from the whole
necessity of their nature, but from attaching too
much importance to one side of it, that many
young people now have the idea that love loses
its fire and its purity by waiting until the organism can bear its fruits. Nothing is more

certain than that the chastity of perfect love is
conditioned towards unity by the will of the
soul and the senses. But this chaste will may
be found before or after the possibility of its
realisation. And love's chastity may then show
itself as well in waiting for complete unity as in
altogether renouncing the same.

It is true that a young man will not experience
the intoxication of love at twenty-five as he
experienced it some years earlier. But if he
feels it for the first time at about twenty-five,
then— according to all the laws of physico-
psychical sensations of pleasure—just at the
height of his sexual existence, and after years of
self-control and labour for happiness, he ought
to be able to experience a richer vital intoxication
than he would have been capable of in the earlier
years of his youth.

It is incontestable that premature erotic claims
are less the result of the needs of the organism
than of the influence of the imagination upon it.
Only a new healthiness and beauty in the method
of treating erotic questions will gradually re-
fashion the now over-excited imagination, calm
erotic curiosity, and strengthen the sense of
responsibility towards self and towards the new
generation, so that premature sexual life may
lose its attraction for the young.

.   .   .   .

All this however concerns only immature youth.

When, on the other hand, a pair of lovers have reached the age referred to as that of full maturity, and their complete union can only further their own life-enhancement and that of the race, then they commit a sin against themselves and the race if they do not enter into union.

But not even in such a case is secret love desirable, in which the woman goes in constant uneasiness for the possible child, and yet—after the first period of happiness—in a growing desire not only for it but for all the other conditions of life which might give sun and fresh air to her feeling, confined, as it were, in forcing-house or cellar.

In most cases it is only a question of time how soon this secret happiness will languish, since the risk is almost entirely on the woman's side and the man is too much in the position of one who receives. For human nature is such that this makes one hard; and love is such that this makes one weak. If the man is not hardened thereby, it is because he is extremely sensitive. And again, if he is so, then the secret union, in which the woman gives most, becomes just as humiliating to the man as a marriage in which the wife keeps him by her fortune or her work. The woman, on her side, will be the more difficult to please, will make higher claims upon the love which is to compensate her for the home and for the child, the two interests through which she would first have felt her powers developed in every direction, or, in other words, would have gained complete happiness.

For a woman's best qualities, even as a mistress, are inseparably bound up with the motherhood in her nature.

There has been and is an infinity of talk about the degradation of woman by her complete surrender without marriage; that the man thus depreciates his loved one in his own eyes and himself in hers; that he is selfish in proposing a union which injures the virtue and modesty of love; that he "sacrifices" the woman to his desire; and so on without end. All this talk is worthless, simply because a woman who loves feels herself degraded neither in her own eyes nor in those of the man; because she has no idea of a "sacrifice," but of giving and receiving. For she desires the completeness of love with a much profounder will than man, since her erotic needs are stronger—although calmer—than his. But she is frequently—and often for a long time— unconscious that her profound desire to be made happy at any price through love nevertheless refers at bottom to the child. The man sees only the woman's longing and his happy smile not unfrequently tells of an easy victory. But he does not know—for a long time she does not know herself—when her love becomes a sacrifice; when she begins to feel her position as a degrading one. The man does not see what her smile conceals; he does not understand her when she is silent, and perhaps he does not listen when she speaks. He thus believes her to be still satisfied, when she has begun to hunger for more.

Woman's need of living and suffering for the race gives her love a purer glow, a higher flame, a profounder will, a more tireless fidelity than man's. The unsatisfied longing for motherhood is released in an ever warmer, ever more self-sacrificing affection for the loved one. Man, on the other hand, who has less and less opportunity of giving, thereby comes to love less and less. When the woman discovers this, she begins to remember what she has given. And then strife, sin, sorrow, and their wages—death—have entered into what was perhaps at the beginning a genuine love; a love which might have had a full and fair life, if it had had the unifying and purifying influence of a common end, a great purpose.

When love possesses nothing of this kind, its power of motion is directed against itself. The feelings of both parties then become the object of a game like that of *parfiler*, which was the rage in the eighteenth century, and which consisted in drawing the threads out of worn-out cloth of gold. The feelings are torn up, ripped open, tied together; tangled, disentangled, and wound up. But feelings are roots, not threads—not even gold threads. It is in the great, wholesome realities of life that the creative force of love, like that of art, finds the productive earth for its growth. Torn out of this earth, love, as surely as art, is like a tree blown down by a spring storm, which may indeed put forth leaves this spring—though all its roots are exposed to the air—but which will not live through the summer.

Clandestine love is in this respect like an upper-class marriage without children and without common pursuits, although the self-sacrificing, self-supporting, clandestine mistress stands far above the kept wife, fashionable and full of pretension.

Thus it is not abstract ideas of duty, but real selfishness, which is one with real morality, that will teach youth to understand the meaning of Spinoza's profound thought, made still more profound by the doctrine of evolution: that "the sexual love which has its origin in what is external and accidental, may easily be turned to hate, a kind of madness that is nourished on discord; but that love, on the other hand, is lasting, *which has its cause in freedom of soul and in the will to bear and bring up children.*"

Through the religion of life and its countless influences, through gradual, scarcely perceptible transformations, will love's freedom more and more come to mean freedom for enduring love.

The spirit of the age, working through the standards of literature and public opinion, transforms with infallible certainty thoughts and feelings in the direction in which the strongest lead them.

It now rests with the young to be these strong ones.

With the growing desire for a many-sided enhancement of life, parentage will also become an ever more important condition of this enhancement. Young people will be no more willing to depreciate by a premature sexual life the value of those years which ought to be devoted to furthering their individual growth, than they will be to diminish their joy of parentage by putting a weak and unwelcome child into the world. For they will wish to possess all happiness fully and frankly. The expected child ought to give them beautiful dreams, not tormenting uneasiness; it must be carried in rejoicing, not in unwilling, arms, and must have received life from the fulness of happiness—not from a mischance.

Here as everywhere, what is the most genuine and lasting happiness for the individual is also for the moral enhancement the race.

When two lovers have this desire and have reached that maturity, when the will has a right to realisation, and is in full agreement with the health and beauty of themselves, of the new generation, and of society, it is right that they should come together, even though it may not be possible for their pure desire of common life and common work to take the form of marriage.

For him who has ears to hear, these figures will speak: they show that the average age of unlawful unions is the right age appointed by nature for marriage. Thus the statistics of Sweden for 1900 show that 6340 "illegitimate" children were born of mothers between 20 and 25 years old, while those born of mothers under 20 were 2028, and of mothers between 25 and 30, 3857. Another eloquent fact is that, even before the extension of compulsory military service, the highest figures of emigration, for men as well as women, occur among the unmarried within a year or two on either side of twenty.

By unlawful unions, the race is often defrauded of the children's fitness for life, which is ruined by the unfavourable conditions in which the children are brought up; and by emigration the best blood of the country is drained away. And even if the latter is occasioned by a variety of causes, no thoughtful person could omit to reckon among them the difficulty of marrying at the right time. Another equally eloquent circumstance fully supported by statistical evidence is this: that prostitution increases in direct proportion as the general social conditions and the economical situation are unfavourable to marriage, and that it decreases as marriage is facilitated. And the majority of prostitutes—as of unmarried mothers—are of the right age for marriage.

The youth of the upper classes ought not, however, in their struggle against actual conditions, to descend to the irresponsibility of the lower classes. Educated young people must set an example to the rest, not only by entering into their matrimonial alliances at the right time, but also in a way that is unimpeachable as regards the claims of the race and of society. The young have a perfect right—like their contemporaries among the people—to assume the responsibility of founding a home, which may be denied to them, before the child is expected. But they have only a right to this kind of defiance if they are willing, as soon as they are able, themselves to provide for the new creatures who will one day replace them in the race. But above all things, educated young people must also take part in the social reform which—speaking broadly—will be the only solution of the marriage question.

Instead of defending "free love," which is a much-abused term capable of many interpretations, we ought to strive for the freedom of love; for while the former has come to imply freedom for any sort of love, the latter must only mean freedom for a feeling which is worthy the name of love.

This feeling, it may be hoped, will gradually win for itself the same freedom in life as it already possesses in poetry. The flowering, as well as the budding of love will then be a secret between the lovers, and only its fruit will be a matter between them and society. As always, poetry has pointed out the way to development. A great poet has seldom sung of lawfully-wedded happiness, but often of free and secret love; and in this respect too the time is coming when there will no longer be one standard of morality for poetry and another for life. Even the poet of

Sakuntala calls that love the most beautiful
which gives itself freely in the "Gandoarva marriage," sanctified only by the fulness of emotion.
But even then the danger was recognised of

> . . . *unknown heart closing against unknown heart.*

Even then it was uneasiness about the fate of
the child which coupled responsibility to society
with love's freedom.

The new moral consciousness is thus an old
thing. But it must nevertheless be called new,
since it is only beginning to be wide-spread. It
is becoming plain to more and more people that
a man or woman—whether married or free—
does wrong to the nobility of self by giving himself or herself to one who is at heart a stranger;
it is more and more becoming intuitively felt
that it is the sense of home in another soul which
gives devotion its sanctity.

The suitor who—dressed for the occasion—
went first to the father to declare his feelings
for the daughter is already such an old-fashioned
type that it is past ridicule. The brilliant wedding festival will soon come to be regarded as
ridiculous, then unbecoming, and finally immoral.
And—like other survivals of the time when marriage was the affair of the family—it has already
begun to disappear, in the same degree as love
has developed. Lovers are less and less inclined
to tolerate a spying upon their finest feelings;
they are increasingly anxious to rescue these from

the prying fingers of society, of family, and of friends. More and more is love venerated as part of nature's mysticism, whose course no outsider can determine, whose sensitive manifestations and uncertain possibilities no one may disturb, a mysticism within whose sphere a fixed time-table would be out of place.

How can Love, one of the great lords of life, take its freedom from the hands of society any more than Death, the other, can do so? "Love and Death, which meet like the two sides of a mountain-ridge, whose highest points are ever where they come together" (G. Rodenbach); Love and Death, which—one with the wings of the dawn, the other with those of the night sky—overshadow the portals between earthly life and the two great darknesses which enclose it—only these two powers are comparable in majesty.

But while there is only one death, there are many sorts of love. Death never plays. When all love becomes equally serious, it will also possess death's right to choose its own time.

. . . .

In the springtime of love, parents can be of significance to their children only when they feel reverence for the marvel which is accomplished in their presence. But it seldom happens that parents have previously been so sensitive that their children then treat them as perfect friends. The period of youth is commonly full of strife, which is brought about partly by the parents' desire of remodelling their children according to their own ideas—against which children are only now venturing to defend themselves,— partly by the children's desire to assert their own ideals, which are always different from those of the parents, for otherwise "the new generation would own no title to exist" (G. Brandes). Parents might save for themselves and for their children endless suffering, if they understood from the beginning that children are significant exclusively as new personalities, with new gods and new aims; with the right to protect their own nature, with the duty of finding out new paths, without forfeiting the right of being respected by their parents in the same degree as the latter on their side retain the right of being venerated by their children—for the best of what they are or have been, what they will or have willed. The only right that parents ought never to renounce in dealing with their grown-up children is that of giving to them the benefit of their own experience. But in so doing they must remember what a poor loving heart forgets easiest of all: that not even their own most bitter experience will be able to save their children from making sad discoveries for themselves. They will probably avoid their parents' mistakes, but only to make others of their own! The only

Love's Freedom

real power a father or mother possesses over the child's fate—but indeed this is an immense one—is to fill the home with his or her strong and beautiful personality; with love and joy, with work and culture; and thus to make the atmosphere so rich and so pure that the children may calmly delay their choice and have a high standard to choose by.

But if parents see that in spite of this their children are tempted to confuse accident with destiny, then they are called upon to show an almost godlike wisdom in order to divert the danger. In most cases, parents consciously or unconsciously play into the hands of the accidental, while they raise obstacles against what is predestined. Their warnings are not directed against what is silent and has nothing to give; no, they advance mean and paltry reasons which the young oppose with all that is best in their nature. Thus they silence their own uneasy intuitions, which their parents might have induced them to follow if they themselves had had a clearer perception of what was essential.

Even in homes where there is most affection, the children, in their stormy period of springtime, are as riddles which their parents often try in vain to solve. A young soul never suffers so much as during the solution of its own riddle. But only such a father or mother as has succeeded in becoming renewed and rejuvenated through his or her children will be able to help them in the solution.   Otherwise the result will only be that the parents on their side will bring stones to the wall which the children on theirs are building ever higher.

Even parents who have not grown into crabbed working-machines; who do not use their authority because they have the means of power, but only because they possess spiritual superiority; who in their home let their children have not only freedom for gladness but also the joy of freedom, will nevertheless many a time fall short in the endeavour to render their superiority serviceable to the children, or by their broad-mindedness to liberate them from the one-sidedness of youth. And in that case they must give up the struggle; for it will not improve the difficulties of the present, but only destroy future chances of understanding.

In the three greatest decisions to be taken in life—those of the fundamental view of life, of one's life work, and of love—each soul must be its own counsel.   In these matters, parents must restrict their authority to saving their children from vital dangers; but they must also be able to discover such dangers, and to differentiate profound from superficial needs, the high-road from the by-road.   If their parents are not capable of this, then the children must perform their duty to themselves and to life, by — sooner or later—going their own way.

If, like a young couple in a similar case, the

children can "smile and be silent," while show-ing their seriousness in their actions, then they will probably be capable of educating their parents. In that case, it will frequently be apparent that the heart of a father or mother was stronger, their soul greater than either child or parents had believed before the test was made. If, on the other hand, it should prove that the faults and prejudices of the parents were the sole cause of the conflict, then these faults and prejudices are not entitled to any more respect because they are those of a father or mother.

But even if it should be the case that the par-ents have no souls capable of profound feeling, but only hearts which can bleed—it is nevertheless the duty of the child towards itself, and towards past and future generations, to give to its own nature the highest possible perfection through love. Parents are only a link in the infinite chain of the race: it is the blood of hundreds of thou-sands that the parents have transmitted to their children, who now in their turn are to pass it on. Children have higher duties towards all these dead and unborn beings than they have towards the single couple who became their father and mother. It behooves the young to let all these dead ones live again as fully as possible through the development of their own being and in the blood of their children. A human being may owe a greater debt of gratitude for his own nature to his grandmother's heart or to his grandfather's imagination than to his own narrow-hearted mother or unintelligent father. So far is it from being an invariable duty to bring joy to the parents, that it may be one's duty to bring them sorrow—in order to bring joy to one's successors. It is a good thing to honour one's father and mother; but the commandment which Moses forgot is more important still: to honour one's son and daughter even before they are born.

When the sense of the dead and of the unborn becomes a conscious motive of human action, through being a force in human emotion, then the claim of the parents to decide their children's life—as well as the claim of the latter to decide that of their parents—will gradually fall to pieces before the majesty of the past and of the future.

.　　.　　.　　.　　.　　.　　.

It results from the foregoing that any doctrine of morality is of little worth which does not involve the need of providing the means of marriage for healthy persons between the ages of twenty and thirty; a possibility which was possessed without exception by the Germanic ancestors whose example of abstinence is now appealed to.

So long as increasingly difficult examinations, the scale of pay in government departments, the division of profits in business, and the general rate of living, stand in the way of young people's chances of marriage, things will remain as they are, in spite of an increasing minority of men who, for their own personality's sake or for that of their love, maintain abstinence until marriage or remain celibate.

The abolition of this sacrifice to the state of society and civilisation is a matter of sufficient importance to the individual, but of infinitely greater importance to society, whose forces are now being wasted by the effects of immorality and checked by those of morality: society, whose strength depends to such a great degree upon young and healthy parents for the new generation.

Even under actual conditions, the chances of marriage for young people might be increased by a judicious realisation of the "own home" idea in country districts; by a shortening of the university course; by the raising of salaries in the lower ratings (they appear at present to be calculated upon the satisfaction of sexual needs through prostitution); by the granting of pensions at an earlier age, so that the higher rates of pay may be reached in middle age—when the burden of educating children is heaviest;—and by increased exemption from taxation for men and women who have to provide for a family.

In addition, a thorough change in social pretensions and habits of life is necessary, above all in the large towns, where building societies for the erection of small flats with common kitchen, offices for providing domestic help, paid by the hour, and co-operative societies for the cheaper supply of the necessaries of life, might considerably assist young people in establishing their homes. It is, however, not only this, but also communal employment that must be promoted, if men of about twenty-five are to be ready to enter upon their various occupations and—after thirty-five years in the service of the State—to be entitled to their pensions, but at the same time under the obligation to retire, except in the rare cases where special talent renders a person indispensable in some leading position. The experience a man has gained, and the strength that is left to him, would find full employment in other social affairs or in personal interests.

It is not against immoral literature, but against the Treasury, the Budget Committee and against private employers of labour that moral reformers should draw up their resolutions. So long as a business man is able to make two or three millions a year net profit while of those employed in his office scarcely two or three are so paid that they can think of marriage before the age of thirty; so long as the head of a government department can reply, to the application of a class of officials for an increase of salary in order to facilitate marriage, by a gracious promise of more frequent leave to go to town; or an employer refuse a female employee's demand for a raise of salary with a gallant reference to the ease with which—

with her advantages of appearance—she might increase her income; so long will the marriage question remain unsolved.

.   .   .   .

All preaching of morality to youth which does not at the same time condemn the state of society that favours immorality, but makes the realisation of youthful love an impossibility, is more than stupidity, it is a crime.

So long as the present low rates of pay and uncertain conditions of employment continue, the blood of men will continue more and more to be corrupted, and that of women to be impoverished, while waiting for the marriage which might have given to society excellent children born of healthy and happy parents. So long as societies thus fatuously sacrifice their highest values will every other kind of social reform be nothing but a work of Penelope, of which the night will undo what the day has done.

CHAPTER IV

LOVE'S SELECTION

In the foregoing chapter it was insisted that love's freedom in the procreation of new life must have a downward limit, in that this freedom can only be allowed to those who have attained the age of sexual maturity. But it ought also to have an upward limit, since a great difference in age between father and mother—like the advanced age of one of them—offers unfavourable conditions for the health, strength, and upbringing of the children. And as, for reasons given in the last chapter, the lawful age of marriage for both sexes must be put at twenty-one, a difference in age of twenty-five years should be the highest the law ought to allow in one or the other case.

No one who sees the meaning of life in its advance towards higher forms would dispute nowadays the obvious duty of not transmitting serious diseases the hereditariness of which is already ascertained by science. But as this has only been ascertained in a few cases, legal hindrances as regards the many doubtful cases would be not only a—perhaps meaningless—interference

with the life of the individual, but also an unfavourable circumstance for continued research
in the most important branch of biology.

What ought to be insisted upon even now is
that each party before marriage should possess
full knowledge of its possible dangers, but that
the choice should thereupon be left to their
own sense of responsibility. No one—at least
not yet—can ask the individual to sacrifice his
happiness for contested possibilities; but in the
interests of the individual, as of that of the
race, we can, on the other hand, demand that
no one shall make his choice in love in ignorance.
And the more the sense of racial community
approaches its renaissance under the influence
of evolutionism, the more natural will all safe-
guards appear with which that choice may be
surrounded to the advantage of posterity. Even
now it is considered quite natural that a medical
examination should precede life insurance. In
the future it may be equally obvious that before
marriage the woman should ascertain from a
female doctor and the man from a male doctor
whether they are capable of fulfilling their duty
to the race. And it is not only a question of in-
suring the new lives, but also of assuring the couple
themselves that they have no organic defects
which in some instances might make marriage
impossible, which in others are easily avoidable,
but ignorance regarding which would in each
case entail unnecessary suffering.

In most cases it is the anxiety of one's self contracting or transmitting diseases to the other party and to the children that the physician has to confirm or dispel. It is beyond all question that healthy selfishness, which desires to preserve its own individuality, as well as the growing appreciation of a worthy offspring, will then hinder many an unsuitable marriage. In other cases love might triumph over these considerations for its own part, the married couple abstaining, however, from parentage. In those cases, again, where the law would definitely forbid marriage, this would doubtless be no hindrance to diseased people having offspring outside wedlock. But the same is true, of course, of all legal enactments: the best people do not require them, the worst do not obey them, but through them the ideas of justice of the majority are cultivated.

Only those who are ignorant of the laws of psychological transformation doubt the possibility of the simultaneous enhancement of the feeling of love and the racial sense. Century after century the emotion of love has been growing, while at the same time men have nevertheless sacrificed it to religious prejudices, superficial ideas of duty, tyrannical parental authority, and empty forms. Now, when the sacrifice is called for on behalf of the highest of possible gains—the conquest of disease by health, the ennobling of the human body itself—now, of all

times, it is asserted that mankind would be incapable of this sacrifice—because in the course
of time the power of love has increased.

On the contrary, it is through the greatness
of their feeling for each other that two married
people can bear the loss of children, when—
knowing that neither of them thus deprives the
race of a material asset—they enter upon their
union with the resolve not to become parents.
Through the same greatness in their love, the
party on whose side the danger lies may gain
strength to sacrifice individual happiness in
order that the other may gain a happiness more
significant to himself and to the race with some one
else. Such sacrifices occur even now more frequently than is supposed.

But above all it is the extension of the instinct
of love through the racial sense which will secure
the ennobling of the race without sacrificing
individual happiness.

The point of view of racial ennobling found
expression even in the Mosaic marriage law.
In ancient Greece also this ennobling was a
conscious factor. But Christianity's insistence
on the importance of the individual and of humanity weakened the feeling of the individual
for the race, as did likewise the doctrine of souls
supplied to the bodies from heaven and returning
thither. It was only through the enhancement
of man's spiritual force, by the mortification of
his sinful body, that Christianity raised the

quality of the race. The doctrine of hereditary sin was its only—half-rational and half-irrational —insistence on our connection with our ancestors. Since Christianity regarded the human species as once for all determined by God—though bungled by Adam—restoration, not new creation, was, as already stated, its fundamental idea. In the very conditions of the renewal of life Christianity saw the root and origin of sin in the world. This way of viewing things must be entirely overcome; and fortunately the church has of necessity lost—and will continue to lose— in every conflict with love. But in this way the advance takes place by a turning-aside from the direct line of development: the enhancement of the race. At the present time many symptoms show that love and the racial sense are beginning to approach one another.

Whenever abstract, logical thought confronts real life with a problem that admits of only two solutions, the latter asserts its proud determination not to allow itself to be confined within definitions or ruled by deductions. Life is movement, movement implies variability, transformation, in other words, development in an upward or downward direction. Never will the upward curve assume a more pronounced elevation than when the desire of procreation has reached the point at which it is directed by the selection of personal love, this selection again being directed by a clear-sighted instinct tending to the ennobling of the race.

That the choice of personal love at present appears often either to lack or to oppose this instinct, is no proof that it will always lack or oppose it. Love's selection has already in certain cases—such as those of near blood-relations, different races, and certain diseases—become an instinct, since law and custom have influenced selection sufficiently long for this to have influenced feeling and instinct. At the present time brother and sister—since they are aware of their relationship—seldom have to suppress a mutual erotic feeling, as such a thing does not arise. No prohibition, but only all the impulses of her blood, hinder the American woman from marrying a negro or a Chinese. The woman who is known to have epilepsy is excluded from marriage less by the law, in this case easily circumvented, than by the fact that no man wants her as his wife. On the other hand, it is known that under conditions favourable to the cultivation of the beauty and strength of the human body, this has in a great degree influenced the erotic selection of either sex—so far as they otherwise possessed freedom of choice. The law of inheritance, which makes it easy for the degenerate to contract marriage, and women's need of maintenance have, on the other hand, falsified the instinct of the latter in this direction. The prevailing customs and ideas of morality have as a rule deprived future mothers of their full freedom of choice and thus to a great extent neutralised the importance

of womanly love's selection for the spiritual and
bodily improvement of the race. To this must
be added that the Christian doctrine of fraternity,
the eighteenth-century doctrine of equality, the
transference of economical power to the third
estate—in a word, the whole democratisation of
society—have broken down the laws and customs
which prevented the mixing of blood between
different classes and races. This has certainly
favoured the selection of personal love, but at
the same time, to a greater extent than formerly,
it has favoured a selection governed by pecuniary
considerations. In the marriages which were
formerly a matter of family arrangement, many
other advantages, besides those of money, were
taken into consideration. But in this case also,
as in that of the marriage of near relations, it
was less and less a clear-sighted solicitude to
preserve noble blood, more and more an empty
pride of birth, a narrow race-prejudice, that raised
obstacles to marriage. It was thus necessary for
love's selection to conquer these obstructions,
which in addition, even from the point of view of
racial enhancement, were often of doubtful value.
But all the more must we deplore the influence
of money in determining matrimonial selection,
above all when this influence makes itself felt at
the cost of the inclination which love shows,
in spite of everything, of making its choice
by preference among equals; an inclination
which—besides other easily explicable causes—

may also imply an instinct developed in the course of generations, tending to the preservation of the best peculiarities in a class or a race.

Since Christianity and the civilisation influenced by it modestly veiled the natural mission of love and obscured it by transcendentalism, mankind began to be ashamed even of self-examination or self-confession in this relation. We ought again to pay attention to family history, though not to such as used to be recorded in old family Bibles, with the dates of birth, marriage, and death, but such a history as should include the circumstances which determined birth and death. We must resume the casting of horoscopes, but not so much according to the signs in the heavens—although perhaps these will regain something of their former importance— as according to those on earth; and not only from the signs at birth but from those long previous to it. Just as alchemy became chemistry and astrology led to astronomy, it is possible that such a reading of signs might prepare the way for what we may call—while waiting for a word of more extended meaning than Galton's eugenics or Haeckel's ontogony—erotoplastics: the doctrine of love as a consciously formative art, instead of a blind instinct of procreation. It would be of infinitely greater significance for humanity if the majority of the women, who now translate their experiences into half-candid and wholly inartistic fiction, were to write down for the benefit of science entirely true family chronicles and perfectly frank confessions.

It is certain even now that the customs and ways of thought, the artistic and emotional tendencies, which make up the atmosphere of love, unconsciously operate upon its selection to the advantage of the race. This also involves the possibility of such influence becoming conscious, when once it is clearly seen in what direction it ought to go, which are the spiritual and bodily properties that it is desired to eradicate or to enhance, and by what means the properties of the new generation may depend upon the choice of parents. But above all, racial considerations will operate indirectly in the same direction, so that love will be less and less likely to arise under conditions unfavourable to the race. Man is not inwardly a logical creature: *les entrailles ne raisonnent pas, elles ne sont pas faites pour ça* (George Sand). But by degrees our nature becomes unconsciously transformed through reciprocal influences: the body together with the soul, the soul together with the body; the desires through the thoughts, the thoughts through the desires. It is true that love's selection will always remain a mystery—from this among many other causes, equally or more important. But the individual and universal qualities which in the main act as an attraction will gradually be more clearly perceived, more sought after by both sexes, and will have more weight in determining their choice.

We have already seen that a displacement of motives, a division of motive power, has during a certain period altered the character of love. Thus, as pointed out above, the influence of the spirit of the age was able during the age of chivalry, and again during the eighteenth century, to separate love both from marriage and from the mission of the race. By the same psychic process a new spirit of the age—full of the aspirations of evolution and determined by the religion of life—may restore this connection and make it closer than ever before. Then will mankind look for a new Blake to glorify the feeling of devotion which fills hearts and souls at the coinciding selection of personal love and of the racial sense, a coincidence which alone gives the certainty that

I am for you, and you are for me,
Not only for our own sake, but for others' sakes,
Envelop'd in you sleep greater heroes and bards,
They refuse to awake at the touch of any man but me.[1]

Religion, poetry, art, and social custom have collaborated to elevate the racial feeling into love. They ought now to collaborate again to make the racial feeling conscious in love. The altars that the ancients raised to the divinities of procreation must be rebuilt. Not for men

[1] Walt Whitman.

and women to assemble around them in frenzied orgies, in the red glow of sunset, but in the golden light of the morning and the joy of creative day.

Family feeling, ancestor-worship, pride of pure blood will regain, in a new sense, their decisive power over emotions and actions.

Thus will love's freedom be limited—but not through idealistic philosophy's abstract conceptions of citizenship and duty, nor yet through the hard-and-fast breeding rules of a Spartan evolutionism.

Freedom for love's selection, under conditions favourable to the race; limitation of the freedom, not of love, but of procreation, when the conditions are unfavourable to the race—this is the line of life.

Love, like every other emotion, has its ebb and flow. Thus, even in the greatest souls, it is not always at the same height. But the greater the soul that the wave of erotic emotion inundates, the more surely does this wave quiver at its highest with the longing of eternity. The child is the only true answer to this longing.

This does not mean that lovers in the moments of rapture divide their consciousness between the present and the future, between their own bliss and the possible child. The life of the soul does not work so awkwardly as this. But the conscious conditions of the soul are determined by emotions—reduced for the moment to unconsciousness; and motives, which are forgotten in the hour of fulfilment, have not therefore been less decisive. The athlete in the moment of victory does not remember the training which preceded his race, but it was nevertheless that which decided the fate of that moment. The artist in the hour of creation does not remember the toil of his student years, but that nevertheless determines the perfection of his creation. The will to ennoble the race need not be conscious in a pair of lovers, who in each other forget time and existence, but without the emotions, which, consciously or unconsciously, have been influenced by that will, they would not be united in an ecstasy of the soul and the senses.

. . . .

Young men are becoming increasingly conscious that the thought of the child influenced them in their choice of love; women are increasingly aware that never was their longing for a child stronger than in the embrace of the man to whom they have been attracted by a great love. More and more often do mothers search the features and souls of their children for evidence of their love. More and more often does one hear the unmarried woman confess the hungry longing for motherhood, which a few decades ago she concealed as a shame.

Every awakened soul perceives that the consciousness of the time comprehends the mission of the race with a new intensity, although

centuries must pass before it can be proved what
influence love's free selection has had upon the
production of beings above the present standard
of humanity.

Even from believers in the religion of life
warnings are still heard against the love which
is a matter of personal choice, which excludes
all else, and which dissolves all former ties.
Evolutionists thus admit that this emotion certainly produces in the individual the highest
possible development of force, the fullest richness
of life, and that this indirectly and in many ways
is to the good of the whole. But at the same
time they assert that love itself often consumes
these enhanced powers; that it ought therefore
only to occupy a brief period of human life and
should not be allowed any decisive importance in
shaping the course of life, since this would be to
the detriment of the new generation. Their
special objection to love is, that just as monastic
life and the celibacy of the clergy during the
Middle Ages and down to the present day have
deprived the race of excellent qualities—since
the most gifted often choose the calm of the
cloister or the call of the priesthood—so now
many of the best men and women are kept from
marriage by the dream or by the loss of a great
love's happiness.

Finally, from the point of view of evolutionary ethics, not only the desire of great love, excluding all else, but monogamy itself has been

attacked. This purely scientific line of thought has at present no conscious part in the utterances of what is called the "new immorality," all the less as the scientific reasoning lays stress upon the point that *if* mankind is to abandon monogamy, which has possessed such enormous advantages, then this must be done with a conscious purpose, to further the development of the whole race, not the passions of individuals.

But if this evolutionistic reasoning be conceded, then it will result in a transformation of society's view of love's freedom of choice, both in the direction of extension and of limitation. Much of what is now called the "new immorality" may then appear as the unconscious self-protection of the race against a degeneration forced upon it by the customs and arrangements of society.

.　　.　　.　　.　　.　　.　　.

Against the future claims of evolutionism, however, the conviction asserts itself that personal love, the great creation of culture, will not disappear; and thereby the danger of polygamy is removed. It must therefore continue to be love's selection which will occasion the ethical "adulteries" just alluded to, but it will be a love determined by the point of view of the ennobling of the race. At present the claims of evolution in this respect have scarcely begun to be perceived, still less have they succeeded in exercising a transforming influence on moral opinion, which will perhaps one day apply in this connection Plato's saying: that what is useful is fit, and what is hurtful is shameful. Where good reasons exist for not outwardly dissolving the marriage, the right may perhaps be admitted which even now a man or woman has here and there appropriated: that of becoming a father by another woman, or a mother by another man, since they themselves have a passionate longing for a child and are eminently suited for parentage, but have been deprived of its joys because the wife or husband has been wanting in these possibilities.

Even now people begin to perceive the psychological justification of the oft-repeated experience that a man—sometimes also a woman—can at the same time and in a different way love more than one, since the great love, the love which is one and indivisible and pervades their whole being for ever, has not been given to them. Even now such conflicts are solved in a new way—there are examples of it known throughout Europe—not as Luther solved it for Philip of Hesse, who kept the wife that had just borne him a ninth child, while secretly wedding a new one, but as Goethe first intended to bring about the solution in *Stella:* that the wife, without any open rupture, should step aside; that the devotion, the tenderness of memories, which united her and her husband, should still render possible their meeting now and then as friends, in a common care for their children, although the husband had contracted a new matrimonial relation to another woman.

From the children's point of view such a solution may come to be looked upon in the future as more desirable—and more worthy of respect— than it seems now.

.   .   .   .

The new sexual morality—where the light, as in Correggio's *Night*, will radiate from the child— may, however, continue to uphold single love as the ideal for the highest happiness and development both of the lovers and of the children.   It has already been contended that this is the direction in which the evolution of love is moving. But we must likewise admit—and always for the well-being of the race as well as of the individual—that love may take lower as well as higher forms without our being obliged to regard the former as immoral.   When the point of view of the ennobling of the race has penetrated the ethical ideas of mankind, the following may be described as immoral, with a force at present unsuspected:

All parentage without love;

All irresponsible parentage;

All parentage of immature or degenerate persons;

All voluntary sterility of married people fitted for the mission of the race; and finally

All such manifestations of sexual life as involve violence or seduction, and entail unwillingness or incapacity to fulfil the mission of the race.

But, on the other hand, society will admit, with a freedom wholly different from that now existing, the union of people, not only in their best years, but also in their best feelings; it will perceive the present hindrances to be an injustice which falls not only upon the individuals but upon society itself—since connubial unhappiness not only interferes with the highest development of many people's powers for the good of all, but it also deprives society of the children to whom life might have been given by a new happiness.

It is through its view of the social importance of love's selection that the new morality will be a transforming force.

That a pioneer of reform who puts his ideas into practice may be a dangerous example is certain. It is possible to be fully convinced of the future of, for instance, the art of flying, without therefore denying the dangers of experiment or encouraging people to jump off church-towers with nothing but a pair of goose-wings on their shoulders.

No thorough reshaping of emotions and customs takes place according to dogmas and programmes; this one least of all. But no other motive power exists which will finally induce all—the small and the great, the weak and the strong—

to follow the line of development, except the increased freedom of choice of personal love, with a correspondingly increased certainty as regards the influence of that choice upon the welfare of the race. For unless love continued to be the condition of morality, the cause of selection, the new humanity would gradually lose advantages already gained. Neither the "breeding institute" nor "freedom of pairing" is capable of enhancing the spiritual and bodily resources of mankind in a universal, permanent, and organic way. Love alone can do this.

It is true that it has yet to be proved that love—other conditions being equal—produces the best children. But this will one day be proved.

This knowledge is for the present only intuition. But so are all truths in the beginning. Moreover, possibilities of indirect proof are not wanting even now. First and foremost this, that love has not its origin in human life, and is not a product of civilisation, but shows itself already in the animal world. Among animals it is capable of resulting in death from sorrow at the loss of a mate, as also in other emotional phenomena of human life. It may even lead to monogamy, although with animals as with human beings monogamy is neither a necessary result of love nor an indispensable condition of development. For many of the higher species of animals are polygamous, while others, below them in the scale, are monogamous. If love did not involve any great advantage, it might doubtless have arisen, but would not have persisted, in the face of the hindrances which its personal selection appears to put in the way of the maintenance of the race. Mankind has thus already brought the emotion of love from its primitive animal stem and grafted it upon the tree of civilisation. It has gradually been ennobled and exalted into one of the highest powers of human life. And how would this growing importance of love be possible, if it enhanced only the happiness of the individual, and not also the life of the race?

The evolution of human love has shown itself partly in an increasingly definite individualisation in selection, partly in a more complete admission and enhancement of individual qualities.

In other words: personal characteristics have tended more and more to inspire love, and love has more and more developed personal characteristics. This again—as already admitted—has resulted in more and more individuals failing to perform their duty to the race, either because their feeling, although reciprocated, could not lead to marriage, or because the feeling in some respect or other has been disappointed. This passionate selection of a single one among the many by whom—from an objective point of view—the duty to the race might equally well have been performed, has thus in a sense become anti-social.

But such lives, wasted as they are from the

immediate point of view of the ennobling of the
race, have yet been able to serve the same end
indirectly. Many of these persons, childless in
an ordinary sense, have left immortal offspring.
Others have shed upon the battle-field, in winning
victories for humanity, the blood which they never
saw flowing in the fine network of veins on a child's
temples. By the greatness of their own ideals
they have enlarged the hearts of their fellow-men;
and their courage has not had to sink before the
possibility of their own failure to realise their
ideals being cast in their teeth. They have
bought their prophetic power at the highest possible price: that of never having had a happiness to
lose; and they bear without bitterness the poverty
which has made them richer in faith.

That many lives—and worthy lives—are wasted
through love is only one manifestation of life's
impenetrable tendency to universal prodigality.
It is one with the great necessity, whose hand
smites and wounds us so long as we curse it,
but caresses and supports as soon as we bless it.

We must not look at the victims—even if we
ourselves are among them—if we would see the
meaning of life in life itself. We must fix our
eyes upwards. And then it is certain—since love
continually and in spite of all is extending its
power—that individual love, with all its victims
and all its mistakes, nevertheless in the long
run assists the elevation of the race.

.   .   .   .

The great Western prophet of pessimism argued that love was nothing but a task imposed in this fashion upon the individual by *der Genius der Gattung;* that only contradictions attract one another and that the offspring inherits the complementary qualities that each has sought in the other. These contradictions—through the hostility of which the parents afterwards make each other unhappy—coalesce and neutralise each other in the child, so that the latter, at the expense of its parents, becomes a well-equipped, rich, or harmonious personality. Carried to an extreme, this saying of Schopenhauer's, like many other such pregnant thoughts, becomes an absurdity. But every one who has observed love must have found—long before he knows, or without ever knowing, that this experience is exalted into pessimism—that all powerful love arises between opposed natures. The harmony that results from similarity is monotonous, poor, and moreover dangerous to the development of the individual, as well as that of the race. But what is contrary is certainly not always conflicting, although it may prove so if the contrariness extends to views of life and its purpose, its value and conduct. Conflicting natures are—in spite of Schopenhauer—not unfrequently equally unfavourable for the child's disposition and for its bringing-up, and the will of the race often fails of its purpose through their very compulsion to unite in a love which is soon turned to hatred.

Again, contrary natures often become conflicting, owing to their turning the wrong side of their qualities to each other after marriage, while in the early period of love they had shown each other the right side of these qualities. That such a marriage is unhappy is no evidence against love's selection, but a great one for mankind's lack of culture for marriage. That every sympathetic dissimilarity between persons has a limit, the overstepping of which leads further and further towards antipathetic dissimilarities, is a psychological lesson which is deeply inculcated by marriage.

The more, however, the art of living is developed, the more will human beings be able to minimise their own loss of happiness through this selection of love to the advantage of the race; for married people will come more and more to delight in and preserve each other's differences; to restrain the antipathetic contradictions in themselves; to make more conscious use of the sympathetic dissimilarities in the other for the completion of their own one-sidedness; to cease from the endeavour, so hostile to happiness, of reforming the other according to their own nature. Even now, moreover, the need of sympathy in love is so awakened, so sensitive, that the blind passion aroused by external contradictions is less and less able to overmaster it. The need of sympathy is now quickly warned when it encounters the irreconcilable contradictions which show that each is on a different plane of existence; that each belongs to a different psychological period or continent or race. This perception even now checks the development of love in many cases, where the contradiction really is a conflicting incompatibility, and not the elective affinity determined by nature into which enter both primary dissimilarities and secondary similarities. The latter results in the lovers' contradictions forming a rich harmony, both in their own life together and in the personalities of their children. When this attraction of contradictions has once missed its mark, one still often sees that it is one and the same type that a person will love a second or third time, or even oftener, with a persistence of selection which makes it true in a way that the object of love has all the time been the same woman or man.

The relentless force of nature's uniting will shows itself not only in the way love brings together contradictions in marriage, but also in the rupture of marriage. A good wife, married to a good husband, loving and loved, is thus seized by a passion, incomprehensible to herself, for another man. Without reflection she gives herself up to her passion, to return again to the husband she has not ceased to love, but who never inspired in her the overmastering emotion whose purpose—according to the will of nature and of the woman herself—ought to have been a child. The same will of nature manifests itself in a number of phenomena, incomprehensible to others. An intellectual man or woman is seized by a passion for a person far inferior. How often has not a "good-looking fellow" vanquished the most high-souled man in the affections of such a woman; how often have not thoughtless beauty and empty gaiety won from a superior man what the personality of an exceptional woman could not secure! The whole secret was nature's will to counterbalance cerebral and nervous genius by healthy, sensuous strength, to the advantage of the race. As sexual love has its origin in the fact that the sexual characters, which biologically are favourable to the race, are the most attractive, this general attraction constantly operates side by side with the individual; and it operates most strongly precisely in that kind of love which is rightly called "blind passion," the kind which thus brings together to their misfortune conflicting contradictions.

But there is no reason to doubt that love's selection in this case will be able to retain its instinctive sureness, although love is continually widening its instincts of psychical sympathy also. The consequence of this is that the number of contradictions which may attract will become less, but on the other hand the fewer possibilities will be more finely adapted; that the selection among contradictions will thus become more and more difficult but at the same time more and more valuable. Love's selection now not

infrequently has for its result that, of two contradictions, irresistibly united by the affinity of souls,
one or both does not offer the best physical
conditions for children. But to make up for this
the selection may turn out excellently for the
enhancement of a particular disposition, the formation of a harmonious temperament, or the fostering of a great spiritual quality. It is not
only by avoirdupois and yard-measure that the
advance of the race must be tested.

Such a race-enhancing selection may, for
example, take place through the tendency of
young women of the present day to feel or retain
love less and less for a man who is erotically
divided, while, on the other hand, the men who
have preserved unity in their love have more and
more prospect of being attractive to women.
Thus, generation after generation, erotic unity
may become more and more natural with men,
as in the same way it has become so with women.
Man's desire for woman's purity has determined
his choice, and this choice has then through
heredity further advanced the feelings of the
next generation, until these have become the
strongest in his erotic instincts. The clearest
consciousness of the injustice of the different
moral demands on man and woman; the most
"liberal" view of woman's right to the same
freedom as man, are in this case unable to vanquish his instincts. When a man learns that the
woman he loves has given herself to another

before him, or that he shares her with another, his feeling often becomes diseased at its root: the will of sole possession that has grown up in him through the love-selection of thousands of years, and has now been further heightened by the desire for unity of individual love.

These indications may be enough to show the superficiality of the conclusions about love's selection which are confined exclusively to physical improvement, although naturally this also is of great value. But that a pair of lovers can have a feeble-bodied child ought in itself to be no more used as evidence against love's selection than would be the physically excellent children of an unhappy couple.

Even if the erotic attraction of dissimilarities is thus the strongest proof of the probability of love's influence from the point of view of the enhancement of the race, it is nevertheless far from being the only one. Another is the astonishing excess of first-born or only children among distinguished personalities in different departments. A third is the proverbial ability of so-called "love-children." A fourth, the result, often favourable to the disposition of the children, of marriages between people of different nationalities. In the first two cases we may suppose that the parents' happiness in love—or at least their sensual passion—was at the height of its freshness and strength at the conception of the child. In the case of "love-children" it is not unfrequently a healthy woman of the people who with genuine devotion encounters the sensual desire of a man intellectually her superior. In the last case, again, it is usually a powerful love which has conquered the obstructions raised by patriotism and traditions against the attraction by means of which the national contradictions are to be blended in the child into a happy unity.

Observation in this connection is misled by innumerable side influences, counteractions, and contradictions as yet unsolved. So long as any wreck of humanity is allowed by "the right of love" to reproduce the species, the lines of conclusion in this subject will continue to intersect one another in all directions. *Not until cases arise where the conditions are comparable in every other respect, shall we begin to approach an objective demonstration in the question of children's decreasing physico-psychical vitality when they are born in unwillingness or indifference, and, on the other hand, of their increasing vitality when they are born in love.* And it is not in the tender years of childhood, but when they have lived their life, that the question can first be finally answered.

That the development of children's inherited dispositions, their childhood's happiness, and the future tenor of their life are determined to a great extent by their being brought up in a home bright with happiness, by parents who co-operate in sympathetic understanding, this need not be dwelt upon. Everyone knows how children from such homes have received the gift of a faith in life and a feeling of security, a courage and a joy in life which no subsequent sufferings can wholly destroy. They have laid up enough warmth of sunshine to prevent their being frozen through even in the most severe winter. Those, on the other hand, who began with winter, sometimes freeze even under the summer sun.

. . . .

It is no more true with regard to love's selection than in any other respect that passion is opposed to duty otherwise than in the intermediary stage of development. In the state of innocence there is no division, since no other duty exists but blindly to follow instinct. When development is completed and "the second innocence" attained, duty will be abolished, since it will have become one with instinct.

It will then be seen that they were wrong who now think that—while God walked in Paradise and founded marriage—the devil went about in the wilderness and instituted love. Dualism will be vanquished by monism when the circular course of development has brought the starting-point near to the goal; when the natural instinct of the race meets the will to ennoble the race, born of culture; when the golden ring from either side encircles the gem with the sacred sign of life: the child. But the treasure which is now regarded as the most precious, monogamy, is perhaps destined not to be encircled by the golden ring until after many new spiral turns. *It will be so when love's selection has finally made every man and woman well fitted to reproduce the race.* Not till then can the desired ideal—one man for one woman, one woman for one man—universally include the best vital conditions, for the individual and for the race. And when we have come so far, the will of erotic choice may also be so delicately and firmly entwined with every fibre of the personality's physico-psychical material, that a man will only be able to find, win, and keep a single woman, a woman a single man. Then it may be that many human beings will experience through love's selection what is even now the fortune of a few: the highest enhancement of their individual personality, their highest form of life as members of the race, and their highest perception of eternal life.

CHAPTER V

THE RIGHT OF MOTHERHOOD

EVERYONE knows that the methods of production of modern society tend more and more to limit woman's domestic work to directing consumption, whereas at earlier stages she used also to produce a great part of the commodities consumed in the home. Everyone can see too that the most profoundly influential cause of the woman's movement has thus not been the assertion of woman's political-juridical rights as a human being, but first and foremost the question of how she is to find employment for her powers of work which are no longer required in the home, and be enabled to find that self-maintenance outside the home which the altered conditions of production have rendered necessary.

Through the ever-increasing connection between the different parts of society, woman's work has had profound influence in other quarters than those of the labour market. Competition between the sexes has produced—as regards manual labour—for men and women those lower conditions of labour which are the usual result of an overcrowding of the labour market, namely, low wages, long hours, and uncertainty of employment. The possibility of marriage has become dependent on the bread-winning labour of both husband and wife. Those married women who are partly maintained by their husbands, have by their supplementary earnings reduced the wages of the self-supporting unmarried ones, and when these in their turn are married, they lack the desire and capacity to look after the home and waste through negligence more than they earn in the factory. The consequence of the outside employment of wives—as of children—has furthermore been sterility, a high infant mortality, and the degeneration of the surviving children, both physically and psychically; a debased domestic life with its consequences: discomfort, drunkenness, and crime.

Among the middle classes, again, the competition between the sexes has directly reduced man's chances of marriage, and indirectly diminished the desire of both sexes to contract matrimony.

The apparently inevitable law that one-sidedness alone gives strength has made the champions of woman's rights left-handed in their treatment of all social questions connected with their "cause." They have pressed forward woman's right to work, while overlooking both the conditions and the effects of her work. Women, actuated by the combined motive power of the spirit of the age and of necessity, have looked for

employment of any kind and at however low
a wage. Among the middle classes, the result
has been that many girls, who were in no need
of supporting themselves entirely by work, have
depressed the conditions of labour for those women
who needed it. Thus the latter are held down
to a minimum which is dangerous alike to health
and to morality. Girls living at home, on the
other hand, have been able to satisfy their increased demands, and this has made it still more
difficult for a man to offer them acceptable conditions in marriage.

It has already been pointed out that the self-
maintenance of women has had and still has a
profound influence on love in marriage. The
Swedish poet Almquist indicated this when he
wrote that only the woman who *"in glad activity
can provide all that is necessary for her living"*
makes it possible for the man to whom she gives
herself *"to say rightly to himself, I am loved."*

But no one can calculate in advance how a
new social force is going to work in every respect;
how even souls are changed with altered needs,
so that new demands and forces arise. The
erotic problem of the youth of the present day
is one of the most illuminating pieces of evidence
of this impossibility.

Woman's competition with man in the field
of labour has, in fact, occasioned a profound ill-
feeling between the sexes. Women feel themselves—rightly or wrongly—cheapened and under-

estimated, and men, on the other hand, consider themselves thrust aside, when woman's lower demands of wages decide the competition in her favour. But this is still the external side of the matter.

It is the new woman—the transformed type of soul—that man objects to. The mannish emancipated ladies will soon, however, have died out. We can therefore pass them by and consider only the young women who have preserved or tried to preserve their possibilities of erotic attraction.

These have, however, lost the calm, the equilibrium, the receptivity, which formerly made of woman a beautiful, easily-comprehended piece of nature, like nature in her unconditional yielding. When a man came to the woman he loved with his worries, his fatigue, his disappointments, he washed himself clean as in a cool wave, found peace as in a silent forest. Nowadays she meets him with her worries, her disquiet, her fatigues, her disappointments. *Her* picture has been refused, *her* book is misunderstood, *her* work is abused, *her* examination has to be prepared for . . . always hers! All this makes the man think her disturbed, unapproachable, and apt to misunderstand. Even if she retains her affectionate attention for him, she has lost her elasticity. She does not choose the conditions of her work; she is obliged to overwork herself if she wishes to keep her work. But love—as has been aptly said—requires peace, love will dream; it cannot live upon remnants of our time and our personality. And thus the value of love—like all other personal values—sinks under modern conditions of work, which drain the vital forces and make people forget even the meaning of the idea of living. Thus the people of the present day are excluded from love: not merely from the possibility of realising it in marriage, but also from the possibility of fully experiencing it.

Nor have these over-tired young women a chance of preserving their charm in outward appearance and manner. This is only done nowadays in a conscious style by ladies of the highest society—and by those of the *demi-monde*—who perform no other duty to the community than the more elegant than worthy one of illustrating the parable of the lilies of the field. But even now few women can afford—and fewer still feel that they have the right to or the leisure for—this worship of their own intoxicating and self-intoxicating loveliness. More and more have to take part in a life of work; while, moreover, women are becoming less attracted by the ideal of perfection of form, and more by that of formation of personality. But this movement involves uncertainty of form, until new forms have been created; and man loves in woman precisely that sureness, lightness, and repose in her own sense of power which are generally wanting in the tentative young woman of the present day. A new kind of young women is, however, already to be met with, who will neither work nor charm exclusively, and who are solving the problem of being at the same time active and beautiful.

Thus the deepest conflict of all lies herein, that young men feel young women to be independent of the love they offer; they feel themselves weighed and—found wanting. Woman's capacity for making a living has thus undoubtedly resulted, as Almquist hoped, in giving man a greater chance of believing himself loved, but at the same time —a smaller chance of being so.

We see two groups of the daughters of our time, as new manifestations of woman's primitive double nature.

For one group the child is not the immediate end of love, and still less can the child sanctify all the means for its attainment. If such a woman has to choose between giving and inspiring a love as great as that of her dreams, without motherhood, and becoming a mother through a lesser love, then she will choose the former without hesitation. And if she becomes a mother, without having attained the full height of her being in love, she feels it as a degradation; for neither child nor marriage nor love are enough for her, only great love satisfies her.

This is the most important step in advance that woman has taken since from the emotional sphere of the female animal she approached that of the human woman. And—however great may be the sufferings that this attitude of the soul may involve for the individual—no one who sees sufficiently deeply can hesitate as to the certainty of this being the true line of life.

This, on the other hand, will not coincide with the path of those women who are now demanding liberty for motherhood, not only without wedlock but also without love.

Those who hoped that woman's independence through work would assure man's knowledge of being loved, did not reckon for woman's dependence on man in and for the tenor of her life. This dependence, created by nature and not by society, still drives many otherwise independent women into marriage without love; and it drives other women, who wish to preserve their independence by not contracting marriage, to the desire of attaining a mother's happiness without it. The new woman's will to live through herself, with herself, for herself, reaches its limit when she begins to regard man merely as a means to the child. Woman could scarcely take a more complete revenge for having herself been treated for thousands of years as a means.

We must hope, however, that woman's lust for vengeance will not long retain this form. Woman's degradation to a means has retarded man's and her own development. But a similar degradation of man would have the same effect, and the children might suffer just as much through woman's misuse of man as through his of her.

The child must be an end in itself. It requires love as its origin; it requires in its mother love's understanding of the qualities it has inherited from its father, not a surprised coldness or resentment of the unsuspected or unwelcome elements in its nature. The woman who has never loved her child's father will infallibly injure that child in some way—if in no other, then by her way of loving it. The child needs the joy of brothers and sisters, and not even the tenderest motherly love can take the place of this; and finally the child needs the father as the father the child. That children, both in and out of wedlock, often lose their father or brother or sister through death or life, belongs to the inevitable, in most cases at any rate. But that a woman with full knowledge and purpose should deprive her child of the right of gaining life through love, that she should exclude it in advance from the possibility of a father's affection, is a piece of selfishness which must avenge itself. The right of motherhood without marriage must not be equivalent to the right of motherhood without love. It is equally degrading to surrender one's self without love in a free relationship as in marriage. In both cases one can steal one's child and thereby lose the right of one day proudly assuring it that it has enjoyed the best conditions for its entry into life. Love—it must be constantly repeated—desires the future, not the moment; it desires union, not only at the formation of a new being, but in

order that two persons through each other may
care for a new and greater being than either of
themselves. A woman may be mistaken in this
love, as she may be in her suitability for marriage.
But this she cannot know in advance. She
experiences these things first in loving. If she
has misplaced her devotion, then it will not save
her to conceal the mistake in a marriage. But
to receive her child from a man with whom she
knows in advance that she never intends to live,
this is having an illegitimate child in the deepest
sense of the word. But this is nevertheless
the way in which a number of women now think
that "the madonna of the future" is to win a
mother's happiness.

.   .   .   .

Work is always a development of force, and
the more it exercises our individual powers, the
greater happiness will it give. No part of the
old catechism is more valuable than that which
is omitted in the new, on the blessings of labour.
The path of every cherished and reasonable work
might be marked by milestones, on which the
good old words should be carved: here "health,"
there "welfare"; here "comfort and consolation
in adversity," and there "preventing lapses into
sin,"—above all, that of doubting the value of
life.

But the man to whom work has given all this
has all the more reason to curse the work of

women, who are able neither to choose their labour according to their talents nor to proportion their hours of work according to their strength. Greater and greater are the multitudes who move forward upon the road of toil, where the milestones bear the inscriptions: ill-health, uncertainty for the morrow as for the future, joylessness, lethargy of the soul, and the sins that thrive in the shadow, above all that of blaspheming life as meaningless.

For others again work has come to mean in our time drunkenness, vice, and superstition. It has made men and women unscrupulous, empty, hard, restless. It has made them destroy for others the remaining treasures of life—sorrow, love, the home, nature, beauty, books, peace—peace above all, since it is the condition of the full realisation of suffering as of joy. The grand words about the liberty and the joy of labour mean in reality slavery and trouble over labour, the only trouble our time fully experiences.

With thoughtless hymns of praise to this massacring labour, society allows one holy spring-time after another to wither without having blossomed—whereas thousands of years ago the cities of antiquity sent their "holy springs" to open up new districts and build new dwellings for men.

Just as true as that the losses of the individual mean the poverty of all, when these losses involve a diminution of health and power; just as certain

as that nothing becomes better without the desire
to improve it, so is it a healthy sign of the times
that starvation wages for conscientious drudgery
no longer fill young women with heartfelt gratitude.   They know, these young women, that their
own nature also can be outraged; that there are
other suppressed forces in woman's being besides
only the desire of knowledge and the thirst for
activity, and that neither the right to work nor
that of citizenship can compensate for trampled
possibilities of happiness.

Far from its being the duty of any thoughtful
person to lull to rest this despondency of the
young, we should render the best service to them
and to life by taking from them everyday con-
tentment and the calm of resignation; for only
the suffering which is kept awake, the longing
which remains alive, can become forces in the
revolt against that order of society which has
added meaningless pangs, hostile to life, to those
that the laws of life and life's development still
necessarily involve in the relations of sex.

.   .   .   .

All confined forces, which do not find employment, may degenerate; and our time, with its
repression of the erotic forces, can show even
among women such signs of degeneration.

It is therefore a necessary self-assertion when
those who are excluded from love seek to preserve
their health and enrich their life with the sources

of joy which are at the disposal of every living
person. Even he who is chained to an unin-
teresting work can find some moments to feel
his way along some path which leads to a glimpse
of the infinite space of science. Almost every kind
of work may bring with it an increase of individual
capacity, and therewith also of joy at feeling one's
value as a workman and one's dignity as a personality enhanced. There is no day which may
not bring with it a glimpse of delight in beauty.
Finally there is no hour—except the heaviest
hours of sorrow—in which a human being cannot
feel the strength and greatness of his own soul;
its independence of all external fortunes; its
power of seeking itself, finding itself, enhancing
itself through all and in spite of all. The words
which Victor Hugo put to a young woman in
sorrow:

N'avez-vous pas votre âme?

are addressed to all who have been badly treated
by life.

And whatever belief or unbelief a person may
profess, it is in the last resort this consciousness
of his own soul's worth which saves him when no
other help is to be found — and there is no other
help.

In this sense it is doubtless true that the human
being, woman as well as man, is an end in herself;
that she has fulfilled her task if she has not suffered
injury to her soul, even if she has gained nothing

else from life; if she has increased the power of her soul, discovered her own individuality and realised it; for this alone is saving one's soul. In this sense it is true that the "mission" of woman as of man cannot be the sexual mission, which does not depend upon our own will alone; nor, therefore, can he who has not fulfilled this be said to have lived in vain. In this sense also there is at bottom a certain agreement between the feeling of self-glorification just described and that of those who think that neither woman's nor man's highest destiny can be love, but only the life of an eternal being above all earthly and social considerations; that the highest reality of every human being is within himself, and that his highest happiness can be only to grow in holiness and godliness.

But for the shaping of life the difference is immeasurable. Here we are confronted once more by the dualist and monist views of life, the belief in the soul as supersensuous, and the belief in the soul as dwelling in the senses; the belief that the soul can attain its highest development and happiness independently of—instead of by means of—its earthly conditions.

According to the latter view man and woman are determined by their sexual life even in the greatest emotions of their soul. Sexual emotions pulsate in the age of puberty's dreams of heroic deeds and martyrdom; they are the warm undercurrent in the religious needs which awaken at that time. Every woman who has afterwards performed a brilliant achievement of love, who has become a great Christian character—like St. Bridget of Sweden, like St. Catherine of Siena, or like St. Teresa—has had the fire of great love in her soul; her blood has been on fire with the longing to serve the race with body and soul. And therefore also her charity had warmth in it, while the victims of so much other benevolence freeze like shorn sheep.

A woman's essential ego must be brought out by love before she can do anything great for others or for herself. She whose existence has been erotically blank seldom finds the way to what is human in a great sense, while, on the other hand, she to whom life has denied the opportunity of manifesting her erotic being in the usual sense, transforms it into an Eros that embraces all life, the Eros of whom Plato had the intuition when he made Diotima proclaim him: a touch of infinite delicacy; for may it not possibly be only woman who—since her whole nature is erotic—can thus satisfy her love-longing from the whole of existence?

But this sense of oneness with the universe—which the theosophist, the mystic, the pantheist, and the evolutionist express each in his own way, but which they all feel alike—is, above all, the gift of a great happiness in love. It is this way of loving of which it is especially true to say, that only he who loves knows God, the great word for unity in the all, in which we live and move and have our being. Not because God created mankind to increase and inhabit the earth, but because they were fruitful and filled the earth with beings and with work, did they give the Creator's name to life and worshipped in the likeness of gods their own creative power, on account of which they also dreamed that they were eternal.

Because fruitfulness, the power of production in all its forms, is the divine part of man, it is impossible for anyone without it to attain "holiness and communion with God" in the meaning of the religion of life, or, in other words, full humanity. Even in its limited form, that of creating a family, it is the unerring means of extending the ego beyond its own limits, the simplest condition for humanisation. It can transform the egoist into a generous man, merely by giving him something to live for. For this reason love has taken the place of religion with innumerable people, because it has the same power of making them good and great, but a hundredfold greater power of making them happy. Therefore all great and beautiful resignation—flowing with sweetness and benevolence—is like a vineyard, made upon the slope of a crater.

But therefore also it is true of all who have quenched the warmth of fruitfulness in themselves, that they have committed the one unpardonable sin, that against the holy spirit of

life.   These women have received their condemnation in Lessing's fable of Hera, who sent Iris to
earth to seek out three virtuous, perfectly chaste
maidens, unsoiled by any dreams of love.   And
Iris certainly found them, but did not bring
them back to Olympus; for Hades had already
made Hermes fetch them for the infernal regions
—there to replace the superannuated Furies.

.   .   .   .

Because the means of life must never eclipse
the meaning of life—which is to live with one's
whole being, and thus to be able to impart an ever
greater fulness of life—it is immoral to live solely
either for sanctity or for work, fatherland or
humanity, or even love, for man is to live by all
these.   His exclusion from one of these means of
full humanity can never be compensated by his
participation in any of the others, just as little
as one of his senses can be replaced by another,
even though the latter be perfected under the
necessity of serving in the place of the lost one.
And the resignation which prematurely contents
itself with part of the rights of its human nature
instead of aspiring to the whole, such resignation
is a falling to sleep in the snow.   It is undeniably
a calmer state than that of keeping one's soul
on the stretch for new experiences; for in that
case one must also be prepared for new wounds;
and he who keeps his suffering awake can be sure
of more pain than he who puts it to sleep with

an opiate. But no criterion is meaner than that of suffering or not suffering. The question is only what a man suffers from, and what he becomes—for himself and others—or does not become as the result of his pain.

Life holds in one hand the golden crown of happiness, in the other the iron crown of suffering. To her favoured ones she hands them both. But only he is an outcast whose temples have felt the weight of neither.

.   .   .   .

A woman of feeling once said that, although love was acknowledged by the majority as life's greatest treasure, mankind has not yet been able to prepare a place for love in life. Outside of marriage it is called sin; within it—as marriage now is—love can seldom live, and if it arises for another than the partner in marriage, then for the sake of the children it must be sacrificed.

It is this observation which made the new women all the more decided to prepare a place for love outside matrimony.

Women—and men too—have begun to examine the ideas of morality in which the small and the great values are mixed together like the cards in a shuffled pack. As far as woman is concerned, all morality has become synonymous with sexual morality; all sexual morality synonymous with the absence of sensuality and the existence of a marriage certificate. In speech and in poetry woman's mission as "wife and mother" is glorified, but at the same time the mission is not considered honourable until it is attained, but, on the contrary, dishonourable so long as it is sought after with the healthy strength which is the condition of its complete fulfilment. A woman may be proud and strong, good and active, courageous and generous, honourable and trustworthy, faithful and loyal—in a word, she may possess all the virtues prized by man—and yet be called immoral if she gives a new life to the race. On the other hand, a woman, irreproachable from the point of view of sexual morality, may be as cowardly, slanderous, and untruthful as she can be without being denied the respect of society.

This confusion of thought is to such an extent one with the feelings, that it may take centuries for new ideas of justice to work a change.

In spite of all, however, it remains a truth that a woman's morality in other respects is more profoundly connected with her sexual morality than is the case with a man. Nature herself established this connection, when she made love and the child more closely bound up with woman's existence than with man's. It must always be a matter of paramount importance to a woman's whole personality to abandon herself to the possibility of creating a new life; and therefore a woman's attitude, not with regard to marriage, but certainly with regard to motherhood, will be decisive evidence of her moral development in other respects and of her spiritual culture.

The same sexual freedom for woman as for man
is to every profoundly womanly woman a demand
contrary to nature. But this does not mean
either that man ought to continue to misuse his
freedom or that woman must continue to confine
hers within "lawful" bounds; nor yet does it
mean that women ought to go on lying to themselves, to men, and to each other concerning their
nature as sexual beings. It is true that many
women exist who have no feeling of this kind, and
that other married women deny the claims of
the senses—because they have had them satisfied
before they became conscious. But when the
development of love has introduced a purer and
healthier view, neither women nor men will consider it a merit or superiority in a woman to
develop in herself the character of "the third
sex." Then everyone will acknowledge that human life, to be in the fullest sense healthy and
rich, must imply fulfilment of the sexual destiny,
and that even if a restriction of the vital forces in
this respect does not entail physical suffering,
then it must involve profound psychical injury
resulting in diminished powers. Nor will one then
wilfully blink at the fact that—among many
strong, well-balanced, active unmarried women—
others are to be found who are equally worthy of
respect, although they cannot attain harmony
without motherhood. And the cause is not want
of self-discipline or seriousness in work, but
simply the fact already stated: that sexual life

in a woman—when it has become strong and healthy—dominates her in a far more intimate way than it does a man. She seldom suffers acutely, often unconsciously or half-consciously, from restriction in this direction; but to make up for this she suffers in a far more radical way, which slowly exhausts her vital forces; and many cases of madness, hysteria, etc., are due to this cause.

Every victim of this kind makes life the poorer; for it is often the warmest feminine natures, the richest in goodness and in soul, the most fruitful in every sense, that go under in this way. And in them the race loses not only directly, but also indirectly, in their children that were never born.

For the present it can be only by an altered criterion of morality that these losses can be avoided, at least so long as there is not one man for every woman. For we can look only for a very slow operation of the measures which may restore the balance that nature seems to intend by an actual excess in the birth-rate of boys over girls; measures, that is, for the better protection of the lives of male children and men. A proposal which was put forward a few years ago in one of the leading civilised countries undoubtedly deserves consideration as an incidental remedy; namely, to arrange an organised and well-supervised emigration of capable women from the countries where they are in excess to others where the reverse is the case; for while their proficiency in work would make these women independent of marriage, they would thus be afforded increased possibilities of marrying, as would the surplus men—at present, in the countries referred to, left to the alternatives of celibacy or prostitution.

In the main it is, however, only the awakening of the consciousness of society that can provide a remedy. But until youth itself awakens the conscience of the time with the tocsin of action, that remedy is likely to be long in coming.

In one respect young working men and women might take their destiny in their own hands, namely, in the purely external point of providing themselves with the opportunities they lack— which in the case of young people of the student class now form the foundation of many a life's happiness—opportunities of getting to know each other under pleasant and worthy conditions of comradeship.

In those cases again where a woman's destiny from one cause or another has rendered the realisation of love impossible, she ought—like the wife in a childless marriage—oftener than at present to enrich her life and partly satisfy her motherly feeling by choosing one among the destitute children, who are unfortunately still to be found in abundance, to provide for and love. Such grafts upon one's own stem often give splendid fruit. The lonely woman thereby avoids falling a victim to that hardness and bitterness, which are not necessary consequences of a checked sexual life, but are all the more so of a frozen life of the heart.

In those cases where a woman suffers a lasting and unendurable clogging of her life through the want of motherhood, she must choose the lesser evil, that of becoming a mother even without love, in or out of wedlock. Necessity is its own law—and he who steals to save his life ought to go free. But she must not be made an example for others who are not placed in the same necessity.

The solution of the right of motherhood, therefore, ought not to be the encouragement of the majority of unmarried women to provide themselves with children without love; not even the encouragement of the majority to obtain them through love when they know in advance that a continued community of life with the child's father is impossible.

But, on the other hand, the unmarried woman, from her own point of view as well as from that of the race, has a right to motherhood, when she possesses so rich a human soul, so great a mother's heart, and so manly a courage that she can bear an exceptional lot. She has all the riches of her own and her lover's nature to leave through the child as a heritage to the race; she has the whole development of her personality, her mental and bodily vital force, her independence won through labour, to give to the child's bringing-up. In her occupation she has had use only for a part of her being: she desires to manifest it fully and wholly, before she resigns the gift of life. She therefore becomes a mother with the full approval of her conscience.

All this, however, seldom applies to a woman before she has reached or exceeded the limit of *la seconda primavera;* not till then will she feel fully sure of her longing and her courage, nor will she have reason to know that life has no higher destiny for her. And even she must not be taken as an example of a final solution of the problem. But in times like ours, when the hindrances to life in this direction have become unendurable, bold experiments are justified— when they are successful.

In order that such an experiment shall succeed, the woman must be not merely as pure as snow, she must be as pure as fire in her certainty of giving her own life a bright enhancement and a new treasure to the race in the child of her love.

If she is this—then indeed there is a gulf, deep as the centre of the earth, fixed between this unmarried woman, who presents her child to the race, and the unmarried woman, who "has a child."

Beyond all doubt the first-named would have considered it the ideal of happiness to be able to bring up her child together with its father. The circumstances which prevent her may be many. The man's liberty, for instance, may be limited by earlier duties or feelings, which bind him, against his will or not. The conditions of life or of work of one of them may prevent a complete union. So may the experience that the personality of one of them is fettered through marriage. Or again, love itself was not what it had promised to be, and the woman was proud enough not to consider herself fallen and in need of being rehabilitated by a marriage which, on the contrary, would under these circumstances be a fall.

Finally, there are exceptional cases, where a superior woman—for it is often the best who are seized by the powerful desire of a child—feels that she cannot combine her motherhood with the claims of love and of intellectual production; that she can suffice for only two duties, and therefore accepts from love the child but renounces marriage.

But there are also destinies entirely contrary to these, where a woman for her own part wished to have a child but renounces it for the man's sake.

In most cases this is because she surrounds his work with such affection that, when it is asked of her, she sacrifices to it her mother's happiness in the spirit of Heloïse. And the more love is perfected, the more does woman thus learn to love her husband's work as her child, while he, on the other hand, loves her work as his own.

But it may also be for other reasons that a woman desires a man to keep his complete freedom; it may be, for instance, that he is the younger, or that she knows she cannot give him a child. Such unions are not unusual in Europe, unions by which two people long make their own lives and the lives of those about them richer. In such a case the woman transforms her motherliness into affection for the man. She gives the best of her powers of production for his use, so that he grows while she stops short. But she thereby enjoys the bliss of a mother with a child at her breast; as the mother feeds herself for the child, so does such a mistress seek the finest intellectual nourishment that she may afterwards impart it: she feels that she steals what she enjoys alone. Perhaps the legend of the pelican, which nourished its young with its own blood, would be a better symbol for these women, who must be prepared sooner or later to see the man choose the young bride who in every respect will answer to his longing. Cases like these, if any, verify Nietzsche's words that "great love desires more than a return," and that "it will create." Here, if ever, woman's nature reveals that its great genius is for love; that the higher a woman attains, the more certainly will her own honour, her own triumphs, her own future weigh lightly as a feather against the joy of being able to develop in all its fulness her great talent, that of loving. And when does she love more highly than in lavishing the whole superfluity of her developed feminine nature on the perfecting of her lover—for another woman?

What every woman needs, in our time more than in any other, has been expressed by Ricarda

Huch in these words: *Courage for one's self, sympathy for others.*

Courage for one's own destiny; courage to bear it or break under it. But also courage to wait for, to choose one's destiny. Sympathy with the many who have lacked one part or another of the new courage: boldness or vigilance or patience.

.   .   .   .

Both these courses which woman's new courage has found out—the man and work without the child, or the child and work without the man—may doubtless be called justified forms of life, when they show themselves life-enhancing. But they cannot be the line of life for the majority. This line follows the direction of the old Indian proverb: that the man is half a human being, and the woman half; only the father and mother with their child can become a whole. And even if women have the right, so far as life is thereby enhanced, to satisfy their erotic longing, they ought never to forget that they never attain their full humanity until through love they have given their husband a child and their child a father.

.   .   .   .

We have not spoken here of the young women who are unmarried wives of men, while waiting till the latter are able to provide a home for the child and a full domestic life. These women may, it is true, experience the grief of having trusted too much to their own or another's heart. But they have been pure in their will and their will has been directed towards the future domestic life, not towards "adventures," whose only value for them has been that they rapidly succeeded each other.

The young women alluded to must, therefore, be carefully distinguished from those who have become the hetairæ of the present day. These neo-Greek women are finely cultured, richly endowed, choice and pure types of the cerebral and polygamous woman. Love for them is an element of enjoyment—somewhat higher than that of the cigarette with which their dainty fingers toy, or of the alcohol which warms their pale cheeks—but decidedly lower than the joy of colour or the intoxication of poetry.

They share with man the joy of work, the desire of creation, delight in beauty, ideas, and freedom in love. Nothing would be more unwelcome to them than possible consequences of their "love," which passes from one relation to another, with a growing sense of emptiness, fatigue, and prostration. Unfruitfulness in every respect, that is their lot and their condemnation; for life has no use for the solitary unfruitful. Sometimes indeed they are not even capable of continuing to live—only to prove again and again that their soul cannot love, cannot create, cannot suffer, and has no other will but to free itself from the tree of life like a damaged bud, a spoilt fruit.

. . . .

The right to an exceptional destiny belongs only to one whose happiness it provides for; in other words, one whom it places in such an agreement between the needs of his own life and the surrounding conditions that the powers of the individual thus attain their highest possible development. And as this is seldom the case when the individual creates for himself a position which places him in conflict with society, no thoughtful person can thus refer to an exceptional destiny the majority of young women now oppressed by compulsory labour, who wish to improve their lot. The most immediate possibility to begin with is to improve the character and conditions of their labour.

Women must be more eager to discover or invent for themselves departments of work which will give them the opportunity of expressing something of their feminine nature, their human personality. It is one of the gladdening signs of the times that this is beginning to be done. Thus, for instance, in Denmark a distinguished lady mathematician—determined by precisely the reasons given above—has abandoned her science and become the first female inspector of factories in Scandinavia. Thus in Germany a lady chemist, for the same reasons, has chosen the same career. A lady lawyer in the same country is devoting

herself entirely to the protection of children;
another—in France—to the profession of advocate
for the assistance of poor women. But there are
still to be found far too many women whose
fortunate situation has given them free choice
in their work and who, nevertheless, have sought
the profession which offers them the surest income
or the largest pension, not the most liberal use of
their personal powers.

But even the possibility of the choice belongs
to exceptional ability or exceptional circumstances.
The majority of women, who must work or wish
to work, have difficulty in finding a calling which
really gives them a backbone, not merely a stick
to hold them up. To render possible a greater
organic connection between woman and her work,
nothing is more necessary than a business and
professional agency or exchange, to which reports
would be sent from different places as to local
needs of practical or ideal work, and then, in
connection therewith, a new kind of mortgage
bank, but one in which the mortgages would be
upon young women's courage, industry, and
invention; a bank, in fact, which would advance
on easy terms of repayment the loans which would
be necessary to enable these at present unutilised
assets to be invested in the wealth of the nation.
The sum of happiness of unmarried women would
rise if their creative instinct were thus at least
directed into a strong and healthy activity, by
means of which they could in some measure satisfy

their need of having something to care for, of
evoking around them comfort and beauty.

No fund would be more worthy of the sub-
scriptions of enlightened patrons than such a one
as this.

It is important, again, that all those women
who are forced to continue working for wages
should enter into the social question at least as
much as is necessary to make them understand
the duty of solidarity and the need of organisation
if they would obtain the higher wages, the shorter
hours, the summer holiday, and the better conditions in other respects which they must win in
order to preserve in some degree their spiritual
and bodily powers and with them that measure
of joy in life which everyone may thus possess.
The first condition for this is that girls who live
with their parents should cease to take work at
other rates of pay than those which the wholly
self-supporting can live on; and that women in
general should cease to think themselves meri-
torious merely because they work—without
troubling about the harm their underpaid labour
may do to the whole community.

But it is not only the will to elevate their own
lives, but above all a more lively feeling for social
organisation as a whole that that these working women
need. Their personal demands for education,
rest, beauty, love, motherhood, must be placed in
connection with those of everyone else, so that
they may begin to claim also for others what they

desire for themselves. Instead of making their own existence poorer by unfortunate experiments, they ought to fill the souls of other women with their dreams of a more beautiful life. And to be able to do this they must be constantly active and on the watch, giving and taking on every hand.

Thus innumerable little streams swell the flood of wills, which shall one day remove the old landmarks between the power to wish and the compulsion to renounce. Thus shall the woman deprived of love be able to forget her own little lot in the destiny of the many, and in spite of the limitations of her own life to feel that she lives by feeling the beat of humanity's heart in her own.

CHAPTER VI

EXEMPTION FROM MOTHERHOOD

To him whose thoughts go beyond the surface of life to its depths, the demand for the right of motherhood is a sign of health, an evidence of the existence in a nation of the strong, sound woman's will to people the earth, without which the nation shall no longer live upon earth. Even if certain manifestations of this will fall short of the life-enhancing purpose, in itself the will is only worthy of respect.

It is, however, significant of the confusion of ideas on this subject that the evidence of health inspires terror in the guardians of morality, while they regard with calmness that tendency of the age which is charged with the materials of tragedy, alike for the individual and for the nation— namely, the desire of exemption from motherhood.

Christianity, with its extension of the idea of personality and corresponding lack of consideration for the race, in opposition to the world of antiquity, made marriage the affair of the individual. The development of love has carried on the liberation that Christianity began. As stated in the first chapter, the champions of Christianity constantly admit the right both to remain unmarried and to limit the birth of children, if both are only the result of abstinence.

To the evolutionist, on the other hand, only the cause, not the manner, is the deciding point. Danger to the possible children or to the mother herself; the fear of pecuniary or personal insufficiency for the bringing-up of the children; the desire of using all one's powers and resources for an important life-work; a Malthusian point of view in the question of population—these and other motives are regarded by the evolutionist as good reasons for limiting or altogether abstaining from parentage. And in this respect the individual is allowed freedom of choice also as regards the method which best agrees with the opinion of science on hygiene, and with his own on morality and fitness.

As soon as it is recognised that the individual is also an end in himself, with the right and duty of satisfying in the first place his own demands according to his nature, then it must remain the private affair of the individual whether he will either leave altogether unfulfilled his mission as a member of the race, or whether he will limit its fulfilment.

But as the individual cannot attain his highest life-enhancement or fulfil his own purpose otherwise than in connection with the race, he acquires duties also towards it, and not least as a sexual being. If life has given the individual a lot which renders moral parentage possible, and conditions which are favourable to new lives, then the only moral limitation of the number of children is one which—in and by means of the individual's own life-enhancement and that of the children—is to the advantage of the whole community.

But when only petty and selfish reasons—such as considerations of the children's inheritance, personal good-living and voluptuousness, beauty and comfort—determine fathers and mothers to keep the number of their children below the average required to secure the due increase of population, then their conduct is antisocial. A person, on the other hand, who is content with few or no children, because he or she has a work to perform, may be able to compensate society by the production of another class of value.

To these now moral, now immoral, motives for having few children or none at all, must be added woman's desire to devote her purely human qualities to other tasks. This, however, does not refer to those wives who are obliged to establish their married life upon their own bread-winning labour as well as their husband's; a necessity which for the present hinders them from motherhood although they are continually dreaming of the future child. It is here a question only of women's personal self-assertion.

Women are no longer content to manage their husbands' incomes, but wish to earn their own;

they will not use their husband as a middleman
between themselves and society, but will themselves look after their interests; they will not
confine their gifts to the home but will also put
them in public circulation. And in all these
respects they are right. But when, in order thus
to be able to "live their life," they wish to be
"freed from the burden of the child," one begins to
doubt. For until automatic nurses have been
invented, or male volunteers have offered themselves, the burden must fall upon other women,
who—whether themselves mothers or not—are
thus obliged to bear a double one. Real liberation
for women is thus impossible; the only thing possible is a new division of the burdens.

Those already "freed" declare that, by making
money, studying, writing, taking part in politics,
they feel themselves leading a higher existence with
greater emotions than the nursery could have afforded them. They look down upon the "passive"
function of bearing children—and rightly, when
it remains only passive—without perceiving that
it embodies as nothing else does the possibility
of putting their whole personality in activity.
Every human being has the right to choose his
own happiness—or unhappiness.

But what these women have no right to, is to be
considered equally worthy of the respect of society
with those who find their highest emotions through
their children, the beings who not only form the
finest subject for human art, but are at the same

time the only work by which the immortality of
its creator is assured.   Another thing that these
women who are afraid of children cannot expect is,
that their experience should be considered equally
valuable with that of women who—after they have
fulfilled their immediate duties as mothers—
employ for the public benefit the development
they have gained in their private capacity.

.   .   .   .

There is no secret and infallible guide to natural
instinct, any more than there is to the tendency
of civilisation.   Both may lead the individual as
well as the race astray with regard to the goal
which both, consciously or unconsciously, are
seeking: higher forms of life.   In motherliness,
humanity has attained what is at present its most
perfect form of life within the race taken as a
whole.   Motherhood is a natural balance between
the happiness of the individual and of the whole,
between self-assertion and self-devotion, between
sensuousness and soulfulness.   A great love, a
power of creation amounting to genius, may in
solitary instances attain the same unity.   But the
immense advantage of the mother is that, with
her child in her arms,—without being conscious of
a struggle and without belonging to the favoured
exceptions,—she possesses that unity between
happiness and duty which mankind as a whole
will attain in other departments only after endless
toil and trouble.   But if this personal self-

assertion, this personal joy in woman's consciousness be gradually released from its connection
with the child, then this unity will be broken up.

An incidental displacement of it was necessary;
for the liberation of woman—like every other
movement of the kind—involved precisely the
disturbance of that equilibrium which had been
produced by the pressure of superior force and by
hereditary inertness, an artificial equilibrium,
which could be maintained only by pressure on
one side and inertness on the other. It was
necessary that daughters should rise up against
their fathers' ideals of wives; sisters against the
brothers' share of inheritance, which had increased
so greatly to their cost; mothers against the view
of their duties which kept them within the sphere
of female animals.

They must carry through that emancipation
which has already made it possible for them to use
their brains—not only their hearts—in fulfilling
their eternal mission: that of fostering and preserving new lives.

Already the educated—nay, even the uneducated—mother of the present day makes use
in her care of children of double the brain power
but of only half the muscular force that her grandmother employed. She knows better how to
differentiate between the essential and the un-
essential; she can by circumspection obviate much
toil and trouble. And when all mothers receive
the practical and theoretical training in nursing

children and the sick, which must be their form of universal service corresponding to the military service of men, then the problem will be even more simplified in the direction of the impersonal and more and more extended in the direction of the personal. The mother must use her intelligence and her imagination, her artistic sense and her feeling for nature, her instincts in physiology and psychology, in order to provide the child with the conditions under which it may develop itself in the best and freest way; but, on the other hand, she must beware of—remoulding the child. She will in this way gain much time which at present is wasted in unnecessary attentions and harmful education.

But avoidance of the personal charge is impossible to the mother without incurring the dishonour of a fugitive.

There are a number of women who think that the feeling of motherhood can exist independently of a mother's care and responsibility for the child, and that the latter may therefore be taken charge of by the community and still retain the treasure of motherly and fatherly affection. These women can never have reflected that, with human beings as with animals, parental affection is formed by care and self-sacrifice; that it rises with these; that the less demand is made upon it, the poorer it becomes. When a father for a time takes the place of the mother, he becomes as tender as she; when a sick child exhausts its mother's strength, it is nearest her heart; and as the child grows up, her affection becomes less spontaneously intimate, although instead it may increase through personal intercourse. State care of young children would mean a withering of the intimacy of parental affection. The tenderness evoked by the child's bodily presence shows, better than any other feeling, the unity of soul and senses. Without the sensuous presence, the psychical impression loses its power, as does the bodily impression without the psychical. The instinct of motherhood, like all others, has been formed through constancy of external conditions. It is acquired through definite sensations and associations of ideas. When certain of these emotions, at first conscious, became unconscious, and were then performed by lower nerve-centres, the higher nerve-centres, which had formerly been occupied, were set at liberty for higher uses. But if the sensations and associations of ideas, which originally formed the instinct, are weakened, then the instinct loses its automatic sureness. What worked easily, "of its own accord," as popular speech rightly has it, becomes once more laborious. With the displacement of the instinct, corresponding dislocations result, though with extreme slowness, in the organ with which it is connected. Thus nursing was perhaps an acquired faculty, which became "natural." It has now become so difficult that among the upper classes the majority, even with the best will, can scarcely perform this function for a couple of months, or perhaps not at all. Science is already enquiring into the possibility of the disappearance of the mammary glands and with them of the peculiar character of woman's breast.

It is often only the future that can decide what is progress and what degeneration. But certainly nothing can be more unscientific than to dismiss all anxiety about the future with the dogma: that the will to live in offspring is so strong that only the degenerate do not possess it, and that with a healthy woman nothing can injure the motherly instinct.

To a thinker of the evolutionist school, every-thing is subject to possible transformation, and nowhere is there anything at work which can "make no difference." There is not a brain, not a nervous system which can evade even the involuntary impressions of the street. These sink into the subconscious soul and thence may arise again after many years. Not one person is the same—or will ever be the same,—when, for instance, he comes away from a lecture, as he was when he went to it. Some psychic waves have always been set in motion and this motion is con-tinued to infinity. If this is even true of a notice on a shop-front, or of a momentary feeling of anger or joy, how much more then must it be so of the impressions which dominate our days and years. Our conceptions are forged from the true or false metal of our moods and become in turn the implements by which the bronze or gold of moods is wrought. All sanctity, all self-culture rest upon man's power of diverting certain thoughts, suppressing certain conceptions, turning aside certain impulses of the will; of introducing other thoughts, intensifying other conceptions, encouraging other impulses; in other words, partly utilising and partly rejecting certain states of mind. In this way, bad habits arise from one class of moods, good habits from another. When these have acquired sufficient strength, new modes of action, new plans of life gradually become "natural"; new instincts are formed, in which willingness and reluctance often stand in an opposite relation to that they occupied at the commencement of the process. Sensuousness and soul are thus both the creations of development, and it is the voluptuousness of many thousands of years that stirs in the mother when she feels her child's lips at her breast; it is the tenderness of as many ages which bends in the shape of every new mother over her child's cot.

However powerful these emotions of the senses and of the soul may have become, there is always the possibility—for the reasons just given—that the mighty stream of tenderness may dry up, if its supply be cut off, and that thus humanity may lose its most indispensable motive power in the development of civilisation.

Our destiny is shaped, not only by what we have experienced, but also by what we have turned aside to avoid experiencing.

Our conscious ego is made up of our states of mind, the images, feelings, and thoughts which through our earlier life have become our inner property; and which by certain processes are connected with each other and with our present ego. The less these images, feelings, and thoughts in a woman's past life have been determined by the sense of motherhood—intuitive or actual,—the less valuable will be the "ego" she has to assert, or the destiny she shapes for herself. And the woman whom no higher reason keeps from motherhood is a parasite upon the parent stem. The majority of these women have not even a deeper meaning in their claim to "live their own life." They fritter themselves away in many directions and do not get much profit by the process—since it is only great feelings which give great rewards.

These women, who thus without more ado renounce motherhood, have they ever held a child, not in their bosom, but even in their arms? Have they ever felt the thrill of tenderness such a soft-limbed creature, made, as it seems, of a flower's soft surfaces and fair tints, inspires? Have they ever fallen in worship before the great and marvellous world that we thoughtlessly call "a little child's soul"?

If they have not, then we can understand these poor women, who do not perceive their poverty, wishing to make the rich as poor as themselves—whereas all the poor should be made rich.

If this "liberation" of woman's personality

succeeds, it may go with her as with the princess in the story, who found herself in the rain outside the kingdom she had given up for a toy.

In a modern poem a woman, when offered as a consolation the thought that childlessness will spare her many sufferings, exclaims:

Spared!   To be spared what I was born to have:
I am a woman and this my flesh
Demands its nature's pangs, its rightful throes,
And I implore with vehemence these pains!
(STEPHEN PHILLIPS.)

When this ceases to be the desire and the choice of woman, then the prophecies of pessimistic thinkers of the voluntary extinction of the human race will be in a fair way to be realised.   But in that case women would not possess the nobility which a logical reading of the world's processes implies: they would only operate like a wheel unconsciously rolling towards the abyss.

.   .   .   .

To every thoughtful person, it is becoming increasingly evident that the human race is approaching the parting of the ways for its future destiny.   Either—speaking generally— the old division of labour, founded in nature, must continue: that by which the majority of women not only bear but also bring up the new generation within the home; that men—directly in marriage or indirectly through a State provision for motherhood—should work for women's support during the years they are performing this service to society; and that women, during their mental and bodily development, should aim, in their choice of work and their habits of life, at preserving their fitness for their possible mission as mothers.

Or, on the other hand, woman must be brought up for relentless competition with man in all the departments of production—thus necessarily losing more and more the power and the desire to provide the race with new human material—and the State must undertake the breeding as well as the rearing of children, in order to liberate her from the cares which at present most hinder her freedom of movement.

Any compromise can only relate to the extent, not to the kind, of the division of labour; for no hygiene, however intelligent, no altered conditions of society with shorter hours of labour and better pay, no new system of study with moderate brainwork can abolish the law of nature: that woman's function as a mother, directly and indirectly, creates a need of caution, which at times interferes with her daily work if she obeys the need; while if, on the other hand, she disregards it, it revenges itself on her and on the new generation. Nor could any improvements in the care of children and domestic arrangements prevent what always remains above these things—if the home is to be more than a place for eating and sleeping—from taking up time and thought, powers and feelings. If, therefore, we are to retain the old division of labour, under which the race has hitherto progressed, then woman must be won back to the home.

But this involves more than a thorough transformation of the present conditions of production; for we are here face to face with the profoundest movement of the time, woman's desire of freedom as a human being and as a personality, and in this we are confronted with the greatest tragic conflict the world's history has hitherto witnessed. For if it is tragic enough for an individual or a nation relentlessly to seek out its innermost ego and to follow it even to destruction—how tragic will it not be, when the same applies to half of humanity? Such a tragedy is profound even when it occurs in the struggle between what are usually called the "good" and "evil" powers in man—a form of speech which followers of the religion of Life have given up, since they know that so-called crime may also increase human nature and human worth; that what is profoundly human may appear as evil and yet be healthy and beautiful, since it involves the enhancement of life. But infinitely greater will be the tragedy when the conflict arises between powers unquestionably good— those in the highest sense life-enhancing—and not even between secondary powers of this order, but between the very highest, the fundamental powers themselves, the profoundest conditions of being.

That is how woman's tragic problem now

stands, if we leave out of consideration the egoists just alluded to and turn our eyes to the majority: woman's nature against man's nature, exercise of power in order to satisfy the claims of the member of the race or those of the personality. If Shakespeare came back to earth, he would now make Hamlet a woman, for whom the question "to be or not to be" would be full of a double pathos: the eternal terror of the human race and the new terror of the female sex before its own riddle; the bearer of the most refined spiritual consciousness of the time, and therefore—while forced by circumstances to make a decision—a victim of hesitancy, doubt, and fortuity. As true as that all life is a development of force, so is it that happiness is an ever more complete use of one's powers, ever richer in promise for the future, in the direction of their greatest aptitude. But when these aptitudes lead in two contrary directions, then the soul is in the same position as the wanderers in the legend of Theseus, whom the "pine-benders" bound to the tops of two trees.

The struggle that woman is now carrying on is more far-reaching than any other; and if no diversion occurs, it will finally surpass in fanaticism any war of religion or race.

The woman's movement circles round the periphery of the question without finding any radius to its centre, which is the limitation of human existence to time and space; the limitation of the soul in the power of simultaneously giving itself up to different spheres of thought and feeling, and the limitation of the body in the capacity for bearing a constantly increased burden.

The heaviest cause of degeneration at the present time—the necessity for millions of women of earning their bread under miserable conditions, and the risk that they may lose, some the possibility, some the wish, for motherhood—may disappear, and nevertheless the chief problem will remain unsolved for any woman who has attained individually-human development.

In however high degree a woman may be bodily and mentally competent, this can never prevent the time her outdoor work occupies being a deduction from the time she can bestow on her home, since she cannot simultaneously be in two places; she cannot have her thoughts and feelings simultaneously centred upon and absorbed by her work and her home. And all that is personal in her home life, all that cannot be left to another, will thus necessarily interfere with her individual freedom of movement, in an inward as well as an outward sense.

If the child and the husband mean anything at all in a woman's life, she cannot allow another to have the affection, the care, and the anxiety about them: she must give her own soul to this.

But then, on the other hand, it will interfere with her book, her picture, her lecture, her research, just as infallibly as would the trouble of in her own person nursing and taking care of the child—

a trouble which she is really able to renounce, though with a great loss of happiness and of insight into the child's character.

In a word, the most momentous conflict is not between health and sickness, development or degeneration, but between the two equally strong, healthy, and beautiful forms of life: the life of the soul or the life of the family.

Many women, who see the necessity of deciding for one or the other, choose the former and thus avoid or limit their motherhood, since they believe themselves to have another, richer contribution to make to civilisation. But would not the race have gained more by the talents of which these gifted women might have been the mothers?

We may pity for their own sake the barren women of the aristocracy or plutocracy, who from pure selfishness have refused to become mothers. But they do an involuntary service to the race, in that fewer degenerate children are born.

Full-blooded women, in a mental or bodily sense, are, on the other hand, the most valuable from the standpoint of generation. When these are content with one child or none, because they wish to devote themselves to their individual pursuits, then it is their work, not the race, which receives the richness of their blood, the fire of their creative joy, the sap of their thought, and the beauty of their feelings.

But it may be—according to a very moderate calculation—that there are annually produced by the women of the world a hundred thousand novels and works of art, which might better have been boys and girls!

It is nearly always the best women who are confronted by the tragic necessity of choosing one sphere or the other, or of dividing themselves in an unsatisfied way between the two; for, the more they increase their demands upon themselves, the more surely do they feel this partition as a half-measure.

Partly by economical necessity, however, partly by the spirit of the age, the choice is more and more often determined in favour of work, when the two alternatives are evenly balanced in a woman's own feelings; for the emancipation of women has laid the stress of feeling upon independence, social work, creation.   This has raised these considerations in the mind of woman to the same extent as it has depreciated those of home life. Want of psychological insight makes the champions of women's rights candid when they declare that they have never depreciated the tasks of the home, but on the contrary have tried to educate woman for them.   Schools of housekeeping deserve all recognition, but as regards creating greater enthusiasm for domestic duties they have not hitherto been signally successful.   It is because their enthusiasm has been directed to every manifestation of woman's desire to work in man's former sphere, that the calling of wife and mother has now lost in attraction.

Viewed historically, the work of emancipation must be advanced by this one-sided enthusiasm. But now it is a question whether woman, in a new way, will be capable of being inspired by devotion to her purely womanly sphere of activity?

For nothing short of this would in the main be the solution of the question. A return to the old ideal of womanliness would be as unthinkable as it would be unfortunate. A continued struggle to get rid of the ancient division of labour between the sexes is thinkable—and equally unfortunate. That woman should apply her new will to her ancient mission would be the most fortunate solution. But—is this even thinkable?

The answer is unconditionally in the negative as regards exceptional natures, such as now, in their increased vitality and capacity for suffering, beat their heads against the limitation of life which prevents their giving themselves wholly either to love, or to the joy of motherhood, or to the mission of civilisation.

Here we are faced by the fundamental cause of the modern woman's nervosity. She lives year in and year out above her powers.

She still retains the old consciousness that a mother ought to be unselfishly absorbed in her mission; that she ought to repose in it with a profound calm; that she ought therefore to allow the inner voices, which urge her to follow her instinct of personal development, to remain unheard. Added to this, she has the new consciousness that

the bringing-up of a child demands the same undivided attention as the production of a work;
that the child is just as sensitive as the work to a
divided mind, a wandering attention.   She wishes,
as an authoress has aptly said, "that she could be
at the same time the mother of past ages: the
patiently bearing caryatid, who was always in her
place, with the bowl ready for the child's thirsty
lips; and the mother of the present day: ever on
the move, seeking out all new paths, quenching her
thirst at all the springs of life."   She becomes
more and more unique, by being ever more firmly
and delicately individualised, and in the process
her desire increases to live her own life in every
direction.   But at the same time her feeling of
community with the race increases, and therewith
her consciousness of responsibility as mother and
human being becomes more and more aroused.
The more "egocentric" she has become, the less
does she remain a family-egoist.   The demands
of her personality become ever more definite, ever
wider but at the same time more fastidious in their
choice, ever more difficult to satisfy.   Her growing
sense of personal dignity imposes on her an ever
stronger self-control—while her whole being is
quivering with an ever more delicate sensitiveness.

And upon this new woman, who is already the
embodiment of unrest, thirst for life, and suffering,
the hungry, violent spirit of the present day flings
itself like a cat seizing a bird.   A hundred times a
day such a woman is forced to subordinate the

claims of personality to those of society; a hundred times the will of her personality has to elude her feeling of responsibility. Perfected methods of work may spare her hands and her footsteps, but they cannot prevent her eyes from watching with increasing disquiet the balance wherein affection, sympathy, and responsibility are weighed against her most intimate longing, her creative joy, her thirst for solitude, and her self-development. And as first one side of the balance rises and then the other, it will always seem to her that the heavier one contains a piece of living flesh cut from her heart; while the side which is—for the moment—lighter has nothing but dead, though perhaps golden, weights.

The brain-woman's time-tables know nothing of collisions. Her train-schedule is clear: nursing institute and kindergarten, school and dormitory for the children, whose number is fixed according to the requirements of society. The meals are served automatically from a common kitchen; the housekeeping is done by adding up the cash-book. In a costume designed for work or athletics, she goes to her study. When the work is done, there is five minutes' conversation on the telephone with each of the children; two hours' exercise in the open air. In the afternoon, ten minutes' conversation on the telephone with her husband, thirty-five minutes' pause for reception of ideas; the evening is given up to meetings of a utilitarian or social nature. On Sundays, the husband and

children are invited, when three hours are set apart
for the elimination of their defects, the rest of the
time for profitable amusement. Such a woman
never has a thought of the children while at work;
never wants to snatch ten minutes' extra chat
with her husband, never has promptings at night.
She wakes refreshed after the hygienic number
of hours' sleep; everything goes like clockwork
—better indeed, for the woman of the future is
never behind or ahead of time. But love's selection will probably not tend towards any great
increase of this type, whose present representatives
seem physically and psychically so little affected
by motherhood, that for their part one is inclined
to believe in the stork! And with the other
poor, weak, and "sensual" creatures the blood will
no doubt continue to be "a strange sap," which
makes the head hot with anguish when it ought
to be cool for thought; which forces the heart to
beat with longing, when it ought to be still for deciding; which makes the nerves quiver with anxiety,
when they ought to be tense for creation.

And it is the consciousness of this which in her
innermost heart makes the new woman shy of the
love for which she longs. A little emotion she
will not give; the great one would swallow up all
the forces of her soul, and what would then become
of the revelation of her personality, of the word
she alone among all beings has within her, the word
for the pronouncement of which she was born?

Mona Lisa's mysterious smile—interpreted by

Barrès as *une clairvoyance sans tristesse*—expresses, as someone has said, the feminine individualism of the Renaissance. It is certain, on the other hand, that the feminine individualism of the present day has a clairvoyance that is sorrowful even to death.

Never has the earth seen a more complicated and contradictory being than this woman, melancholy and wistful, cold and sensitive, thirsting for life and tired of life at the same time. The blood dances otherwise in her veins, sings another song in her ears, than it has in those of any other woman since time began. She sees through her husband and is a stranger to him; his desire seems brutal to her finely-shaded and contradictory moods: she is not won, even when she allows herself to be embraced. She fears the child, since she knows she cannot fulfil its simple demands. When fate attempts to tune these fragile beings to their full pitch, they break like harp-strings under a rough touch. They are only able to live partially—but thus they do not find life worth living.

Even if such a woman chooses this partial life and gives herself entirely to work, she will nevertheless be still disturbed, in the domain of personal self-assertion, by the woman's nature she has in the main suppressed; for she will often be confronted by the choice of not succeeding at all or of succeeding by the means of man, the means she abhorred in him before she herself discovered that it is the struggle for existence which gives the bird of prey its beak and claws.

She is forced to lament in the choice between relentlessly seeking her own or failing; between the necessity of being hammer or anvil, of dividing herself in order to give, or collecting herself in order to create.   Until woman took up a position in the world of public competition, she did not suffer from this necessity.   It was thus that—in a literal as well as a spiritual sense—she could afford to develop affection, sympathy, goodness. It is therefore a melancholy truth that woman's nature, as it has become when removed from the struggle for existence, is profoundly opposed to the condition which in the present economical and psychological circumstances brings success in this struggle, the condition, namely, of forcing one's way over others.

This conflict often begins in a field where woman cannot renounce her relation to motherhood— that is, where she herself is the daughter.   Even in this character she has a choice to make, pain to inflict and to suffer.

When we thus see the woman of the present day placed between insoluble conflicts on every side— or agonising, if solved—we are no longer tempted to agree with the poet's dictum that woman's name is weakness.   For in every fibre we feel that her name is pain.

.   .   .   .

Those men who, from the observation that woman's professional and brain work seems to stand in inverse proportion to her fecundity, have drawn the conclusion that woman must "return to nature," leave her brain unemployed and exclusively bear children, are easily refuted. There is no satisfactory evidence that mental work in itself need injure woman's capacity for easy and happy motherhood. In the animal world, as among savages, the females easily bear motherhood together with other great burdens. In civilised communities, on the other hand, it is partly through a lower class, whose bodies are overworked, partly through an upper class, who overwork their brains —or else do not work at all,—that the physical difficulties of motherhood have arisen. That the world's greatest female geniuses have had few children or none, is in full analogy with the great male geniuses—while these men as a rule have had gifted and distinguished mothers, an experience which alone is sufficient proof that woman's "weak-mindedness" may not be the most favourable state of mind for the enhancement of the race. No conclusive evidence can be adduced against the statement that, when brainwork is moderate and combined with proper care of the health, it may have good effects also in women. The same is true of bodily labour. But as both are carried on at prsent, the woman, no more than the man, has been able to keep within the limit of her powers. Therefore at present woman's studies and bread-winning labour involve dangers which have been increased under the spur of the dogma of equality, which has driven woman on to show that she could bear everything that man bears—that is to say, more than man or woman can endure.

But when once studies and labour have been somewhat organised, they do not in themselves involve anything that will make the unmarried woman any less fit to be a mother of the race; on the contrary, they are certain to involve much that will make her more valuable. It is thus not for the unmarried woman that the conflict is presented in the form of a choice between renouncing—even in the uncertain possibility of motherhood—the development or use of one's purely human powers. And when perfect candour as regards the sexual life has become the custom between the sexes even from childhood, it will also be possible for women, during work, study, or exercise, to have those considerations for health which modesty has hitherto led them to neglect. In this way, but not through the employment itself, many a woman has lost her chances of motherhood.

Thus the conflict does not commence until marriage; and for the exceptionally gifted, as we have already said, it may be tragic. For the majority it will not become so unless the wife is obliged to earn her living outside the home and at the same time wishes fully to perform her duties as mother, or when she wishes to attend to her personal business but is prevented by a large family from so doing.

The question is thus for the majority: either the abandonment of the work which produces a living, or the limitation of the number of children.

The first alternative will be dealt with later. As for the second, it is here that the main conflict takes place.

It is from the point of view of the ennobling of the race, as well as from that of the nation, that men implore women to "return to nature"[1]; it is from that of civilisation that women now refuse nature their allegiance.

Nothing—even from the national point of view —is more justified than woman's unwillingness to produce children by the dozen or score. The former consumption of wives, for a man between fifty and sixty, was seldom less than three wives in succession and as a rule half the children of each of them. Limitation of the number of children— apart from other sociological points of view—has above all the advantage, that many children of poor quality return a low interest upon the capital of working-powers and other expenses that their birth and bringing-up cost, while a smaller number of fully efficient children return a high rate of interest in the shape of increased working-powers, as is sufficiently shown by the prosperity of France.

[1] As far as England is concerned I will here only remind my readers of Galton's contributions to this subject ; of Geddes and Thomson's *Evolution of Sex;* of Havelock Ellis's *Man and Woman, Sex in Relation to Society*, etc.

But when we turn to the question, up to what point the limitation may be unattended with danger either to the nation or to the individual, then opinion is so sharply divided that to any unprejudiced examination it must seem premature at present to lay down the line of development of the woman's question as coinciding with the limitation of the number of children. Even if it be finally agreed that a nation's welfare demands of the women who ought and can be mothers, the birth and upbringing of but three or four children, it is not decided that the enhancement of the race is thereby sufficiently provided for.

Besides which, the new woman does not want three or four children, but only one or at most two.

Besides the danger, in this case incontestable, from the point of view of the nation, and the possible danger from that of the race, there is here a great danger for the children themselves. Their childhood's happiness demands a circle of brothers and sisters and the difference in age between the children should preferably not be more than two years. Not only their happiness but their development is aided by this. The position of an only child, or of only son or daughter, usually results in childhood in great selfishness, while in later years, on the other hand, it produces frequently a heavy burden of duty, and thus, in both cases, brings danger to harmonious development.

One or two children have a poorer, and also a more dangerous, childhood than those who among a number of brothers and sisters learn the value of mutual consideration, of shared joys and troubles. Thus, without any risk of loss of individuality, awkwardness is polished and sensitiveness strengthened, which otherwise in later life would cause great losses of power. For a circle of school-fellows can only imperfectly take the place of the nursery's first education in social humanity.

Besides which it may easily happen that parents lose an only child, or the only son or daughter.

Thus perhaps from the point of view of the nation, always from that of the children, and most frequently from that of the parents, the normal condition for the majority of healthy, well-to-do married people must be, that the number of children shall not fall short of three or four.

But in this case a mother must reckon that her children will occupy about ten years of her life, if she will herself give them the nursing and care which will make them fully efficient. And during these years—if her contribution in either direction is to have its full value—she must neither divide her powers by working for a living nor by constant public activity. During these years, she may continue her own general development; she may take occasional part in social work; now and then she may have time for mental production. But any continuous and exhausting work outside the home will, at least indirectly, diminish her own vital force and that of her children.

Thus the majority of women will never avoid a

conflict, lasting for years, between the renewal of the race and their own outward self-assertion, in whatever direction the latter may go; just as little as they can avoid the conflict of the double burden, now laid with increasing frequency upon women: that of bread-winning and the increase of the race.

When to all this is added the need, for both husband and wife, of mutual converse, and finally the cares of housekeeping, then every thoughtful person must see that woman—and with her society—is confronted by a problem in the form of "either—or," not of "both—and."

Only by society undertaking the support of those women who by well fulfilling the duties of motherhood have produced the highest social asset, can the question of married women's bread-winning be solved.

And only if women put their personal creative desire into their mission as mothers during their children's first years, will the problem be solved of woman's self-assertion and of her simultaneous devotion to the mission of the race.

.   .   .   .

No, is the answer of Charlotte Perkins Stetson[1] and of many others with her; the solution is State care of children.   Look at all the wretched homes, where the children lack the most necessary mental

---

[1] See *Woman and Economics* and later works by this American authoress, who has many adherents in Europe as well as in America.

and bodily conditions for healthy development. The collective rearing of all children would
be both better and cheaper. Only those women
who are liberated from the toils of the nursery
and the kitchen are really free. To the woman
accustomed to public activity, the tasks of the
home are monotonous and tiresome. On the
other hand, as a calling freely chosen, the care of
children would satisfy those who have the gift for
it. The majority of mothers are only ape-
mothers to their little children, and, as the
latter grow bigger, this vague affection is replaced
by an obstinate misunderstanding.

This is what one hears over and over again at
the present time. And the more it is repeated,
the more certain do women become that all
these half-truths are—the truth.

Thus it is the mothers who are not good
enough to bring up their own children, that are
expected to provide the new illustrious leaders of
the community. It is the parents who themselves
lack the talent and inclination for bringing up
children, that—directly or indirectly—will have
to superintend and select the persons who, in their
place, will perform the duties of parents. In other
words, they are to discover and appreciate qualities
that they do not themselves possess. The trouble
that a woman cannot take for the children to
whom she has herself given life, is to be borne by
other women for ten, twenty, or thirty children,
who are not their own.

Even to-day, there is sometimes to be found a kind of primitive type of womanliness, so widely maternal, with such a superfluity of strength, of tenderness, of talent for organisation that it is too powerful for a single home; a type which really possesses the immense wealth of spiritual elasticity, joy, and warmth, that is necessary in order that every such child should have its full share of these. But most women probably do not possess any more of these things than is just sufficient for their own children. And with these "elected mothers," quickly worn out as they would be, ten, twenty, or thirty children would be as badly off mentally as they would be bodily if a single mother's milk had to be divided among them all. It is even now a serious loss to society that so many human beings are enfeebled for life by insufficient nourishment in childhood. But according to the plan we have been discussing, which now has so many adherents, everyone would be starved in childhood as re-gards affection. It is even now a serious loss to culture that school-life makes children uniform. Still more irreparable would be the harm if their fashioning were in the hands of a thorough-going State care of children.

The danger of uniformity is inseparable from the present tendency to a hard-and-fast organisation of society, with an ever greater need of co-opera-tion, an ever closer connection, an ever more intimate feeling of relationship between its com-ponent parts. The organisation must go on, because, amongst other reasons, it is only in this way that the individual can now gain increased freedom for development and the use of his personal powers. But if these increased possibilities of satisfying personal needs and using personal powers are to be of value to the individual—and through him to the whole community—then we must also have some individualities left who will be capable of taking advantage of their possibilities.

And now it is certain that the home—with its changing conditions of good and evil—is first and foremost the best means of forming an organically developing sense of solidarity with the whole community. Life itself creates in the home an interdependence among its members, a sympathy for others' destiny, a contact with the realities of life, and with the seriousness of work, which no institution can create. It is by the efforts of a father and a mother that the joys of home are provided; it is affection for all which counterbalances the mutual rights of all; which gives to each his weight and his counterpoise in a way so natural that the methodical arrangements of an institution would never be able to imitate it. And furthermore, different homes, with the variety of different impressions they offer, are the best means of forming different characters and peculiarities. However straitened and poor in every sense a home may be, it nevertheless, as a rule, provides more personal freedom of movement and results in less uniformity than a collective system of bringing-up.

If this is even true of those homes where there can be no question of education in a higher sense, then in better homes the watchfulness and warmth of affection, its understanding and sensitiveness, will be the forces which will induce and protect individuality of character, and which will most surely discover what ought to be counteracted and what left alone for self-development. To this must be added the insight which the parents' knowledge of themselves and of each other gives into their children's character, an insight which no stranger can possess.

To this it is objected that, if every quarter of a town and every few square miles of country had its "State nursery," parents would often be able to see to their children, as well as to take them home and thus have an opportunity of using their influence. But apart from the circumstance that the relationship would then in most cases resemble that of the French *petite bourgeoisie* visiting their children *en nourrice*—that is to say, that affection would be shown in a desire to amuse and deck out the child, to caress and play with it—the most important point is forgotten. This is that time, more time, and still more time, is one condition of education, and quiet the other. Souls are not to be tended like maladies, in fixed hours of treatment.

There is no sphere—as parents are still too apt to forget—in which the psychological moment is

more important than in education. The action
which a mother has seen in the morning, should
often be first mentioned by the child's bedside at
night; the confidence which at the right moment
might have burst from the child's lips, will never
be given if the father has not availed himself of
that moment; the words which pained the mother
this week, must perhaps wait till next before a
natural opportunity of effectively combating them
occurs. The caress for which a little head fever-
ishly longs this evening, will perhaps to-morrow
leave it indifferent. The word of affection which
might have been all-powerful at one moment, is
powerless a couple of hours later. And above all,
direct advice or correction is worthless in comparison with the unpremeditated words that parents
let fall in the course of the day, with the result that
the child simply sees the full human life of its
parents.

Only living together on week-days and holidays
deepens the immediate influence of parents; only
this makes it possible for the parents to distinguish
in the child the accidental from the essential, the
newly-acquired from the intrinsic in its changing
moods.

And finally, when we think we have found that
children receive too much warmth at home, and
that they ought rather to be hardened against
life—have we then not observed such "hardened"
ones? Have we not seen how they are beautified
when they are admitted to a corner in a home;

have we not discovered that, though in intelligence they may be far in advance of their time, their feelings are still on a level with those of the savage?

So far from homes being too warm, they are seldom sufficiently warmed by the only love that lasts for life, that of knowledge and comprehension. Never yet was a human being too much loved, but only too little, or not in the right way. The whole spirit of the age is now opposed to the fatherly and motherly feelings of older times, which were related to the blind affection of animal parents. The affection that is left must be intensified, not weakened.

The child's splendid, unconscious happiness is in making others happy; in being answered by the smiles it produces; in showing outbursts of affection and receiving affection in return; in feeling the security and pride of itself owning and belonging to its father or mother; in allowing this delight to show itself in play and caresses and being met with the same delight without its being empty. For in a home, where some seriousness prevails, a child soon learns that affection also means work and sacrifice for others. From such affection the psychically personal tie of blood is formed, while the "natural" one grows weak, as it is not renewed by the apparently unimportant daily, hourly influence of the intangible, invisible things, through which, as even the *Edda* tells us, the indestructible ties are formed. In a word, the home of one's childhood is for the development of human feelings, what one's native place is for the development of patriotism. Even now home-life suffers in a disquieting degree from the school's increasing grasp of the older children; from the indifference to and disconnection from the home which occurs when it sees the children only at meal-times, on Sundays, and during the holidays. But if even the little children were to be placed in the same situation, then this evil would be extended to the most decisive years of their lives.

To turn now from parents and children to the new foster-mothers of the town and country nurseries, how is it intended that these shall suffice for their own children, if they are mothers, how—if they are motherly—are they to content themselves with the children of others, which they will furthermore be compelled to lose over and over again? Have the women who want to be "freed" ever given a thought to the sufferings of these others?

The only possibility of endurance for such nurses will be to give the children only that general kindness that is not enough for them. Love they will not be able to give. No word is more abused than love, not least by the interpreters of Christianity, who attenuate it into a wafer for the nourishment of all, under the name of universal love. But there is no such thing as universal love, or love of humanity; there cannot be such a thing; it would be as much a contradiction in terms as a quadrilateral triangle. There is a charity which pours itself out like oil upon all wounds; there is sympathy in joy and sorrow between individuals; mutual help and mutual responsibility in society; a common feeling of rejoicing or suffering with our nation or with humanity at great moments. But all love from one human being to another which deserves that name, is in the highest degree individual; it is a selection, a separation. If it is not this, it is nothing. A woman chooses her children even when she chooses their father; and she often shows her preference among the children themselves. An individually developed mother rightly asserts her privilege of not loving all her children equally. She gives them all the affection they need in the same degree; she is capable of the same broad justice towards them all, but she has for one of them a more personal love than for the rest. The profound tragedy in the relations between parents and children is precisely this, that this relationship is often as passionate as personal love, but without the latter's understanding; that it involves the claims of a great emotion, but not the power that an individual feeling has of becoming intensified in the same degree as the claim is increased.

Individual love is alone sufficient for a child's needs. An "elected mother" may perhaps once, or several times, be able to feel such a love for one or more of the children entrusted to her. But she cannot have this love for all of them, and she will herself be torn asunder when one after the other the children she loves are taken from her.

The mothers for the State institution must furthermore be found by thousands, if the whole of society is to be constructed on this plan. And then it will be with them as with the clergy, who in the earliest congregations were called by the Holy Spirit, but afterwards by the congregation. It would be more and more rarely the proved personal aptitude and inner necessity that would decide the choice, but in its place the accepted standard of professional training.

It is by means of these professional mothers, as is now the opinion, that children would have better conditions of life than in their own homes, where, in spite of all shortcomings, personal responsibility and personal affection render imperfection in the higher grades of education less dangerous than perfection in a lower grade.

Exceptional circumstances exist, to provide for which the crèche, the kindergarten, the asylum, and the industrial school must continue for the present. But instead of trying to make these expedients universal, we ought to endeavour to eradicate the causes which render them necessary. This would be road-making in the right direction. The other is a short cut, which will infallibly take us longer round.

It is true that poverty now gives many children unhealthy homes. Attack the causes of poverty

then, instead of taking away the children and leaving the parents in misery.   It is true that much
parental affection is injudicious.   Then educate
people to be parents.   It is true that parents now
increase the inheritance of certain children at the
cost of the others.   Then lessen the possibility
of this.

But do not deprive all children of their rightful
inheritance: home feelings and memories of home,
home sorrows and home joys, all that gives its
peculiar tone, colour, and perfume to every human
being's disposition.

Do not abolish the most important of all collective education, that of the children through
the parents and of the parents through the
children.

Doubtless, love's freedom will bring about more
complicated family relations than at present.
From this point of view there seems to be an
evident advantage to the children in State institutions, where their lives would not be so immediately
affected by dislocations in those of their parents.
But to deprive the majority of children of their
homes, because the minority might thus lose
theirs, would be a worse expedient than that of
connecting the home more closely with the mother
and developing human beings so that they may
remain friends even when they have ceased to be
husband and wife, and may thus continue to be
capable of co-operating for the welfare of the
children.

In a word, it is not the family that ought to be abolished, but the rights of the family that must be reformed; not education by parents that ought to be avoided, but education of parents that must be introduced; not the home that ought to be done away with, but homelessness that must cease.

The State rearing of children would work like the feeding of foundlings on Pasteurised milk: they sickened when they were thus deprived of certain indispensable bacilli. The people who were brought up on the germ-free milk of universal benevolence, in the untainted air of uniform order; who had their origin in the love of the majority, their nourishment from the automatic machine of the institution, their education in the mould of the school, their occupation as wax-makers in the social hive—these unfortunate creatures might find existence so tame and so empty that those of them whom weariness of life had not driven to suicide before the age of twenty might use their atavistic longing for happiness in burning down the institutions and rebuilding homes for human beings.

Can people not understand that State care of children would force upon the young generation life's last and hardest experience, that of not being the most important or the nearest to anyone, and that this heavy fruit—under which old trees may give way—might deform the young ones for ever? Do not people see that, even if many homes are

now hell, we should not sink to the lowest
circle of hell—which Dante's fancy made ice-
cold—until the warmth was quenched which the
hearths of home still throw out, and their place was
taken by the steam-heating of the institution?
When existence is made up of beings with starved
hearts, frozen souls, obliterated characteristics—
what materials will these afford for constructing
the society of which they will form part? Will
they even care to produce children as raw material
for the human factories; or the necessaries for
the maintenance of that life in which the elements
of personal happiness are wanting? Will they
even have the energy to take a decision about the
order of society which robs them of life's greatest
values?

.   .   .   .

So wonderfully strong is in man the need of
having some place of his own, of being among
his own, feeling himself at home in one poor
corner of the world, in a single poor heart, that
this feeling has even the power of clearing a
morass into a spring by subterranean ways.

On a railway journey in the South I once saw
a woman, whose face, figure, and manners betrayed
the completest downfall.   This mother had a
beautiful six-year-old daughter.   Never was it
more horrible to see a child at her mother's knee;
never did an amulet seem more powerless than the
saint's image that a pitying hand had hung about

the child's neck. But when the child leaned towards her mother, she was embraced by the
drunken harlot with a tender emotion, which
restored to her a spark of human dignity. And
when the child read in the looks of her fellow-
travellers the disgust her mother inspired, her
dark eyes glowed with angry sorrow and she took
up before her mother a position of protesting
affection. No one could doubt that this child
ought to be taken out of such unclean hands.
But I wonder whether a better guardian would be
able to give her the great emotion which at that
moment dilated the child's soul? If in a case
like this one can even hesitate about the line
between disadvantage and advantage, then in
many other cases one will be convinced that it is
not necessarily where a child has the best food, the
cleanest bed, the most uninterrupted care, that it
will thrive best, but rather where its soul may be
expanded by the warmest and greatest emotions.
Moreover it is one of the sacred mysteries of life
that most parents, in themselves and towards one
another, are worse than the child sees them; for
the last being before whom a wretch casts off his
protecting rags of human dignity is his child.

Against the wickedness of parents, however, as
against their ill-treatment, the child must be
protected, and that in a much greater degree than
now by a constant extension of the right and
duty of society's intervention in these cases. But,
when it can be avoided, the children ought just as

little to be deprived of the protection of home as
the home should be deprived of the protection
children give to it, by compelling the parents to at
least some measure of self-discipline, self-control,
and self-sacrifice, whereby their souls are extended
beyond the individual ego.   In the day when the
"hardening" atmosphere of the State institutions
encompasses all children, human virtue will sink
with even greater rapidity than human happiness.

.   .   .   .

All that has been said above does not imply any
blindness to the fact that even the best homes are
now penitentiaries in comparison with what they
may become when the formation of a home has
become a science and an art.   At present the
home is fortunately—or unfortunately—neither
inspected nor rewarded with prizes.   But perhaps
this time is coming—as already in France the
seventh child is brought up at the cost of the State,
and decorations are proposed for those women who
have borne and brought up the greatest number
of efficient children.   Then, if not before, will
the "liberated" women perhaps regain some interest in the development of their powers in the
direction of the home.

What now frequently diminishes externally the
value even of good homes, is that they are arranged
to promote a kind of "aspiration," diametrically
opposed to genuine life-enhancement, whose first
condition is that the home in a material respect

should bear a relation to the health and comfort of its own members, not the habits of life of outsiders. What again detracts in a spiritual respect from even the very best homes is that their members still retain the family rudeness and want of consideration of older days, a rudeness which—owing to the new sensitiveness, the deeper strength of personal consciousness—causes even from childhood daily pain that, as infallibly as the grosser faults of bad homes, poisons air and food.

People still allow themselves within the home circle a scornfulness of each other's peculiarities, a silencing of each other's opinions, a prying into each other's secrets, a betrayal of each other's confidences, which in daily life place the members of the circle on a footing of armed neutrality. In good homes, affection, and in inferior ones fear, stops them from breaking out into open war; for in both cases all know each other's vulnerable spots so well, that they are perfectly well aware how severe the conflict would be for themselves as well as for the others.

But so long as homes, even the best ones, have these faults, institutions must exhibit similar results—since both will be formed of the same human material. The institutions, on the other hand, would not possess the advantages which in the case of homes outweigh the faults. These faults may be gradually diminished by a higher spiritual culture. But nothing could compensate

for what mankind would lose by the abolition of
the home.

.   .   .   .

The conclusion is thus that—however differently
the conflict must be resolved in exceptional cases
between woman's personal claims and her motherly
feelings—in the main those women who, in order
to serve humanity, renounce motherhood or its
cares, are conducting themselves like a warrior
who should prepare for the battle of the morrow
by opening his veins the evening before.

CHAPTER VII

COLLECTIVE MOTHERLINESS

AT a Scandinavian meeting on the woman's question, a cantata was sung which proclaimed that the human race under the supremacy of man had stumbled in darkness and crime. But the race was now to be newly born from the soul of woman, the sunrise would scatter the darkness of night, and the advent of the Messiah was certain.

That men during the period of their ascendancy had nevertheless produced a few trifles—for example, religions and laws, sciences and arts, discoveries and inventions—that the darkness of their night was thus at least illumined by a Milky Way, all this her majesty Woman was pleased to forget.

If man were sufficiently vindictive to set about finding out what woman has accomplished in the course of ages to justify her towering self-esteem— or in other words to justify her challenging the comparison with these works of man—then he would find only one thing.

When nature formed the instinct of the race, woman remoulded it as love; when necessity made the dwelling, woman transformed it into the home. Her great contribution to culture is thus affection.

And this work is in truth great enough to counterbalance man's contribution—but not to make it worthless.

.   .   .   .

Fortunately we hear less and less about man's "tyranny" having robbed woman of the chance of also proving her powers within his sphere of activity. It is more and more recognised that in the struggle for existence necessity decreed that woman's social work should take the form of home work. The same necessity has now—in the main—liberated the powers that were confined in home work, although woman has never, at any time, been excluded from the use of her mental gifts. Such use was, however, obviously an occasional one, so long as the total of her activity belonged to another sphere.

It is from the point of view of their now emancipated personality that women—and many men on their behalf—demand the right of employing these personally-human powers in social work. They point in particular to the neglect of the State in that sphere of duty, which is already theirs in the home, namely, that of protecting and improving the existence of the young and of the weak. And men are beginning to see that, the more fixedly society is organised, the more indispensable will be the co-operation between all its parts, if the social organism is really to fulfil its purpose, the welfare of all; they see that the new forms both of State help and self-help, which are now being sought after with increasing consciousness of purpose, cannot be adjusted to actual needs unless woman is able to co-operate with man in every department and take part in the legislation which is to decide the welfare of herself and of her child.

But that the organisation of society has now progressed so far that man is beginning to look for woman's help, must not be taken by women as a reason for putting the whole blame for the slow development of society on men. This slowness results in an equal degree from the hitherto existing nature of woman and of man, from the limitations of both, and from their both being bound by the laws of development. Progress towards higher conditions depends in an equal degree on transformations in the nature of both, the ideals of both, the means and aims of both in the furtherance of culture. The very beginning of these transformations is the education women give to the new generation, which is afterwards to make the laws, to arrange the work, and to determine consumption according to the needs they bring with them into life and the virtues they have learned to love at home.

Our time is probably more conscious of its own shortcomings than any other. But nothing is more revolting to one's sense of justice than when this consciousness takes the form of women's megalomania as regards their own omnipotence for altering the course of the world.

Following on nature's rough division of the race, nature and civilisation in conjunction have produced a finer one, that of creator on the one side and material on the other. Next to being one's self a creator, it is a great thing to be worthy material in a creator's hand. And enhancement of culture in a spiritual as well as a material sense is brought about by the creators' success in dealing with their material. When that material is human, this means that the creators—or leaders—are successful in converting the rest into real collaborators with will and judgment of their own. Flocks driven on by shepherds, or masses of humanity led by one no more remarkable than themselves, have never had lasting effects on the course of civilisation. Such effects only follow when a creator fires the multitude with the enthusiasm of new aims, or teaches them to ennoble the means by which they may attain ends worthy of aspiration.

Thus, if women are to give the development of society a direction wholly different from that which man has given it, this will depend on the appearance among women of leaders who shall point the way to higher aims and employ purer means.

But what gives us reason to expect this of women? The reason cannot be sought elsewhere than within the sphere of their own creations, love, motherliness, the home, domestic economy. If it can be shown that women have brought all these to the full perfection of which they are capable, then there will really be good reason to believe in their miraculous power in the organisation of society.

But even if we fully admit the hindrances which man's ordering of society, his legislation, his nature have placed in the way of women—is there a single thoughtful woman who can maintain that she herself, or that women in general, have nevertheless done all that they could within their own special sphere; that they have used to the utmost the opportunities they have possessed? What conscientious woman does not perceive that the majority still bungle the great discoveries of their sex, by the way in which they act as guardians and educators of children, as lovers, wives, makers of homes, housekeepers! In every department they lack art and science, clearness of view and circumspection. Frequently they do not possess the first conditions for intensifying and refining a happy love; that of bearing and bringing up worthy children; that of attaining the greatest sum of material comfort for the members of the family with the least expenditure of force and of means; that of arranging the spiritual balance-sheet so that the highest possible enhancement of life will be the net profit. Exactly as the majority of men only slowly and partially receive and trans-

mit the thoughts, the works of beauty, the discoveries that their leaders bring them, so also do
women slowly and partially receive the leading
ideas in their sphere.

There must then be something, not only in man's
nature but in woman's also, which hinders perfection and delays progress.

If such be the case—and the supposition need not
be considered too bold—then also we may perhaps
wonder whether mankind would really have progressed so far, if women had had the lead during
past centuries. And if we have ventured thus far,
we may also be bold enough to ask: whether these
same women—who have been so far from perfecting
their own work—when they come to take part
in the organisation of society, will immediately
perfect what man has bungled; twist the sword into
a ploughshare and bring about the Messianic kingdom, where peace and righteousness shall kiss one
another.

It is not until she has renounced all communion
with the glorification of woman and the assertion
of woman's superiority, that a woman with a
sense of intellectual propriety can occupy herself
with the question of the social work of her sex.

.   .   .   .

Those who conduct the woman's movement
form in every country a "right" and a "left,"
each with an extreme wing.

The particular cult of the right is woman as

an ideal being. In addition, its dogmas include Christianity, monogamy, and the rest of the existing arrangements of society. It seeks to place woman on an equal footing with man within the old forms. To the extremists of this group, duty, labour, and utility are the great words of life; love and beauty do not come within the scope either of woman's rights or of her obligations. To whitewash the stains on the existing social edifice; to give themselves more space by building out a wing on the right—this is their chief concern; the main building itself they would preserve unaltered.

The left has also its deities—but "woman" is not one of them. Its view of life is radical; that is to say, evolutionist and social. It seeks to reform the existing institution of marriage by a new morality, and existing society by a higher organisation, which will express a deeper sense of solidarity. It thus looks at the rights and liberty of woman and of man in connection with the welfare of the whole community. From this point of view, it regards woman's freedom to love and right to motherhood as of equal importance with her right to vote and liberty to work.

Here, however, a difference comes in between this and the extreme left, which would give woman complete personal freedom of movement by leaving the children in charge of the State.

Thus the extreme wing of the old feminism meets that of the new on this point, that to both woman's activity is an end in itself to the extent that her right is independent of whether this activity raises or lowers the vital efficiency of the whole organism.

In everything else the opposition is diametrical, except on the plane where all the groups meet: in the demand for woman's juridical and political equality with man.

Those who demand political rights for woman in return for her liability to taxation and her cares as a mother, have a well-founded claim. But the position becomes still stronger when the claim is based upon the need of society that every member of it should co-operate to further the satisfaction of his own requirements. For modern society corresponds more and more to the idea of an organism increasing in complexity, every part of which becomes more and more important to the whole, determines more and more by its needs and powers the welfare or failure of the whole, and itself receives more and more profit or harm from the condition of the whole organism.

Society means human beings—men, women, and children, dead, living, and unborn—neither more nor yet less; human beings banded together in order thus the higher to enhance the life of the individual and of all. This combination takes at first simple, then more and more complicated forms of organisation: simple, so long as their needs are so, since only his needs move man to organise. An increasing civilisation means a more and more perfect satisfaction of increasingly complicated and higher needs. But as it is our needs that set us in motion, any hindrance of movement will also produce immediate suffering through our not being able to get rid of the cause of our displeasure; and indirect suffering through our losing the sense of pleasure that movement might have brought.

When the aim of society is seen to be that each of its members shall employ and develop his powers to the highest possible extent for the highest possible ends, then it will no longer be in abstract constructions of constitutional law, but rather in the laws of human life, that the criteria of social well-being will be sought.

The order of society must then favour the life-enhancement of the individual; the limitation of individual liberty must favour the life-enhancement of the whole—this will be to the evolutionist the motive for now extending, now limiting, the freedom of movement of the individual.

The parallelism with the human organism is evident. The formation and activity of the individual cells determine the structure of the whole; the degree in which their needs are satisfied determines the well-being of the organism. The total vital needs of the organism limit the cells' expansion of force and self-determination, for without the health of the whole organism the cells would also languish.

Every powerful movement of society—and the demand for women's suffrage is already such a one—is brought about by the will of many individuals to modify society in some respect, in order better to satisfy their own needs and therewith those of the whole community. Such a movement is always opposed in the beginning from the point of view of the agreement, equilibrium, and health of the community. And since a transformation in a society never occurs uniformly in time or degree; since the need of new forms is thus for a long time not widely spread, the conservatives, as a rule, are right at the beginning of their opposition; they are right even until the transformation has been taking place so long that the health of the whole organism demands that the class of society, religious body, or group of opinion in question should be given the freedom of activity without which it is ill at ease; for the uneasiness of many injures all. Conservatism is thus finally in the wrong by reason of the ever-repeated experience, that when the vital force is increased in any important organ, it is also increased in the whole organism.

Woman's suffrage ought above all to be demanded from the point of view of the social value, and consequent right to freedom of movement, of woman's powers. Its opponents answer: " We never thought of disputing either one or the other. Woman has already the same power as man in degree, though not in kind, just as truly as the heart is an organ equally essential to life as the brain. But the whole organism would go under,

if the heart insisted on usurping the functions of
the brain. Woman has become the organ of the
emotions in human life—but the emotions cannot
have a leading mission in public affairs. In that
field woman must either be untrue to herself or
lose her significance. It would be an immense
loss to civilisation if she were forced into the paths
of masculine egoism, instead of putting her whole
strength into the rearing of future men. Thus
new generations of great-minded and far-seeing
men would reform society in accordance with
woman's ideals, and woman would not lose her
ideals in party strife, where the chief thing is
victory by any means and the end is lost sight of."
"If," it was thus said by a thoughtful young
working woman,—"if the child saw both its father
and mother striving for power, with all the hardness and relentlessness this implies, then idealism
would soon become extinct, whereas, on the other
hand, women, by unequivocally making the highest
ideal demands upon fathers and brothers, husbands
and sons, could bring about by degrees an ideal
condition of things."

This view, which gives to woman the function
of one central organ in the social organism and to
man the other, does not, however, correspond to
the reality. Just as the individual is determined
from head to foot by his sex, so also is society
from top to bottom bi-sexual; every function of
government affects, therefore, all women just as
much as all men. At present, however, only the

latter possess the power of directly remedying what hinders and furthering what enhances their life, through also taking part in the functions by which they are affected.

Since every "cell," which indirectly or directly makes up the social organism, is male or female, it is unthinkable that a higher organisation of society would not finally of necessity manifest this its bi-sexual character. Like the family—the first "State"—it is probable that the final State will appear as a unity combining the male and female principles. Or, in other words, it will be a "State-marriage," not as hitherto merely a State-celibacy! Simply by performing the functions themselves, instead of allowing the male cells to do so on their behalf, the female cells may now as members of society experience their highest possible life-enhancement. So long as women were content to let men represent them, woman's non-enfranchisement did not disturb the well-being of the organism. Now, on the other hand, the disturbance has set in and can be removed only by change. But what the health of the organism demands in the highest degree, is that—when the female cells begin to perform their social functions—they should preserve their sexual character, for otherwise no higher form of development would be attained. Not the male sex, but the government of society may with truth be likened to its brain, as representation may be compared with its nervous system. The society of the present day suffers from one-sided paralysis, so long as half of it is excluded from the possibility of making known its needs through the nervous system. And society suffers from this condition just as much as the body would from a corresponding state. We can best see this by observing that society where the whole body is paralysed and only the head acts, namely Russia. There only the wounds bear witness that the organism as a whole is alive. But all the societies of Europe now include within themselves a Russia, that part of the community which Camilla Collet rightly called "the Camp of Silence." From the same inner necessity that prompted a number of the men in those countries whose condition once was like that of Russia to shake off the care of a parental government and take upon themselves the liberty of making known their own needs, of themselves deciding the conditions for their well-being, must women—and the labouring classes—win this right. This does not mean that the female half will work more perfectly or with less danger than the male. But it means that the whole organism will work more, will fare better, and will be developed to a higher condition. Those at present in possession are challenged by women as by working men, when they assert that they fully secure the interests of the unrepresented and direct their forces satisfactorily. And it may not be they, contented as they are with their power and with themselves, but the discontented that we should listen to, if higher conditions are to be attained.

To these general considerations must be added, in the case of the smaller nations, this: that the more alive and thoroughly active the whole social body is, the more power of resistance it will possess in the struggle for its existence. Those nations, in which every person can protect his own interests in and with those of the community, will—other conditions being equal—surpass the others, as an army of athletes would overcome one of invalids.

.   .   .   .

Society is confronted by tasks of increasing complexity. A force hitherto unused, that of woman, now become socially conscious, offers its co-operation in dealing with them.

All thinking persons desire new conditions with growing earnestness. But new conditions do not arise, as the socialist is far too willing to believe, through new external relations alone; nor through new ideas and discoveries, as the man of science with his bias is too apt to think. New conditions arise above all through new human beings, new souls, new emotions. Only these form new plans of life, new modes of action; only these revalue the objects which are then pursued day by day by innumerable individuals. A new idea becomes feeling and motive power, at first with one individual, then with a few, then with many, and finally with all. He who has been able to witness this with regard to any particular idea, knows that it comes about as in the spring, when first a solitary birch-tree on the sunny side unfolds its golden-green banner: then the veil of yellow, reddish-brown, and green is drawn closer and closer over the grey, till finally all the tree-tops are rounded and full, all colours subdued to one shade, and one scarcely remembers what it was like in the play of shifting colours, when the wild cherry gleamed white among the green, the dandelions spread themselves in wild profusion among the grass, the lilies of the valley peeped out from the sheath of their leaves, and the cuckoo called in the summer.

Emotions are the sap which rises when the human landscape thus changes colour and form. Therefore no profound spiritual transformation has ever taken place unless women have taken part in it. It is upon this great power of woman, already indirectly effective, that we may with reason base the hope of her direct exertion of force becoming even more effective—if with it she preserves her womanly character.

Precisely as the stricter sexual morality made woman's love more soulful—till she can now claim love's freedom, since she has a new contribution to make therewith—so the hindering of woman's external activity dammed up her emotional life. Under the division of labour into a "manly" and a "womanly" field, woman's peculiar character became more established; her feeling became intensified in the direction in which she is now ready to use it in the immediate service of humanity. Tenderness distinguishes her whole way of thinking and feeling, of wishing and working. Thus has she reached that dissimilarity to man, which she must now maintain in a public capacity.

It is as natural as it is fortunate that woman should come forward with her claims to participation in social duties and social rights just in our time, when the idea of interconnection, the sense of solidarity, has become increasingly conscious in every nation, as well as between the nations. For a clearer idea of interconnection will have the effect of saving woman from a number of man's mistakes; a profounder sense of solidarity from a number of woman's weaknesses—while the best traits of the womanly character will be invaluable for intensifying the sense of solidarity. The man and woman of the present day have become more sensitive to their own sufferings, and this is the first condition for becoming more sensitive to those of others. But now the problem is also really to intensify and to refine the feeling for others to such a degree that the social organism will no longer be able to endure that any of its members should suffer a hindrance to life in any avoidable way. It is in this respect that woman's deeper sensitiveness, her richer tenderness, are given their great mission. It is true that—as was remarked in connection with the evolution of love—it is becoming more and more impossible to speak of "man" or "woman" in general, since individualisation makes each sex more and more dissimilar within itself, while development makes them more and more mutually alike. Average women and average men have more understanding than feeling. But when feeling is found in a man, it is more violent and more transitory, whereas it is more intimate and more effective in a woman. The majority of men as of women seldom think. But when man and woman think, man's method is, as a rule, that of deduction and analysis, woman's that of intuition and synthesis. She unites instinct and reflection as the poet does: the thought of both forms a connected line of light only in the way that a row of lamps seen in perspective does so. Her actions—like his poems—have the unconscious purpose of inspiration.

These general characteristics are reversed, it is true, in many individual cases. It is thus certain that the most conspicuous revelations of Christian charity have occurred in men. This, however, does not alter the fact that "the milk of human kindness" flows more richly in women than in the majority of men.

This superiority is the natural result of motherliness, which has gradually been developed in the female sex into immediate feeling for all that is weak and in want of help, all that is budding and growing.

But it follows from this that if woman, by her participation in public life, is to provide a great, new, progressive element—then not only must she not lose the power of sympathy she already possesses; she must, on the contrary, intensify and extend it. Motherliness is not to be found in all those who are already mothers, and we have arrived indeed at the strange position that—while man is beginning to see how much society needs the motherly feeling—a number of women are no longer willing to become mothers, since their personal development and civil occupation would thus be interfered with. Nothing is more necessary than that woman should be intellectually educated for her new social mission. But if meanwhile she loses her womanly character, then she will come to the social mission like a farmer with a complete set of agricultural implements but no seed.

In all private activity the individuality is the best seed, while, on the other hand, in the social field women will probably for a long time be most valuable owing to their universal-womanly character; for unfortunately it is still true in public life that individuality is frequently a hindrance to co-operation, which takes place rather through partisanship in interests and views than through the working together of diverging characters. It is only in rare cases that a non-party man has the chance of interposing in a decision. At present, woman may be able to influence society not as a single personality, but rather as a new and powerful principle, a great contribution of a hitherto unemployed element. Doubtless individual women—through mental superiority, intellectual development, strength of will, and powers of work—will bring a great increase of general human value to social work. But it will nevertheless be upon the difference in kind between the nature of man and woman that we must base our hope that women's participation in the work of society will have far-reaching results.

When women think themselves able to accomplish what the whole aggregate of man's courage, genius, devotion, self-sacrifice, and idealism has hitherto not been able to do; when in every difference of opinion on man's and woman's nature they attribute to him every feminine failing in addition to his own, while claiming for themselves all man's merits, then one can be certain only about woman's superfluity for the time being.

Woman's right to participate in public life would, however, be in a bad way, if she could not bring to it something really indispensable, new, and peculiar to herself.

This new thing is her idealism and enthusiasm, however finely and easily they may blaze up, since woman is so much more inflammable than man, so much more eager to translate her enthusiasm into action.

For only such an enthusiast and idealist is of account who can carry the flame of his zeal in his bare hand, in spite of burns, keep it alight in spite of gusts of wind, and thus step by step come nearer his ideal. But such enthusiasts and idealists—whether male or female—are rare, much rarer than genius. They are the wine and the salt of life, whereas the virtues that the majority can show are only the daily bread on the table of society.

If then we look at the majority, the sense of justice in man and the feeling of tenderness in woman may be the greatest virtues. This does not mean that men do not both submit to and commit immense injustices, or women immense cruelties. But it means that the feeling which has been the strongest motive power in man's public actions— in revolts and in revolutions—is the sense of justice, while the feeling of tenderness sets a hundred women in motion for one that is moved by an outraged sense of justice. Nothing is more common than to hear even from the lips of a boy the words: "It served him right"; while from a girl we should hear: "I 'm sorry for him anyhow!"

It is the masculine feeling alone which has decided the structure of society. Not until woman's feeling has the same scope as man's; not until each can counterbalance what is extreme in the other —his what is too weak in hers, hers what is too hard in his—will society in its fatherliness and motherliness really provide for the rightful needs of all its children.

Someone has maintained that the social brain in the course of ages has developed more than the individual: by thinking and feeling more in common, the capacity has also been increased of finding means for furthering the common weal.

It is probable that women's brains will show their efficiency above all in finding means of enhancing and preserving life, which has so much greater significance for woman than for man; for every life has cost some woman infinitely more than any man; every mangled body on the field of battle or of labour has once made some woman happy with its child's smile, and leaves some woman in tears.

But in order thus to become inventive, women must remain what they now are: passionate in the force of their love, rapidly vibrating; otherwise they will not counterbalance the partialities of man in the work of civilisation.   There are perhaps no more remarkable pages in J. S. Mill's book, *On the Subjection of Women*, than those in which he maintains the faculty of woman—guided by her individual observation—for intuitively finding a general truth and, unfettered by theorising, for unhesitatingly and clear-sightedly applying it in a particular case.   Woman, he says, keeps to reality, while man loses himself in abstractions; she sees what a decision will mean in an individual case, while he loses sight of this in face of the general truths he has abstracted from reality, which he tries to force into abstraction.   These qualities of woman make her more unflinching, more rapid, and more immediate in her actions, while at the same time her more intimate and passionate feeling gives her more perseverance and patience in the face of trouble, disappointment, and suffering.

And this opinion of Mill is confirmed by that of Ibsen, whose fundamental view of woman is precisely that she becomes stronger in self-assertion and tenacity of purpose when it is a question of values of personality, but at the same time more devoted and self-sacrificing in the personal sphere. He regards her as less fettered by religous or social dogmas, but with greater piety and a deeper sense of community than man; he sees in her more unity between thought and action, a surer grasp of life and more courage to live it.   In a word: he thinks that woman more often is something, because she has not tried to be it; that she more often attempts the unreasonable, because she cannot be satisfied with the possible.

Thus woman became, not more perfect, but— fortunately for the fulness of life—different, when first life differentiated the natural function of mother and father; made them into separate beings, neither being superior or inferior to the other, merely incomparable.   It is this differentiation which must continue—not least in politics; for otherwise women's votes would only double the poll, without altering the result, and their participation in politics would thus only be a waste of their precious powers.

Thus even in public life woman must preserve the belief in miracles, the courage of apparent foolhardiness which her love gives her; that courage of which the most beautiful images are already to be found in national legends. What private life has taught her, she must now teach in turn to public life.

This is the most difficult of all tasks; for here she must preserve the sudden anger or enthusiasm of her feeling, but purge it of arbitrariness and injustice. She must trust to her feeling's unconscious sureness of direction, but secure it against the risks of foolhardiness. She must allow her feeling its mobility, but free it from the connection with caprice and untrustworthiness. She must keep her eyes for the individual, but yet be capable of lifting them to the universal.

To be able to do all this, woman must be willing to learn of man where he is the stronger, without letting man's scorn of womanly weaknesses or his pretensions to superiority mislead her into seeking a kind of strength which cannot be hers; for she could thus lose only what is already her own.

. . . .

Unfortunately, all the signs are not favourable to the hope that woman will pass through academies and carry on the service of the State without injury to her rapidity of view, delicacy of observation, and liberality of soul. "The conclusions of science," "the laws of history," "the demands of social security," "the opportunity of compromise," and all the other things that men pile up in the way of reform, are also alarming to woman's courage, make her too ask for proofs instead of feeling strong in her intuition.

In the university, the government department, and the business office the soul of woman also may run the risk of becoming tied by red tape, officially dry, amenable to public injustice, sober in the face of enthusiasm. Such official and business women will be as apprehensive as men of being suspected to be dreamers and agitators; they will be as logical in proving the unreasonableness of those who think for the future. In a word: when women bear men's burdens they will also get their bent backs; when they earn their bread in the general field of work, their hands will also be hardened. But we may hope—and everything depends upon this hope—that woman will attain her social power before she has yet lost her special characteristics, and that she will then give her whole mind to bringing about new conditions, in which she will be able to keep her hands soft and her attitude upright.

If this hope fails, then woman's entrance into public life will not change, for a thousand years to come, its tendency to put safety before boldness; to allow prudence to chill enthusiasm, facts to clip the wings of inspiration, and practical considerations to quench ideas. The demands of humane feeling will continue to be blunted by the sharing of responsibility among many; nay, we shall even see woman uniting herself with the

majority in curing the madness of idealists or—
if this is impossible—in rendering them harmless.

It is thus not by hymns of praise in honour of her
sex, but by great and inexorable claims on herself
and on all other women, that each individual
woman can best co-operate in the education of her
sex for public life. Only the spiritual education
that each one gives herself will prevent in the
political field false estimates of value and a con-
fused sense of justice; for in truth political life
in this respect gives nothing to him who has
nothing; on the contrary, it is there, if anywhere,
that the words of the Bible are applicable: from
him that hath not shall be taken away even that
which he hath. Public life in itself widens neither
the view nor the heart of anyone; of this our par-
ish and district councils, our municipalities and
our parliament give sufficient evidence.

It is not only want of education, but in an equal
degree half-education, that has the peculiar shady
side; and such is the education still provided for
the majority by school and high-school: ability to
pass examinations without formation of personality, specialised knowledge without spiritual culture.
The sign of this half-education is that it swallows
up the individuality and makes the instincts
shallow.

This evil will above all be fraught with danger
to woman's peculiar gift, intuition. The whole
existing plan of education aims at rendering more
acute the characteristics of man, and is successful

therein, so that he is strong though one-sided in his half-education. Woman, on the other hand, becomes weak in hers, since it detracts from her characteristics without giving her, however, those of man. We often find in an unlettered woman an instinct for essentiality which the half-educated have lost or to which at least they no longer dare to trust themselves. And, above all, this is true of the qualities essential to woman herself. Thus women who are working in the service of the community often show their resentment of the gladdening power of other, young and attractive, women even within the sphere of social activity. Only the form and contents of the long catechism could convince them of a young girl's seriousness. Whether these beauty-haters belong to the pietists of Christianity or to those of the woman's movement, they are agreed in the opinion that the attractive woman is also the less valuable, and that men show their lack of discernment in so easily allowing themselves to be charmed by her. Man's sense is, however, not so far wrong, even though he often takes appearance for reality. For what man looks for above all in woman—and loves most deeply, when he finds it—is the joy of goodness. It is this which is made visible in all real charm and gains its rightful victory; and only when women possess this joy of goodness and know how to communicate some of its charm to public life, will their participation in the latter tend to beautify it.

In judging of the position of affairs at the present moment we ought to remember that it is not only mothers-in-law but also daughters-in-law, not only the mistress of the house but also the cook, who would receive the franchise. But none of these groups seems inclined to regard the others as at present endowed with the greatest imaginable perfections—in private life! It may not, therefore, be too presumptuous if an outside observer should wonder whether it will be given to them to exhibit greater perfections in political life.

In a word, we must remember that developed women are not more numerous in proportion to the undeveloped than the former kind of men are to the latter. The same or other prejudices, self-interests, and stupidities, which on the part of men delay progress, will also stand in its way on the part of women. Just as one now sees herds of male "electoral cattle" in the wrong place, so will one see crowds of electoral hens—and the wrong place does not mean either the right or the left, but the place to which one is driven without personal choice and where one nevertheless remains without a feeling of shame.

Woman will, however, have the advantage of being able to learn from man's mistakes, and she learns more quickly than he. But only the power of being one's self active where one has the responsibility, and the right of deciding where one is to act, are educative. Developed women will

naturally exhibit one-sidedness, like developed
men; not until each sex comes forward with its
own peculiarities will legislation and administration become universal.   But universality is not yet
connection.   Whether one strums with one finger or
with all ten on an instrument, this does not make
music.   Not until each finger does its work—
and can play together with the others—does
harmony result, whether one is speaking of in-
strumental or of social music.

Before social politics have replaced the politics
of self-interest and class instinct, it is probable
that the vital forces of many will be wasted, and
among them those of many women, if in the mean-
time women enter political life.   But neither the
argument that women are too good, nor that they
are too immature, will weigh heavily in keeping
them from political work; for they will hasten development in the degree in which they preserve
their worth; they will attain the maturity they lack
in the degree in which they participate in development.   Only by being used can tools be gradually
adapted and perfected for what they have to do;
only by performing its functions does the organ
become developed for its purpose.   And to this
must be added the equally weighty argument that
the women even now necessary for development
are, no more than the men, to be found on one
side only of a dividing line of money or birth or
education.   Only the great democratic principle—
equal possibilities for all—involves in spite of its

defects the best prospect of the right man or the
right woman arriving in the right place. It is
more important to the community that one man
or woman through right of election or eligibility
should reach the prominent position for which
nature intended them, than that a hundred others
should make mistakes as electors. Even if women
are at first on the side of reaction—and in Sweden
this would certainly be the case—their direct
influence would nevertheless be less dangerous
than their indirect and irresponsible influence is
now; for there would be a possibility of their
being convinced by public life that, as long as a
dominant social and economical group maintains
the conditions which make innumerable other
members of society the victims of militarism and
industrialism, of prostitution and alcoholism—so
long will all social work be casting seed into the
snow. But even if women did not allow themselves
to be convinced, but only became a support to
those at present in power, this still ought not to be
a hindrance to their enfranchisement. Just as
nothing makes us more persevering than working
for justice, so there is no better evidence of the
purity of our own claims than when we adhere to
them in spite of our knowledge that their attainment will for a long time be to the advantage, not
of ourselves, but of our opponents.

.   .   .   .

Everyone with eyes to see is more and more

clearly aware that in our time new paths must be found. Women too are more and more frequently among those who see this, although the majority of women, by their ignorance, their lack of understanding, their petty aims, still place obstacles in the way of the pioneer work of their male kinsmen and fellow-workers.

But even among women fully conscious of the importance of social questions, there is little perception of their significance. This perception must be raised, but, above all, the idea of collective motherliness must be intensified, by fundamentally distinguishing it from that of benevolence. The latter may be justified in the individual case. But all social work, which is directed to the whole community, must aim at attaining so far in *right*-thinking that all *well*-doing may disappear. Collective motherliness must act more as an eternal subterranean fire and less as the soaring but soon burnt-out flame of a sacrifice. It is not enough that the instinct of mutual help and sympathy is more immediate in woman than in man. Just as affection is not sufficient for the care of children, if insight into the vital laws of the body and soul is lacking, so also do women need an understanding of the biology and psychology of society in order to fulfil their individual tasks in national economy, and to understand the problems which are summed up under the name of social organisation.

Only thus can sympathy with the victims of

society lead women to an ever stronger opposition
to the system which permits these sacrifices.
They must thus begin—and that very soon—by
obtaining power to restrict this, at any rate where
it applies to the bringing-up of children and the
education of the young; to places where women
work or are brought to justice; where the sick and
aged are cared for; where laws are made for all
these. The majority of women—who are still on
Christian ground—preach at the best charity as
the duty of the favoured and patience as that of
the unfortunate. But no more than the individual
mother will be satisfied with charity for her own
child, but will have full justice—which implies full
possibilities of development, full satisfaction of
wholesome needs, full employment of personal
powers—even so will collective motherliness refuse
to be satisfied with less on behalf of any child of
the community.

Not until the idea of poor-law relief is exchanged
for that of self-help, aided by society but without
sacrifice of pride, not until charity is exchanged for
justice, patience for assertion of rights, will there
be a prospect for the many of an existence com-
patible with human dignity. We need not fear
that the virtues of charity and patience will therefore disappear: everyone will doubtless have only
too much daily use for them—not only towards
God, but towards himself and his neighbour.

But as regards the life of the community their
time is gone by—or at least will be so, in proportion

as the belief in a fatherly providence above is exchanged for a knowledge of the power of human providence upon earth. When women's brains and hearts begin to exercise this providence in such a way that their views of life and their social work no longer conflict with one another, then and not till then will these brains and hearts become a reforming force.

Now, for instance, the majority of women are afraid of socialism, as to which however only one opinion should prevail: that as a party policy in the near future it is the most indispensable motive power of development, while as a principle—when cleared of the mutually conflicting dogmas of different schools—in its widest meaning it expresses the ever firmer coalescence of society into an ever more intimate unity, in which the sincere assurance of the old hymn, "the good of one, the good of all," will gradually be realised in and through the whole organisation of society. When this has made the fine image of the suffering of every member through that of one come true—then will the social State be attained.

The fear of socialism now hinders the leading women of the upper classes from supporting the others in conflicts which can result only in the victory of the cause they themselves wish to further. They are alarmed at the mere word *claims*, behind which they see the great hosts of the labouring classes streaming on with their red flags. They therefore prefer to speak of the duty of voting rather than of the right to vote. They hope it may be possible to carry on politics as peacefully as a college of teachers, that a public meeting may be as amenable to discipline as a school class. But this lack of a sense of proportion misses both the end and the means.

Women are thus desirous—and with full reason— of abolishing prostitution. But the first condition is a wholesale raising—for at least fifty per cent. a doubling—of the present wages of working women and shop assistants. This increase can take place only by means of trade-unions, and then strikes will be necessary. But the Christian champions of the woman's movement have a horror of both these things.

The latter desire—and with full reason—to stop the abuse of intoxicating liquors. But they do not see that this is not to be brought about by pro- hibitions and tea-meetings; that only by better opportunities and an increased appetite for the joys of home comfort, education, beauty, and nature can the intoxication of life take the place of the intoxication of alcohol. But these enhanced possibilities of life will result only from the stubbornly waged class-war, of which Christian women in general disapprove.

A number of women wish to abolish war. But the same women are not able in education to re- nounce those kinds of forcible methods which keep alive crude passions and low ideas of justice; they still believe that the souls of children are to be cleansed like mats, by beating. It is in vain that all the most eminent educationalists, as well as many of the foremost criminologists of our time, have again and again condemned corporal punishment—which one of the greatest contemporary authorities on jurisprudence has called the "fruitless bloodshed" of the centuries—since experience has incontrovertibly shown that physical fear never produces morality in the true sense of the term. Women, however, continue to lighten their work in the nursery by employing fear. In other words, they themselves practise—and train their children in—acts of violence, such as correspond in the life of nations to the wars these very women wish to abolish.

These examples might be multiplied. They do not prove that woman is more ignorant or more inconsistent than man in her social activity. But they prove that women, like men, will be of very little value in their public capacity, so long as they follow the methods of piece-work rather than of continuity.

.   .   .   .

To begin with, therefore, it would seem that individual women, and not the majority of the sex, will represent that collective motherliness which is to be at the same time far-seeing and warm-hearted. And these women can no more expect to go on from one victory to another, than can individual men. Those who—with their souls glowing against all injustice, their hearts warm and anxious with sympathy—enter into cold reality, must be prepared to experience what has been the lot of innumerable reformers in thought and action among the other sex: that they have won the best for themselves—martyrdom; but not the best for society—victory. And it is a poor consolation that it is often the best who become martyrs and the next best who are victorious. The former are those who throw themselves into the fight, urged by justice or love of humanity or passion for liberty—without asking themselves whether they will conquer, or at least without knowing what will be the answer to this question. The latter again are usually those who within themselves have answered it in the affirmative; for this conviction of success gives them the power of arraying an army behind them, and the courage to inspire it.

The precursors among women will also find out how unspeakably difficult it is to aristocratise the democracy, which does not mean simply cleaner hands and better manners, but purer actions and finer thoughts. And if they retain their sensitiveness—as they must—the leading women will thus have to suffer not only from their own wounds, but from the shame of seeing so many of their own sex as incapable as the men of sacrificing their own advantage—or the imaginary advantages of their country—when humanity and justice demand it. And it will be the fate of these women—as of so many men before them—that the pure will, the rich personality, which cannot bend, will be forced to break.

Everyone who has had anything to do with politics must have seen something of these trage-dies in which a noble heart is broken piece by piece, and know how cruel these bloodless struggles really are.

Will the best women endure to witness such tragedies? Will they endure to see how year by year politics and the press—indirectly, if not directly, under the sway of financial interest—succeed in producing the greatest possible number of half-measures and the greatest possible amount of stagnation, accompanied by inevitable self-surrender on the part of the best, and unconditional self-satisfaction on the part of the others? Will they endure seeing how in questions of culture, where selfishness can mean nothing, omniscient stupidity decides the great vital interests of the nation?

A gathering of people on great national festivals can together feel and act more greatly than each individual for himself. But in the everyday life of nations the individual is often better than he becomes in co-operation with others. What col-lective stupidity, collective cowardice, and collec-tive untruthfulness together produce without shame in public life, would cause almost everyone who makes up the mass to hesitate in his private life. To rescue the effectiveness of the private conscience—but at the same time to preserve the power of the collective, conscience for great moments—this should be the great task of political morality.

. . . .

Women must be prepared to find that their participation in public life will cost them, not only various unjustified prejudices, but also many hardships. They must, moreover, understand that it will take much time away from their home; for the whole thing is not so simple as merely handing in one's voting-paper, reading the leading article instead of the feuilleton, and going to an election meeting instead of to supper. If one hands in a voting-paper without knowing how one has voted, one's participation is of no great importance. If one wants to know how one is voting, this involves the sacrifice of time; and when once one has begun to take part in public affairs, one is often forced by circumstances further and further into their vortex.

Fathers of families, who "take up" politics, are even now the despair of those families. And what if mothers of families begin likewise?

This is the kernel of the question. As mother of a family the woman who takes part in politics must make her choice between an outward direction of her activities which will be unfortunate for the home and children and a lack of independence which will be personally painful to her. She can sacrifice her private pleasures, not her private duties. But it is this latter temptation which will present itself to the woman of the poorer classes. The wife of a working man wants to go to an election meeting with her husband— but what of the little children? There is no servant. The neighbour's wife? She too wants to go to the meeting. The crèche? It is closed in the evening, for its manageress also takes an interest in public affairs! There is therefore no way out of it but that the wife must be content with her husband's judgment.

In the suffrage question—as always when it was a question of woman's rights—attention has been too one-sidedly directed to the point of view of the unmarried woman of the upper class. But these are so far from being the most important that we might rather assert that a mother of the working class, who—with all the trouble and privations this involves for her—has cared well for her children both bodily and spiritually, has made a happy home for them and her husband and therewithal has acquired for herself education and insight in social questions, affords so extraordinary a social power, that the most just of proportional suffrage methods would be to give her—and all other mothers of remarkable children—a double vote.

We are here again faced by the difficulty already pointed out: that it is precisely the most excellent women, the most indispensable for the task, who will have to choose between the duties of collective motherliness and those of motherhood, as well as between the latter and those of individual development. During her children's earlier years no mother can well fulfil both these motherly calls. She will be forced to acknowledge that, if anyone could be said to cross the river to fetch water— and with one of the Danaids' pitchers at that— then it would be one who should set aside her children for her social mission.

Here and there we already meet one or another of these strong, proud, and beautiful mothers of the twentieth century, who have lost nothing of their full-blooded womanliness, but rather doubled it through a personal quality which year by year embraces the kernel of their being more closely.

Human being and woman, citizen and personality—less than this the social mother of the future cannot be. She has destroyed all bridges which might take her back to the womanly ideal of older times: the powerful but narrow-minded housekeeper, the thoughtlessly devoted wife. But at the same time she has nothing in common with the shortsighted woman's rights woman, who takes pride in being a restless working-machine or a specialist rewarded by diplomas but otherwise half-educated.

She has learned something from the older as well as from the new type. But she resembles neither, for only completeness of life is to her the meaning of life.

. . . .

Many a little girl, leaning over her history book, must have been indignant at the way humanity used to be reckoned in past times: so many men —"besides women and children"!

It was long before women began to be counted at all, and they are still only half-counted. Children are still under "besides." But some day we may perhaps have come so far in our feeling for what is coming on, that we shall invert the order and reckon "so many children—besides women and men." We shall then give evidence in our treatment of children of our reverence for these profoundly wise and mysterious beings, whom we never fathom. We shall see behind the figure of every child the infinite line of past generations, before it the equally endless ranks of those to come. We shall remember in our actions that the child is the sum of these dead ones, the hope of those unborn. We shall let the child reveal itself and receive its revelations with a discretion at present unsuspected.

The tragedies of the childish soul are still waiting for their Shakespeare, although the child is already appearing in literature as never before. And here, as ever, literature is the precursor of the great movement of liberty which shall bring the children's declaration of rights and make an end of the spiritual and bodily ill-treatment of children, which must appear to the future as monstrous as negro slavery does to us. It may be that children too will have their right to vote, as well as their own representatives in the legislature and in the courts of law.[1]

It should be the collective mothers who would thus finally liberate the children of society. It will then be seen that the octave of the child's soul was just as indispensable as that of woman or man, in order that the great harmony of humanity might be complete.

When this happens the third kingdom will have arrived, whose Messiah the age now awaits. But it is not in the lap of collective motherliness that he will be borne.

Again and again saviours will be born to humanity. But always of some young woman with forehead pure as a lily and deep eyes. And Bethlehem will always be there, where a young mother kneels in prayer by her child's cradle.

[1] Every English reader knows what Dickens achieved in this respect. I will only remind them here of Hannah Lynch's (anonymously published) *Autobiography of a Child*.

CHAPTER VIII

FREE DIVORCE

THE desire of the young to abolish prostitution by means of love's freedom has already been adduced as one of the proofs of the higher development of sexual morality. Another such proof is the desire of the present day to abolish adultery by means of free divorce.

The preachers of monogamy are afraid that this desire will prepare the way for an open polygamy, instead of that which at present is at least secret. In the press and in the pulpit, in schoolrooms and lecture-rooms, modern literature is blamed for this "new immorality."

And yet we all know that long before our time, married men and their sons in country houses were too often ready to seduce the wives and daughters of their dependents as well as the servants of the house. The wives and mothers of these gentlemen were frequently not ignorant of this—but they were praised for their wisdom when they pretended to suspect nothing. It was a matter of common knowledge that not a few married men and married women had mistresses and lovers

287

within their own social circle; and every one knew
that in the towns many men, during or before
marriage, had illegitimate families.

Serious preachers of morality doubtless reply
that they no more condone this secret adultery
than they would an open one; that they see in one
and the other a manifestation of that power of sin
which only religion can vanquish. We have the
right then to ask, whether within their own ranks
—among clergymen, missionaries, readers—no
similar transgressions occur.

The honest ones answer Yes, but point out that
this causes shame among their fellow-Christians,
and that these believers themselves acknowledge
that they have sinned. Such men of the world,
who play the hypocrite to retain their respecta-
bility, do the same thing. But the great danger
to society first comes in when free-thinkers with no
qualms of conscience commit, and authors without
moral indignation describe, the sin. This it is
that degrades the ideal of morality.

Here we are at the very cross-roads of the old
and the new morality.

The champions of the latter go on to ask whether
all adulterers—children of this world as well as
children of God—in their innermost consciousness
really feel themselves to be sinners. The need
which impelled them was perhaps so imperious
that it justified them before their own conscience
in choosing a lesser evil in preference to a greater,
when—from one cause or another—they could

not or ought not to satisfy the need in their marriage.

And if this be so, then the exponents of the new morality may have grounds for their opinion: that self-control cannot and must not be the only answer to all the problems of sexual life; that a solution must be found which shall by degrees prevent men from wasting, either in unchastity or in a celibacy disguised as marriage, the strength which belongs to the race. The solution can only be this, that we not only assert love's freedom to unite without external tie, but also man's right more freely than at present to loosen the tie, when real union is no longer possible.

When speaking of love's selection, it was put forward that a growing insight into the value and conditions of the enhancement of the race might produce cases where a marriage could be openly broken without therefore being dissolved. But the true line of development will quite certainly be this: that divorce will be free, depending solely on the will of both parties or of one, maintained for a certain time; that public opinion as regards a dissolved marriage will take the broader view that it has already acquired in the question of a broken engagement, which at one time was thought just as humiliating as a divorce is now.

With ever-growing seriousness the new conception of morality is affirmed: that the race does not exist for the sake of monogamy, but monogamy for the sake of the race; that mankind is therefore

19

master of monogamy, to preserve or to abolish it.

Even the advocates of free divorce know well enough that it will involve abuses. But at the same time they know that there is no better proof of man's incredible indolence of mind than the uneasiness produced by the thought of possible abuses resulting from a new social form, while the ancient abuses are tolerated with the dullest tranquillity.

Whatever abuses free divorce may involve, they cannot often be worse than those which marriage has produced and still produces—marriage, which is degraded to the coarsest sexual habits, the most shameless traffic, the most agonising soul-murders, the most inhuman cruelties, and the grossest infringements of liberty that any department of modern life can show.

We may answer that abuses do not prove anything against the value of any particular social arrangement, so long as its right use serves well the purpose for which it was introduced.

The majority thinks that this is still the case with marriage. The minority, on the other hand, considers that its constraint now tends to defeat its original object, an enhanced sexual morality.

This minority thinks that, as soon as love is admitted as the moral ground of marriage, it will be a necessary consequence that he who has ceased to love should be allowed a moral as well as a legal right to withdraw from his marriage, if he chooses to avail himself of this right.

And this same minority is aware that love may cease, independently of a person's will; that therefore no one can be held to the terms of a promise, the performance of which lies outside his powers.

Nothing is more natural than that love's longing for eternity should prompt lovers to vows of eternal fidelity; nothing is more true than that it is a satanic device of society to seize upon this promise and base thereon a legal institution (Carpenter). Nothing is more necessary than to abolish the legal claims that people have on one another, supported by promises of love and vows of fidelity.

The more people understand the laws of their own being, the more will the conscientious begin to hesitate about making promises which perhaps some day they will be forced by inner necessity to break. An increasing number of people find it impossible to contract marriage, or to ask it of the other party—or to continue in marriage or ask its continuance of the other—when their love has died or has awakened for another. A generation ago, an engaged person could refuse his or her betrothed's petition for liberation with the answer that he or she had love enough for both. In corresponding circles at the present day, such a speech is unthinkable. But then a public engagement was still regarded as a binding tie and the marriage took place. After a long engagement it was a "point of honour" for the man not to let a woman run the risk of being unmarried, and she was satisfied if he only paid his debt of honour.

Such coarseness of feeling is fortunately becoming more and more rare, although it is far from disappearing. People see more and more that they have no more right to marry simply to fulfil a duty of fidelity than they have to steal in order to fulfil a duty of maintenance; that there is no more obligation to abide by a marriage which one feels to be one's ruin than there is a duty to commit suicide for the sake of another.

The love of older times was above all afraid that the other party should not feel sufficiently bound. The finest erotic feeling of the present day shudders at the idea of becoming a bond; trembles at pity and recoils from the possibility of becoming a hindrance. This state of the soul knows of no other right than that of perfect candour. To place legal limits to each other's liberty, so that neither shall cause pain to the other, is under these conditions meaningless; for each suffers just as much through a union maintained without full reciprocity.

Thus the question of divorce presents itself to modern souls, in cases where there are no children. And when there are children—as is of course the rule—they think that the mistakes of parents do not absolve them from the duty of co-operating in the rearing of the children to whom they have given life.

But they maintain that this need not always be effected by means of continued cohabitation. On the other hand, this may often be necessary, and in such cases they subordinate their personal claims of happiness to those of the race. One who holds these opinions regards him who gives the same answer in every case—whether this answer be "freedom at any price" or "renunciation at any price" —simply as a moral automaton.

. . . .

It is true that modern men and women are less able to bear unhappiness in marriage than were those of former times. This shows that connubial idealism makes greater demands than formerly.

The conscious will to live, of our time, revolts against the meaningless sufferings through which the people of bygone days, above all the women, allowed themselves to be degraded, benumbed, and embittered. A finer knowledge of self, a stronger consciousness of personality, now puts a limit to one's own suffering, since the danger is understood of taking hurt in one's soul. This determination of individualism makes it impossible for the modern woman to be fired by the ideal of Griselda—if for no other reason, because she feels how all-suffering meekness increases injustice. The "good old" marriages, sustained by the willing sacrifice of wives, are disappearing—that is happily true! But no one takes notice of the new good ones that are coming in their place. If those who now grudgingly reckon up divorces would also count all happy marriages, it would be seen that new formation has proceeded further than dissolution.

It must be evident that the question of divorce is the pursuance of the line of development of Protestantism. With the formation of a right and a left party, as usual in the treatment of a problem of culture, the Reformation succeeded only in asserting the right of the senses in human life. That it is the right of the soul in sexual life that is now most intimately affected by the question, people will not understand. Against the right of the individual they set up that of the child. If there is none, then a certain number of Christians are willing to admit that divorce is sometimes justified. Unhappy parents, on the other hand, must remain together for the sake of the children.

But the erotically noble person of the present day cannot, without the deepest sense of humiliation, belong to one he does not love, or by whom he knows he is not loved. Thus for one or both of the parties a marriage that is persisted in without the love of one or both causes profound suffering either through this humiliation or through lifelong celibacy.

This is the kernel of the question, which is avoided by all who, in their care for the children, forget that the parents must nevertheless be con-

sidered as an end in themselves. It is not asked
that for the sake of the children they should commit other crimes; thus a woman who committed
forgery to support her child would be disapproved
of. But other women are judged leniently who
"for the sake of their children" feel themselves
prostituted year after year in their marriage.

That married people are to be found who continue to live as friends, since the erotic needs of
both are small; that others do not feel the humiliation of cohabitation without love; that the former
as well as the latter are probably acting best for
the children in keeping together a home for them—
this does not prevent others under similar circumstances from suffering in such a way that life loses
all its value. And these are they who end either
in adultery or divorce.

Even if an enemy of divorce admits these difficulties, he replies, that the individual must still
suffer for his erotic as for his other mistakes, since
only so can people be taught not to commit
mistakes.

But the true state of the case may be, that just
as in old times murders increased in proportion
to the number of executions people witnessed, so
unhappy marriages may become more frequent,
the more there are at present; for it is, above all,
the whole spirit that prevails around us which
determines our action. If the young are accustomed to see their elders content with false and ugly
relations, they will learn to be so likewise. If they

see around them an aspiration towards ideal conditions in love—an idealism which is revealed now in a beautiful married life, now in the dissolution of one that is not beautiful—then their ideals will also be lofty. Those again, who have once made a mistake, will perhaps be more clear-sighted if they choose again.

But neither those who make mistakes nor those who witness them can be saved by the misfortunes of others from that great source of error, erotic illusion. And until erotic sympathy has become more refined, these mistakes are the most innocent of all. Every lover believes himself to be exempted from the sacrifice of illusion and no experience of the irretrievable erotic mistakes of others has ever opened the eyes of one blinded by love.

As it is recognised that society ought to make the lives of all as valuable as possible, this involves the claim that innocent mistakes should cause as little ruin as need be.

In marriage as in other fields, the modern principle must be put in force, that punishment should improve the faulty and prepare the way for a higher idea of justice. But this higher idea is that marriage should be contracted under gradually improving conditions, not that it should continue under gradually deteriorating influences.

Marriage under constraint forces people to continue their cohabitation and to bring children into the world in a revolt of the soul which must leave its mark in their children's nature and thus influence their future destiny. But this is not a "well-deserved punishment" for a mistake: it is the profoundest violation of the sanctity of the personality and of the race.

Here as ever the only logical alternative is full individual liberty or unconditional surrender.

The Catholic Church maintains—and rightly from its own point of view—that, since even marriages entered into with the warmest love and under the most favourable conditions may turn out unhappily, it is impossible to base the morality of marriage on the emotion of love. Nothing that is founded upon emotion can be permanent. Nay, the richer, the more individually and universally developed a personality is, the less immutable will be the state of its soul. Thus even the highest need an inflexible law, an irremovable tie, to prevent their being at the mercy of winds and waves through their emotions, while inferior beings need them so as not to be driven out of their course by their desires. The concessions of Protestantism, therefore, lead to the dissolution of marriage, since when love is made the basis of marriage it is built upon sand.

Marriage, which the Church therefore made a sacrament and indissoluble, had already become the legal expression of the husband's right of private ownership over his wife and children. The course of development has consisted in an unceasing transformation of this religio-economical view, and development cannot stop until the last remnant of this conception has been destroyed.

Therefore the believers in Life refuse to admit either the half-admissions of Protestantism or the logical compulsion of Catholicism. They demand that the step from authority to freedom shall be taken outright, since they know that the external authority which simplifies life does not create the deeper morality. Compulsion fetters legal freedom of action, but thereby only makes secret crime a social institution.

And even if a husband or a wife has outwardly overcome a temptation, this will not prevent that individual when in the embrace of the lawful spouse from being filled with feeling for another. Have they then avoided adultery? Not according to their own finest consciousness—that consciousness which Goethe aroused in his great poem on elective affinities. Duties performed may as surely as those left undone produce incalculable and tragic results. They are foolish who think they can lead another soul across the bridge, fine as a hair and sharp as a knife-edge, by which every one goes his solitary way over the abyss to salvation: the way of the choice of personal conscience.

When custom and law deprive a human being of full freedom of choice in the matters of most profound personal concern—his belief, his work, and his love—then existence is robbed of greater values than those the compulsory fulfilment of duty can bring in.

.   .   .   .

In love, the idea of personality has now brought us to the view that "property is theft"; that only free gifts are of value; that the ideas of connubial "rights" and "duties" are to be exchanged for the great reconstructive thought, that fidelity can never be promised, but that indeed it may be won every day.

This will give the motive power for the attainment of ever higher forms of erotic organisation a power which the Buddha-like calm of indissoluble marriage has left unused.

It is sad that this truth—which was already clear to the noble minds of the Courts of Love— should still need proclaiming; for one of the reasons given in these Courts for love being impossible in marriage is this: that woman cannot expect from her husband the delicate conduct that a lover must show, since the latter only receives by favour what the husband takes as his right.

When divorce becomes free, the attention to each other's emotions, the delicacy of conduct and the desire to captivate by being always new, which belong to the period of engagement, will be continued in married life. As in the early days of love, each will allow the other full freedom in all essential manifestations of life, but will exercise control over his own casual moods, whereas marriage now as a rule reverses this happy state of things.

The security of possession now puts to sleep the

eagerness of acquisition; the compulsion to win anew will brace the energy in this as in every other connection.

A fidelity thus won will be the only sort that will be thought worth having in the future. A craving for happiness more sensitive than the present may one day marvel at the legally insured fidelity of our time, as at its inheritance of wealth. In both cases it will have been seen that only one's exertion of force brings happiness and gives that felicity of victory before which hands stretched out to steal shrink back.

The believers in Life are everywhere distinguished by their determination to give to every relation the value of the unique, the stamp of the exceptional, that which has never been before and will never come again. Like the worshippers of Life of the Renaissance, those of our time have begun to recover the power of strong enjoyment and strong suffering which is always the sign of increasing spiritual unity, a new gathering of force through a new religious feeling.

To this view of life the permanence of happiness will be less important than its completeness while it lasts.

Spinoza, who described jealousy as no one else has done, has also uttered this deep saying of love: The greater the emotion we hope that the loved one will experience through us, and the more the loved one is moved by joy in his relation to us, the greater also will be our own happiness in love.

People of the present day have begun to distinguish the idea of this "greatest joy" from lifelong proprietorship; and therewith jealousy in its lower form has begun to disappear.

Jealousy like other shadows belongs to the rising and setting light and disappears like them in the full clearness of noonday. But its tone of feeling has become quite different since man has discovered that, if the sun stands still in the zenith for him, it is a miracle—not a right. The most highly developed people of the present day say "I am loved" or "I am not loved" with the same simplicity as they say the sun shines or does not shine. The difference is in both cases immeasurable, but in one case as in the other, necessity removes the feeling of humiliation. The grief which comes when a lover no longer feels that he brings joy to the beloved or when he sees another bring it, is natural and worthy of respect. It ceases to be so when it manifests itself in the will of an avaricious proprietor, the brutal instinct which often survives not only the feeling of the other but also its own.

But although the psychological differentiation in our time involves greater possibilities of finding some one who will satisfy some side of the erotic longing,—while it is more and more difficult to find one who wholly satisfies this ever more complex desire,—the danger of such division of self is counterbalanced by the growing wish for the longing to be wholly satisfied. Love by thus making ever greater demands becomes at the same time ever more faithful.

Those who dread the dissolution of society through the insistence upon the rights of love, do not reflect that its right to break up marriage is allowed to the feeling, which has not only the red glow of passion, but also the clearness through which two people have become conscious of each other as a revelation of the whole unsuspected richness of life.   A revelation which included all the fulness of comprehension, all the serenity of confidence;   where both have given with equal exactingness and generosity—not meagrely or hesitatingly, but so that each without reserve has rushed to meet the other—this is the only happiness that love's noblemen will now experience. It will be more and more difficult even to experience it once—how much more so then to find it many times!

A great love is never like the erotic thunderstorms which move against the wind—that is to say, against the whole disposition of the personality in other things.

All valuable feelings—whether entertained for a person, a belief, a place, or a country—are conservative.   The consciousness of this gives the preacher of liberty his boldness.   He never perceives how liberty may be abused, since he knows what it costs to loosen a heart from what it has once embraced.

To a volatile nature, the happiness that a more

steadfast one experiences in love is as unfathomable as the bliss of the mystic becoming absorbed into the fulness of his divinity is to the polytheist.

Here, as everywhere, to the believer in Life, happiness is one with morality. Since happiness consists in the greatest emotions, its first condition is to intensify and enlarge all feelings, and above all that which leads to marriage.

But in addition, the whole standard of personality depends to a great extent upon whether we consider fidelity a life-value. He who desires fidelity centres his moods and his powers upon what is essential and protects them from the gusts of the accidental. Only this gives style and greatness to existence. The desire of fidelity is therefore one with a person's feeling for his own integrity, his inward consistency, the attitude and dignity of his spiritual being.

When fidelity is preserved for these profound reasons, it will also be broken only for the same reasons. A fidelity, on the other hand, which rests upon conventional notions of duty, will be in the fire like a fire-escape of straw.

It is moreover forgotten, in all discussions of the dangers of free divorce, that under the influence of love the whole disposition of the soul is towards fidelity. Great love absorbs all associations of ideas and thus without conscious exertion intensifies and enlarges the personality. Fidelity will be a necessary condition of love, but a condition whose psychological continuance is not favoured by coercive marriage.

Fidelity towards one's self—also in the new sense of the word—thus involves not only the ability in case of need to destroy the bridge between one's self and one's past. It also implies the building of better bridges to strengthen the connection between our personality and our present. It implies not only the capacity to have finished with a destiny; but also that of not having done too soon with a person. It may certainly involve the necessity of a new experiment in life. But still more certainly it involves the need of not allowing the incidental numbness of one's feeling to seduce one to new "experiences." This expression—in place of the old word "adventures"—implies, moreover, an intensification of feeling: where formerly only the excitement of "adventure" was looked for, a richer element of life is now sought. But it is often a fatal error to suppose that this is to be gained in new relations, when on the contrary it might have been won by an intensification of the former ones. By more attention to and respect for the other's personality one may often discover more than one had expected; for some people are like certain landscapes or works of art: they do not begin to make an impression until one thinks one has done with them. But piety is required to await the revelations of soul as of a work. Piety implies contemplation, and this demands peace. But peace is difficult to find in our time, whose misfortune is precisely disturbance and amusement.

That our time like every other has its particular epidemics in the erotic sphere, is certain, and disturbance is just the condition in which the most dangerous of these find a favourable soil. It is therefore a part of the erotic art of living that a married couple should now and then pass some time undisturbed in each other's company—or separately and alone—in order thus to strengthen the health of their feelings. Here as in other things external precautions against infection are unimportant in comparison with care of the general health.

Only he who, after unceasing effort and patient self-examination, can say that he has used all his resources of goodness and understanding; put into his married life all his desire of happiness and all his vigilance; tried every possibility of enlarging the other's nature, and yet has been unsuccessful, —only he can with an easy conscience give up his married life.

. . . .

The life-tree of a human being is formed, no more than are the trees of the forest, according to a strict measure for the length of the branches or a pattern for the shape of the leaves. Like nature's trees, its beauty depends upon the freedom of the boughs to take unexpected curves, upon the disposition of the leaves to exhibit an infinite diver-

sity of shape. Only he who does not permit the
tree to grow according to its own inner laws, but
clips it according to those of gardening, can be
sure of not preparing surprises for himself and
others, when one branch unexpectedly shoots out
and another equally unaccountably withers. No
one can answer for the transformations to which
life thus may subject his own nature; nor for
the changes which the transformation of another's
nature may effect in his own feeling. He may
possess the rarest disposition to fidelity, the most
sincere desire to concentrate himself upon his love,
to "let his personality grow around it, as about
its core"—it nevertheless does not depend upon
his will alone whether this core shall shrivel or
be corrupted.

Therefore the desire of fidelity can not, must not,
and ought not to imply more than the will to be
true to the deepest needs of one's own personality.

In other spheres than that of love, people admit
this freely. Nobody considers it an unquestion-
able duty for a young man to find at once the view
of life or the career in which he can continue for the
rest of his life. What young people are rightly
warned against is the wandering without method
among different opinions or undertakings; for
only that belief or that work which one seriously
tries to live by and live for can really employ the
powers of the personality and thus show its efficacy
in enhancing them. But the most profound
seriousness cannot prevent a continued develop-

ment of the personality from one day compelling
the man to abandon that belief or that work. It
probably would not occur to a thoughtful clergyman to appeal to such a man's promises at con-
firmation, or to a thoughtful father to bring forward
his own choice of a career as an example to his son.

Lifelong tenacity was demanded in those days
when it was assumed that a single doctrine, a
single set of circumstances, was entirely adequate
for personal development for a whole lifetime. The
crime of deviation was then logically punished
by excommunication or by fines. But the profounder view which we have acquired in the
matters of belief and occupation must also be
extended to the third. We ought to perceive that
unconditional fidelity to one person may be just as
disastrous to the personality as unconditional continuance in a faith or an employment. Those
who are now patching the sack-cloth of asceticism
with a few shreds from the purple mantle of personality are spoiling both. Either state the claim
of renunciation clearly, like the Catholic, or admit
the whole claim of personality. But the whole
problem is unfairly stated by those who make
"personal love" the moral basis of marriage, but
go on to speak of this love as though it were a
question of light-heartedly taking partners for a
game, where nothing is more usual than that each
woman finds the right man and each man the right
woman—and so everything is in order. If life
were so easy, there would be reason for the pro-

nouncements, which are now so profoundly coarse, that only the man or woman without character, the aimless personality, is incapable of vowing a lifelong love and keeping the promise; nay, that a true personality can "command itself to love its child's father or mother."

He who asserts that our true personality will always follow the duty laid down by society and constantly be able to fulfil the claims of fidelity, and that those who cannot do this are guided by a false subjectivity and not by their personality, makes the idea of personality equivalent to that of member of society, the whole equivalent to the part. The personality, the unique and peculiar value, is certainly connected through part of its nature with the standards of right upheld by society. Yet it never becomes equivalent to them.

The only thing therefore that a psychological thinker can demand is that love should not divide the personality in any phase of a human being's development, but should always be its true expression.

But only one who is ignorant of the idea of personality can believe that the relation, into which a person at the age of twenty puts his whole feeling, must necessarily correspond to the needs of the same personality as it becomes at thirty or forty. Only one so ignorant can persuade himself that the destiny of our love will necessarily resemble our lofty theory of love, our pure desire of constancy. If even our own will has little to do with the love we feel, how much less then will it influence that which we receive or lose!

Thus the problem of fidelity is not solved merely by imposing the claim of constancy upon one's self; for in the first place, in love there are two who must desire the same thing, and in the second, each of these two is manifold.

No human being is sole master of his fate when he has united it with another's. The possibility of becoming a complete personality in and through love depends in half upon the pure and whole desire of the other to share in developing the common life.

It is this which is overlooked by the eloquent preachers of "constancy as the expression of the personality," and this makes their words about the duty of lifelong love as meaningless as a harangue about the duty of lifelong health.

It is a beautiful sight when two married people enjoy the happiness of their love for the whole day of human life. It is also a beautiful sight when life sets like a clear sun upon the horizon, and does not lose itself like a weary river in the sand. But these are beautiful ideals not commands of duty.

Love, like health, can certainly be neglected or cared for, and by good care the average length of life both of human beings and of their loves may be raised.

But the final causes both of love's birth and of its beath are as mysterious as those of the origin and

cessation of life.　A person can therefore no more
promise to love or not to love than he can promise
to live long.　What he can promise is to take good
care of his life and of his love.

. . . .

This may be done, as already pointed out,
through the conscious will to be faithful, the firm
resolve to make love a great experience.

But perhaps the majority as yet do little to
preserve their happiness.　In this case, life works
for them, as God "gives to his servants, while they
sleep."

If ever the doctrine of the importance of the
infinitely small has its application, it is in respect
to the power the little things of everyday life have
of uniting or dividing in marriage.

That hardships and memories, joys and sorrows
shared bind people together even without the
continuance of love; that in the deepest sense of
the word they cannot be separated, since a great
part of the one's nature remains in the other's—-
this in reality forms the binding tie, but not ideas
of duty, whether clear or obscure, strict or free.　If
in one case a married life has so dried up the feelings
of both that a gust of wind drives them apart like
two withered leaves, in another it may have given
the feelings such deep roots that, even if all the
leaves that the spring-time gave are torn away,
even if life seems as empty and cold as naked
boughs in winter—it is still lived in common.

It is thus a physiological and psychological fact that the man or woman who for the first time has communicated to the other the joys of the senses retains a power over her or him which is never really set aside. It is even said that long after a man's death a woman sometimes bears children to another man which resemble the first. As such influences are more decided in the case of the woman, her fidelity has also for this reason become more of a natural necessity than man's—although the same influence, if in a somewhat less degree, applies to him.

Even if no qualms of conscience for others' sufferings are mingled with a new happiness—in many other senses the two, who in each other seek to forget the past of one of them, will perhaps for ever find a third between them.

Marriage, in a word, has such sure allies in man's psycho-physical conditions of life that one need not be afraid of freedom of divorce becoming equivalent to polygamy. What this freedom would abolish is only lifelong slavery.

.   .   .   .

It is evident to every thoughtful person that a real sexual morality is almost impossible without early marriage; for simply to refer the young to abstinence as the true solution of the problem is, as we have already maintained, a crime against the young and against the race, a crime which makes the primitive force of nature, the fire of life, into a destructive element.

But the consequence of early marriages must be free divorce.

As soon as one approaches the outer side of the marriage problem, one is met by the experience which the four great Norwegian writers, Ibsen, Björnson, Lie, and Kielland, some years ago jointly and publicly announced: that at present the majority do not marry for love. And R. L. Stevenson may have hit the mark, when he calls the marriages of the majority "a kind of friendship sanctioned by the police" and compares the "fancy" which decides them to that which sometimes takes one for a particular fruit in a dish that is being handed round.

But even if we one day come so far that early love-matches are the rule, we shall still be faced, as regards them, by the system which at present obtains among the upper classes: that marriage is binding upon the lovers before love is consummated. There is therefore a truth worthy of consideration in the words of the brothers Margueritte, in their contribution to the question of free divorce; that as the young girl has not experienced what she binds herself to at marriage, the majority of divorces begin on the wedding night.

Free divorce is therefore an unconditional demand of such young people who know that unforeseen transformations may take place in the sphere of the soul as in that of the senses, and who now frequently seek in the secret possession of love a security against a precipitancy which the legal bond of marriage may make irretrievable.

The young know, if any can know, that no form of love is more beautiful than that in which two young people find each other so early that they do not even know when their feeling was born, and accompany each other through all their fortunes, sometimes even to death—for now and then life vouchsafes this crowning fortune. Never do greater possibilities exist for the happiness both of the individuals and of the race than in a love which begins so early that the two can grow together in a common development; when they possess all the memories of youth as well as all the aims of the future in common; when the shadow of a third has never fallen across the path of either; when their children in turn dream of the great love they have seen radiating from their parents.

These happy ones—like the old couple in Bernard's fine fresco in the *mairie* of the Louvre *arrondissement* in Paris—will one day look up to the stars of the winter twilight, united in a more intimate devotion than either the playtime of the spring morning or the midday toil could afford.

If this wonderful love were really the first and only one which fell to the lot of every young man and woman, and were it always possible for them to realise it at the right time—then there would neither be a problem of morality nor of divorce.

But the youth of the present day knows that this love is not the fortune of all. It has learned so much, from literature, from life, from its own soul, of the transformations of love, that one is tempted to wish for these young people the romantic belief of their fathers and mothers in a love which became extinct as easily as now. The difference is merely this, that whereas formerly they were content with a faded glow, we will have continual fire.

It is known now that, although youthful love may be the surest basis of marriage, it is more often the reverse. Here, if anywhere, is the scene of accidents. The one we have grown up with, the girl or youth we are thrown with just when the erotic life is waking; the one we were teased about; the one we hear is "in love" with us; the one we meet when the happiness of others fills the air with longing—these and other accidents, but not personal choice, often decide youthful love.

Then the imagination sets to work to transform the reality in accordance with the ideal we have formed for ourselves—and even this is often the result of accidental influence. It is therefore not surprising that most people, when after ten years or so they meet again the object of their first love, give a sigh of gratitude to the fate which made that love "unhappy."

When it has not been so in the usual sense of the word, one of the parties may often be most to be pitied, and it is just those young people who unhesitatingly realise their love in the belief of its lifelong continuance, that in coercive marriage ɪre made the victims of their own pure will, their ɪealthy courage, their bright idealism.

For the younger, in the richest sense of the word, ɪ person is, the more certainly does he possess the ɔoet's gift which transforms reality according to his ɪreams. The fine curve of a pair of lips renews ;he marvel of the legend: that every frog that ɪumps over them is changed into a rose. Even if a ɪim suspicion awakes, when every serious thought or ɪntimate feeling is met by empty silence or equally ɪmpty loquacity, the imagination easily convinces ;he instinct that silence means "profundity of ɪntelligence," or speech "candour." At every age, ɔut especially at this, love is a great superstition. ɔecure as sleep-walkers in the presence of danger, ;ts votaries fling themselves into a decision. And ;t is this simple rashness of innocence that the ɔurrent conception of morality subjects to a life-ong punishment. The cautious ones, on the ɔther hand, often find in time the great rewards —thanks to their own smaller value.

More things happen in a human life than ɪarriage and finally death. Much may happen ɪ a human soul between marriage and death. ɾhe current assumption that everything which ɪeparates a person from the partner in matrimony ɪ evil and ought to be overcome; everything which ɔinds him to her good and ought to be encouraged —this is part of the wisdom which reduces life to the ɪmplest terms, which is cheap and therefore most ɪ use; for a higher wisdom demands a higher price.

Nothing is commoner, especially for the woman whose first experience of love is in marriage, than that she is in love with love and not her husband. Sometimes woman is betrayed by her senses, but more often by the morning dew of sensibility, which youth and love spread over even the driest of men's souls,—a dew which disappears with the morning. Another illusion, which in these days of intercommunication causes many mistakes in love, is the peculiarity of a foreign nationality, which has the effect of a personal originality—until it gradually betrays itself as only another kind of conformity than that one is used to.

In other cases again, the husband is all she sees in him. But a young woman herself often goes through, during the years from twenty to twenty-five, so complete a transformation of feelings and ways of thought, that after a few years of marriage she finds herself in the presence of a man who is a perfect stranger to her.

This period of illusions in first youth is answered by another towards the close of youth. If a woman has not before experienced love, this is the psychological moment at which almost every illusion is possible. Her now universal demands of love, the longing of her mature woman's nature, have countless times made a noble creature cast these pearls—if not exactly as described in the biblical image—at least into an empty space where they have just as surely been unappreciated.

On man's side, there are other or corresponding

possibilities that early marriage may be founded
on self-deception.

But even when love is real and well-founded,
there yet arise, from the charm of contradictions
already referred to, innumerable occasions of incurable discord.

Thus there are natures so simple that they become crippled, so uncomplex that they are foolish,
so homogeneous as to be heavy. These are they
who usually love once for all, with complete devotion. But, especially when they are women,
Goethe's words are often true of them: that a
woman's greatest misfortune is not to be charming
when she loves. Only complete security gives
these natures the calm of equilibrium, the courage
of self-confidence, which calls forth the "smile of
inward happiness" whereby they also become
attractive. But these natures, who of all most
deserve happiness, usually meet with some person
of constantly changing moods, who reacts with
extreme sensitiveness to every impression, but
can never love deeply, and therefore is soon unable to bear that simplicity and seriousness in
life and death which at first charmed by their
contrast.

Such people are often poets or artists, who in
love seek only constant stimulation. To them
loving means "waking in the morning with new
words on one's lips," and their erotic fortunes
therefore show a rapidity of revolution comparable
with that of the moons around Mars. Just as for

certain natures, a connection originally frivolous may become permanent, held together by depth of feeling, so for this class of natures—on account of the superficiality of their feelings—no kind of connection is serious.

It is not unfrequently those who give the finest descriptions of their soulful moods and their exquisite feelings, who in their acts of love are narrowly selfish or relentlessly harsh. For it is the impressions of culture stored in their intelligence which determine their conscious utterances, but, on the other hand, it is their subconscious ego that decides their actions. And this ego is often centuries behind their cultured consciousness. He, on the other hand, who is reticent and curt of speech or dull and awkward in manners may at bottom possess a delicacy which he can show only in actions, the others only in words. But unfortunately in our time opportunities for speech are many and for action few—and so women pass over the latter for the former. How many a woman has not afterwards—before some act of the man of words—asked herself how it was possible for her ever to love that man! How many a one, before the actions of the silent, has not sighed, What a pity that I was never able to love him!

But in one case as in the other, through the law of contrasts, she was united to him and feels in this union the death or paralysis of the best possibilities of her being.

The most misleading of illusions are, however,

those which are fostered by the actions love
produces; for it is not these which determine the
quality of a personality. While love is fighting for
its happiness it may transform an ordinary person
into something higher than himself, as also into
something lower. When the tension is relieved,
it is seen that in the former case—especially as
regards men—love was able to

. . . unmake him from a common man
But not complete him to an uncommon one. . . .

It was no organic growth of the personality,
but only a straining of self that love called forth.

But she who loved him will watch till her eyes
are weary for what she has seen but once!

Those who have loved them deeply learn from
these, in one way or another, inadequate persons
the most dearly-bought truth in the knowledge of
human nature, a truth that the heart acknowledges
last of all: that even if we poured out our own
blood in streams for any one—we could not thereby give him a drop of richer or more noble blood
than is found in his own heart.

Many have learned this secret in that kind of
marriage, where secure friendship and faithful comradeship abounded; just those feelings, in fact,
which are recommended as the infallible remedy
for love's mistakes.

How often has not one of these married
people active for and with the other, found out

that they never bring their mate into spiritual
activity, that the soul of one has never reached the
soul of the other? Outside observers think them
suited like "hand in glove." The image is significant, for a glove is empty and meaningless when
it does not enclose a hand. But like hand to
hand they are not suited! Therefore it not unfrequently occurs that some day one of them is
seized by a passionate longing to meet with another
hand, which shall be strongly and quietly grasped
in his own and thus double its power; that the
voice, which has continually spoken into empty
space—whence a faithful echo has unfailingly
answered—will finally be dumb from the longing
to receive an answer from another voice, in words
that were never heard before.

Not a few marriages include men who have had
such fine thoughts, dreamed such fair dreams of
woman, that they have desired to win her senses
only through her soul and have disdained to offer
her other than their best, the richest treasures of
their personality. But perhaps such a man has
a wife who understands only money-making and
desires only the pleasures of love. If he offers all
the glories of his soul, she does not even suspect
when a mood is at its height; for her silence is
never eloquent; she is incapable of waiting for
another's thought; has no patience with what is
difficult of comprehension, and will always receive
the unusual with dull misunderstanding or gay
superiority.

The gulf perhaps began to open between them when one became aware of the other's absence at a moment when he himself was most present; or when one felt that their bodies stood between their souls, the other that their souls stood between their bodies; or when one felt a restriction of liberty from the other's superior spiritual or sensual force; or when one found that he could never show his innermost being without its putting the other out of humour. Thus two persons, each one innocent, may make each other profoundly solitary while sharing the same bed and board. Neither receives from the other what his innermost nature needs—and what one gives is only a constraint upon the other's nature. Not a note in the soul of one is tuned to the same pitch as the other's; not a movement in the blood of one is capable of enrapturing the other's. Now it is unbearable dissimilarities, now unbearable similarities, that cause the trouble; each finds in the other "all the virtues he detests but none of the faults he loves." With all this, perfect outward peace may prevail; nay, respect and devotion in a certain sense. That this is the fortune of innumerable marriages is overlooked in general, since married life usually continues—unless a third appears.

In the ideas of the Church, the incapacity for marriage of one party freed the other from the duty of fidelity. In the more spiritual view of the future it will be equally evident that the same right exists to dissolve a marriage which has

remained unconsummated in a spiritual sense;
and there may be just as many possibilities of incapacity to fulfil the spiritual claims of marriage
as there are men and women; therefore also just
as many causes of divorce.

.   .   .   .

In the preceding pages only certain typical cases
of unhappiness have been referred to.   The many
tragic exceptions are here left altogether on one
side.   So also are those causes of divorce which the
preachers of monogamy call the "real misfortunes":
drunkenness, bodily cruelty, and the like; for
with the customary realism of "idealism," they
admit these as valid reasons for divorce.   It is
significant that among the lower classes people still
often think themselves bound to bear these misfortunes as a part of the miscalculations of marriage
as unavoidable as those more complex sufferings
which the champions of monogamy exhort people
on a higher plane to endure.   The pangs a soul
suffers may, they think, be borne with God's help,
whereas unfortunately God is not in the habit of
interfering when a man beats his wife; and the
longer a soul has suffered, the more certain are they
that it can continue to suffer.

Nor do they perceive that a relationship may
have seemed good — perhaps even have been
good,—until, after a lapse of years, a moment has
arrived which has stripped the soul of one of them
naked, sometimes in all its loftiness, more often in

all its baseness. If the latter, then what was possible before becomes from that hour unthinkable.

That the soul may be confronted by such an alternative, of life or death, they will not admit. The soul, they say, is "a spirit," an "invisible and imperishable entity." That its conditions of life are just as variable and complex as those of the organism is, to a certain sort of "idealism," meaningless. With God's help, they say, everyone may save his soul. But such help is in this kind of peril as uncertain as it is in peril of the sea—and even in the latter case it is not "the votive tablets of the drowned, but only those of the saved, that one sees in the temple" (Nietzsche).

.   .   .   .

It is, however, especially when a man or woman is divorced in order to contract a fresh marriage that an outcry is raised over the weakness of the age in bearing suffering. Indeed, it is not even acknowledged that marriage may involve any suffering. Even those who have hitherto found a married couple extremely ill-suited, forget at once that they did so—should either of them "allow a third person to come between them."

They forget not only their own former judgment but also the fact taught by experience, that when two married people are wholly one, there is no room for a third between the bark and the tree. In the contrary case, a third comes between them sooner or later. Sometimes it is the child, sometimes a life's work, sometimes a new feeling—but something always comes, thanks to nature's "abhorrence of a vacuum," which is never more fatal than in marriage. Within the dimensions of the soul, as within those of space, no one can take the place of another, but can occupy only that space which another has left empty or not been able to retain.

In the latter case it is fair to admit the indirect share of literature in the inconsiderateness of those without an erotic conscience. The idea of justice in love has had to be extended. But during this removal of the boundaries, which literature is carrying out, a general insecurity has set in.

Poetry performs with the fullest freedom its duty of investigating the secrets of love, according to which souls and senses are attracted and repelled in answer to that law of elective affinity which our time is seeking more and more eagerly to discover, in order to be able to direct the erotic forces to a higher development. Literature is the foremost of these discoverers; and this in itself is enough to justify that complete freedom, without which, moreover, it cannot become what Georg Brandes has called love-poetry: the finest instrument for gauging the strength and warmth of the emotional life of a period.

That literature is often the power which gives rise to erotic agitation, is self-evident. And thus it always co-operates in some measure in the misfortunes which are caused by loves of the imagination or the intellect, misfortunes which are avoided by the firm and mature personality. The weak, on the other hand, are those who in their loves as in their beliefs adopt the course that another's influence gives them.

Like lawn-tennis—which in certain circles makes or mars marriages—love is favoured by summer air and idleness. But at all seasons there are men and women for whom everyone is a ball that sets their fancy or their vanity in motion. No form of self-assertion is more justified than that of opposing one's vigilance, one's will, and one's dignity to this use of one's personality. What stimulates the game is not the power of the senses alone. No, this game is the sole inventive faculty of spiritual poverty, the mark of erotic ill-breeding. Only a refined person can rejoice at the stimulants to life in every field, the means of which he does not himself possess. As yet few people have attained a culture like that of the Athenian beggar, who thanked Alcibiades for giving him the jewels that Alcibiades indeed wore—but that the beggar was free to rejoice at. To attain in regard to human beings this sense of joy, free from all covetousness, is the flower of fine breeding.

But the nervosity of the present day stimulates, on the contrary, erotic kleptomania. People steal one another, now from the same kind of hysteria which makes thieves of Parisian ladies in the fashionable stores; now from the same crudity which makes the child pluck every flower he sees;

now from the same desire which urges the collector
constantly to acquire new specimens.

When in regard to human beings the pleasure of
the connoisseur rather than that of the collector
has been attained, then the greatest of all joys—
that of human beings in one another—will not be
so often disturbed by erotic complications. To
appeal to the liberty of the personality in frivolous
concessions to eroticism is the same gross abuse of
the idea as to use the name of this liberty in sailing
a leaky yacht in a storm.

The liberty of the personality involves great
risks to win great rewards; but it does not involve allowing one's self to be driven into dangers,
where for a trifle one stakes one's own life and that
of others. To drift into relations where one has
not the hundredth part of the consent of one's
innermost ego, is not proving but wasting one's
personality; for every action which is less than
ourselves, degrades our personality.

Again, it may be disastrous to perform acts
greater and stronger than ourselves. He who
ventures upon an exceptional course must—like
the alpine climber—possess an abundance of
strength and the sense of security which it lends;
for otherwise, in both cases, the enterprise will
be successful only if everything occurs according
to the most favourable calculation. In an unforeseen misadventure the inadequate ones are
those who are lost. Therefore, in one case as
in the other, public opinion is unwittingly right

when it glorifies the daring that succeeds, but condemns that which fails.

Most people are not equal to the consequences of their resolutions. On the contrary, like unseated riders they are dragged by their actions through degraded circumstances that they had not counted upon. Thus many a pair of lovers who have broken earlier ties, have been only a warning example—since their action was destructive, not enhancing to life.

Ruin may be the climax of life; but inefficiency is always defeat; and of all the rashness of this life, the rash project of an exceptional lot is the saddest.

Few people who have passed their youth have courage or strength for such new experiences as imply a real enhancement of life. The majority ought rather to employ their personality in the task of worthily bearing and making the best of their lot—and, in spite of all that is asserted to the contrary, that is also what most people do and will continue to do.

Those who trust only in compulsion to restrain a man's desire to desert his wife, forget to what a degree spiritual influences have even now facilitated divorce, in spite of the coercive law. One seldom finds in our day a high-minded husband or wife who insists on retaining the other against his or her will, except when it is clear to one partner that divorce, if conceded, would result in the certain ruin of the other. As a rule it is now only the narrow-minded or the low-minded who exercise the right of refusing divorce. If this right were abolished, this would not entail the abolition of the influences which even now keep married people together—although in most cases they might be free if they wished it.

Those who thoughtlessly separated, when greater facilities are given, would be the same class of people who now, in coercive marriage, secretly deceive one another.

To the serious, divorce will always be serious. Before a person of feeling and thought consciously hurts another who has loved or loves him, he himself has suffered terrible pain. Gratitude for a great devotion in a free connection has often proved more powerfully binding than the law could have been. Nay, to anyone tender of conscience the ties formed by a free connection are stronger than the legal ones, since in the former case he has made a choice more decisive to his own and the other's personality than if he had followed law and custom.

And even when no feelings of affection exercise their retentive power, many people prefer to remain as wreckage on the same shore, rather than be washed away towards a new and uncertain fate.

Human nature is credited with far too great simplicity and elasticity when it is taken for granted that one experiment in life would succeed another if divorce were free. In this case it is life itself, not the law, which fixes the insurmountable limits. To the deeper natures which have broken away from a life-connection, the pain of it has often been so great as permanently to deaden the colours of life.

. . . .

In connection with the modern demand for exemption from motherhood we have already rejected the expedient of securing love's freedom through the rearing of children by the State. At the same time the importance and value of the parental home was insisted upon as strongly as possible.

Here, on the other hand, is the place to point out the one-sidedness of the notion that nothing is more important than that the parents should remain together for the sake of the children— since everything must finally depend upon how the parents remain together and what they become through remaining together.

The more degrading cohabitation is to the personality of each parent the less valuable will be the influence for the children of the parental relation.

Only one who sees in marriage a system directly ordained by God, a form of realisation of the divine reason, can maintain the proposition that in such a system the good must outweigh human defects. Those who hold that the maintenance of marriage is always the sound and moral course, must take upon themselves the burden of proving

that the dull connubial habits of divided mates
are a pure source for the origin of new beings;
that their mutually conflicting influences are
better able to further the welfare of the children
than a tranquil bringing-up by one of them;
that the happiness of one of them in a new union
is more dangerous to the children than his unhappiness in the former one.

To those, on the other hand, who hold the faith
of Life, the question of the children is always a
fresh one in every fresh divorce. Here again
we must rise to the conditional judgment, and
leave behind the chess-board morality with its
equal squares of right and wrong. The danger
to the children arising from a divorce depends on
all that has gone before and all that comes after.
He who dissolves his marriage in the face of his
inner consciousness of the harm that the children
will thereby suffer, commits a sin which will
infallibly be succeeded by the remorse that
friends are sometimes eager to adduce as
extenuating circumstances. He, on the other
hand, who "sins" with an easy conscience, has
made his choice with the welfare of the children
in one scale of the balance. This calm of conscience is then not indifference, and, therefore,
does not prevent the possibility of his suffering
deeply through the consequences of the decision
which he nevertheless does not regret. It may
be that in most cases where there are children,
the less painful course, even for him who is most

convinced of his personal right, is to endeavour
to the utmost to preserve a common life which
allows the children to grow up under the joint
protection of a father and mother, and for the
sake of the children to give this life a worthy and
kindly character.

In former times, people mended and patched
things up endlessly. The psychologically developed generation of the present day is more
disposed to allow what is broken to remain
broken. For, except in the cases where the cause
of rupture has been outward misunderstanding or
belated development, patched-up marriages—like
patched-up engagements—seldom prove lasting.
It has often been profound instincts that caused
the rupture; the reconciliation violated these
instincts and sooner or later such violation
revenges itself.

Thus, it happens, that even exceptional natures
have a greater burden than they can bear, and
then it is not the living together but the dying
together of their parents that the children witness.

Neither religion nor the law, neither society
nor the family, can decide what a marriage kills
in a human being or what it may be the means of
saving in him. Only he himself knows the one
and feels the other. Only he himself can determine
how far it may be possible for him to have so far
finished with his own existence that he can completely pass into that of his children; to bear the
pain of a continued married life so that it may

enhance the powers of himself and the children.
A mother can do this oftener than a father, but
in no case is there any standard that others can
use to determine when an excess of suffering is
present. More than this, there is strictly no
suffering, but only suffering beings who in every
case create the suffering anew according to their
type of soul.

Only one thing is certain: that no one is more
outside the question than the very one who
causes the suffering. Thus nothing can be more
unreasonable than to leave to the judgment of one
of the parties the decision we have just mentioned.
The knowledge of being able to refuse a divorce
now involves want of consideration for the other's
moods of dejection, which would never occur if
consideration were necessary to prevent separation.
Such attentions are especially significant at the
beginning of married life, when most young married people solve the small and great problems
of accommodation with more or less difficulty.
The birth of the first child, moreover, is often
accompanied by abnormal states of feeling, which
lead to hasty conclusions as to incompatibility
and antipathy. The opponents of free divorce
think that it is just during these years that pre-
cipitate divorces might take place. But they
do not reflect that either partner in his sense of
proprietorship now gives himself a loose rein in a
way that would be unthinkable if such security
did not exist. Thus the young certainly keep

together, but not unfrequently destroy their finest chances of happiness. The need of mutual caution during these dissensions should have a much deeper influence in keeping a couple together than has at present the knowledge that they cannot be free. After the advent of children, the danger is small—except in the case of heartless natures—that a sufferer will too hastily think his powers of endurance are exhausted. The interdependence which children create between their parents when these together care for and love them, is sometimes indissoluble. In most cases it is so strong as to form the real tie, without which laws twice as strict as the present ones would have no power to keep together two unwilling beings.

When speaking of love's selection, we pointed to the signs which indicate that the feeling for the race—the feeling which from time immemorial has linked together man and woman at a common hearth, has raised the altar near it and round them both the town wall—is approaching its renaissance. Consciousness of the children's rights is indubitably on the increase, together with a knowledge of the rights of love. And against the assaults of this most turbulent and dangerous sea the race-feeling will continue to stand as a wall protecting society, though in a new form to give it new powers of resistance.

But the opponents of divorce think, on the contrary, that the sense of happiness through the

children—especially in the case of the father—
has now become so weak that most fathers would
free themselves from all responsibility if they
only could.

If this be so, society itself is to blame. It not
only countenances sexual relations entirely independent of the mission of the race; it frees the
man from responsibility for his illegitimate children
and thus assigns to him a standpoint below that
of the beasts. The instincts favourable to offspring, which in animals have remained undisturbed, cannot attain their full strength until
man is completely answerable for every life he
creates. As soon as society decrees that the fact
of two persons becoming parents makes their
union obligatory, the relationship itself will
gradually intensify their feeling and the man will
wish to possess and preserve the elements of joy
for which he must always bear the burdens.
Even if man's fatherly feelings should be slow in
awaking—and if a number of fathers of the
present day should thus really avail themselves
of free divorce to leave wife and child—there are
still the mothers, who do not, as a rule, lightly
leave their children, but who, on the contrary,
now suffer the deepest misfortunes and renounce
the greatest happiness so as to remain with them,
and who—even if they tear themselves from them
—are hardly ever able to release themselves.
When the law gives to every mother the rights
which now only the unmarried mother possesses,

but imposes at the same time on every father the obligations which now only the married have— then it may be that the child will become a new and more valuable possession in the eyes of the man. If he only feels the influence he may obtain through his wife's respect for his fatherly qualities; if his importance in the child's existence comes to depend on personal force, not on legal might, then the quality of fatherhood may be in a high degree ennobled. And with this affection will grow, according to the immutable law, that the more man gives, the more he loves.

If matriarchy, in a new form, refined by the whole of development, should become the final phase—as in the opinion of many it has been the starting-point—of the family, then this would involve that paternal authority became conditional, depending on the value and warmth of the paternal feeling. At present many fathers are merely an accident in their children's life, an accident which never even looks "like an idea." And this is not only true of those fathers who, with the support of the law, withdraw themselves from all responsibility, but also of many others, especially of those who are driven by work or public business and who remain inwardly strangers to their children.

For the present, it may be regarded as certain that free divorce would, above all, afford this advantage, that a number of wives, who now keep broken-down husbands, could work for food for their children instead of for liquor for the children's father; and that a number of mothers, who now are obliged for the sake of their children to suffer the deepest humiliation, would be able to free themselves; and in both cases the children would gain. On the other hand, the father who took advantage of free divorce to desert his family for frivolous reasons might, as a rule, be easily spared by that family.

In most cases, the children are even better off through a divorce, when the cause of it is differences of temperament and opinion between the parents. Each of them separately may be a person of merit. When they separate on the ground of dissension, both have a sense of something to atone for with the children. This prompts them to try to make amends, and thus the children receive—from each separately—far more than they did when the parents were united, when the children were witnesses to their conflicts and saw the worse side of the nature of each. The children are spared the pain of being the subject of their father's and mother's quarrels; of being compelled to take the part of one of them; of being torn between two diverse wills, between the jealous endeavours of each to win them exclusively. They, in part, avoid being brought up from two different, mutually-counteracting points of view, where one is trying to take away from the children the ideas that the other has given them.

But of all this the opponents of divorce take

no account. The main thing is that the parents shall keep together, however chill or dark with thunder may be the air in which the children grow up.

This point of view misses the reality as much as that of those who call for divorce as soon as love is over. Keeping together may, in certain cases, give the children a happier and richer childhood than the state of things after a divorce. It has been maintained with reason that discord between the parents is sometimes compensated for by the value of the manly nature of the one and the womanly nature of the other, which—even if they do not co-operate—still work well side by side; and that children who, through dissensions at home, have early been forced to think and choose for themselves, often become stronger characters than those who have grown up in happy homes.

While, on the one hand, we hear children whose parents have separated complain that they did not have the patience to remain together, on the other we hear those who have grown up in unhappy homes regret the continuance of their parents' married life. If this had been dissolved, the children might have had at least one good home, perhaps two, whereas now they have none.

But, of course, each one can know only what he has suffered from a series of events, not what he might have suffered if circumstances had been different; and thus the children's opinion cannot in either case be regarded as decisive, when laying down the principle.

The experience, therefore, which we have, of the position of children whom death has deprived of their father is more important. While the widower, as a rule, marries again, if his children are small, the widow, in most cases, remains unmarried. And it may be regarded as certain that statistics of able men would give a remarkable result in respect of the sons of widows.

A divorce often puts the child in a corresponding position of tenderness and responsibility towards his mother. But while society bows to the "stern necessity" of a single battle making more children fatherless than the divorces of a generation—and calmly relies on the mothers' ability by themselves to make good citizens of their sons —it shrinks from the same stern necessity when it is a question of saving a living person from lifelong unhappiness.

The children's chief danger in a divorce is that they are often divided between father and mother and thus lose in part the companionship of brothers and sisters which is so eminently productive of happiness. Next to this, the greatest misfortune is not that the father and mother no longer live under the same roof, but that they are no longer able to meet. This misfortune could often be avoided, if friends and relations would refrain from the pleasure of deciding how the divorced couple ought to hate and variously torment each other. If people saw the merit of two human beings—who were able to separate as friends and to meet again as such—being also capable of this; if the presence of either parent with the children never led to their being influenced to the detriment of the absent one—then children, even after a divorce, would not feel the want of their essential relation to both their parents. Now, on the other hand, divided as they often are between two mutually hostile parents, separated thus from each other and—lacking common memories and other ties to bind them—gradually becoming strangers to each other when they meet, the children lose so much by a divorce, that parents in most cases can gain nothing which makes up for the losses of the children and thus prefer to bear the burdens of living together rather than lay those of divorce upon the children.

In the question of divorce also, the great fundamental idea of protestantism must be applied in the recognition of the individual's full freedom of choice, since no case can be decided generally, and since here also the right and wrong can only be discovered through the searching of each individual conscience.

A child has often—in moments of great crisis—blocked the way which led from the door of the home. But the home within that door did not for that reason become brighter or warmer for the child.

· · · · · · ·

In the preceding, the position of the children in divorce has been considered from the point of view of discord between the parents. If, on the other hand, the divorce is brought about by a new feeling on the part of one of them, then this father or mother must be prepared one day—when the children can understand them—to justify the step by showing them how the new love has made him or her a richer and greater personality. The children have a full right not to be sacrificed to the degradation of their parents. In every case, the children are the most incorruptible judges of their parents.

But the fact that a person has already brought children into the world does not give to these children an unconditional right to demand that a father or mother shall sacrifice the love that may advance themselves, and through them the race, to which they may thus give more excellent children or more excellent works than they have been able to produce hitherto. Many a woman has borne children to her husband without having seen her child; many a man has given the community his industry but never his work—until great love accomplished their innermost longing and the child or the work that was thus created became the only one indispensable to the race.

The claim of society that a father or mother, radiant with possibilities of happiness, shall sacrifice these for the sake of the children, will be reduced when the sense of the value of life has grown and the duty of parents to live for their children is more often interpreted to mean that they must continue to be fully alive, with powers of renewal. On the other hand, this very rejuvenation of parents at the present day may often result in their living so rich a life together with their children that they will need no other renewal than that which is most productive of happiness to all parties; namely, to enjoy their "second spring-time" in the children's first.

If, on the contrary, the result of this prolonged youth of the parents is that a father or mother changes the course of his or her life, then the children must suffer—until they can understand that perhaps in a deeper sense they do not suffer thereby. Sometimes the new partner has exercised a richer influence on the children than their own father or mother—as may also be the case with a step-father or step-mother. At present, however, this possibility is often destroyed by the common opinion just alluded to, which also decides that the children ought to hate, where, if left to themselves, they would perhaps have learned to love.

The selfish demand of grown-up children that the life of their parents shall in and with them have reached its climax and be personally concluded, is as cruel as it is unjustified, since there are souls which do not lose their blossom when the fruit appears, but are able at the same time to bear both fruit and new blossom. Children receive with life a right to the conditions which may make them fully fit for life; no less than this, but at the same time no more. What their parents may be willing to sacrifice of their own lives beyond this must be reckoned to their generosity, not their duty.

.   .   .   .

If great love may thus be admitted to possess a right superior to that of the children, the question obviously arises, how is this love to be distinguished from the accidental?

A mistake is already a hard thing in a marriage where there are children, for the obstacles that have to be surmounted in such a case are so serious that only great love can overcome them— that is, if the parents are such that they really mean anything at all to their children.

It is precisely by its genesis, in despite of all obstacles, that the predestined love often reveals its nature and thus becomes what is called "criminal." Even if those who are possessed by this emotion allow duty to interpose oceans between them, they will, nevertheless, come together in every great moment of their lives until the last, convinced that

"his kiss was on her lips before she was born."

When people have acquired more knowledge of the laws of psychology, they will discover, as Edward Carpenter has said, that there is also an astronomy in the world of emotion; that inter-dependence arises there also, in obedience to eternal laws; sympathies and antipathies which keep all the "heavenly bodies" at the right distance or proximity; that thus the path of love follows an equally irresistible necessity as the orbit of a star and is equally impossible to determine by any influences outside its own laws. And without doubt there will some day be discovered a telescope for this field also, which will at last reveal to the short-sighted the fixed stars, planets, nebulæ, and comets of erotic space, and will prove that its constellations are ordered by a higher law than that of "crude instinct." But until we attain this astronomical certainty we must be content with the degree of knowledge that art criticism can give.

Great love, like a great artist, has its style. Whatever subject the latter may handle, whatever medium he may use, he gives to the canvas or the marble, the paper or the metal, the impress of his hand, and this reveals itself in the smallest thing he has created. So in every age and every country, every class and every time of life, great love is one and the same; its signs are unmistakable, though the fortune it leads to and the individuals on whom it sets its mark may in one case be more important than in another.

But this mighty emotion—which arouses one's whole being through another's and gives one's whole being rest in another's—this emotion seizes a man without asking whether he is bound or free. He who feels strongly and wholly enough need never wonder what it is he feels: it is the feeble emotion that is doubtful to itself. Nor does he who feels strongly enough ever ask himself whether he has a right to his feeling. He is so exalted by his love, that he knows he is thus exalting the life of mankind. It is the minor, partial passions that a person already bound feels with good reason to be "criminal." For him, on the other hand, who would call his great emotion a sinful infatuation, a shameless egoism, a bestial instinct, one who loves thus has nothing but a smile of pity. He knows that he would commit a sin in killing his love, just as he would in murdering his child. He knows that his love has once more made him good as in his childhood's prayers to God, and rich as one for whom the gates of paradise are opened anew.

Art is interpreting a universal experience when it always depicts Adam and Eve as young when they are driven out of Eden. One wonders that no artist has shown them—at a maturer age— outside the walls of paradise, tormented by the sense of now possessing wisdom enough to preserve the happiness for which in youth they only possessed the means.

For there not unfrequently arrives a time in human life when enlightenment enters before coldness has set in; when the blossoms are still rich although the fruits have already begun to mature. It is then that great happiness is often seen for an instant and then disappears. Sometimes she is never seen, for she comes softly and—like a playmate—lays a hand over one's eyes, asking: Who am I? One guesses wrongly and happiness is gone before one can bid her stay. To her favourites only does she come with her hands full and open. To the majority the words of the dying Hebbel are true: *We human beings lack either the cup or the wine.*

Love's deepest tragedy is that a number of people have first to learn through their mistakes before their souls and senses are ready for the great love which of two beings makes one more perfect.

In poetry as in life it is sometimes the first love, sometimes the last, that is extolled as the strongest. Neither need be, and either may be, this. The strongest love is that which—at whatever age it comes—most takes up all the forces of personality.

It also sometimes happens that not until a person ought to have done with love, is he really ready for it. The fewer are then the chances of finding the love he wishes to give and receive. And fewer still the chances that he can give himself up to them, with the concurrence of his whole being.

For it is one thing to have the right to one's great emotion; another to have the right or the possibility of one's full happiness.

Love may be never so free in its social aspect;

no freedom of morals or of divorce can release the sons of men from the inevitable sufferings of their own nature, nor from the inevitable conflicts of their connection with the past. These sufferings and conflicts have been made so deep by life itself that there is indeed no necessity for the law to make them deeper.

The most usual form of the conflict is that a person is bound by or broken by casual love—whether wedded or free—when the predestined intervenes in his existence.

That so many more unhappy marriages continue than are dissolved may be due less to a sense of duty than to the fact that only a few are capable of great emotions. Peer Gynt's symbol—the bulb—illustrates the erotic nature of the majority. It flowers as readily in sand as in water, in the open as in a pot. But should an acorn be planted in a pot, it is inevitable—on account of the vital conditions of the oak—that it should one day burst its prison or die.

And in such a case, it is unfortunate when a Christian ethical view stands in the way of serious and genuine chances of so renewing life that it may be more valuable to the community as well as to the individual himself. People who are equipped with rich possibilities still allow themselves to be decided by unconditional consideration for others' feelings, which, taken from Christianity, have been grafted even on evolutionism, and which, especially through George

Eliot, have obtained their great but one-sided expression.

That the race not only needs people willing to lose their lives in order to gain them, but also people with courage to sacrifice others in order to win their own—this is a truth which nevertheless must be indissolubly bound up with an evolutionist view of life, to which the will to preserve and enhance one's own existence is a duty as undeniable as that of preserving and enhancing the lives of others by self-sacrifice. To have the courage of one's happiness, to be able to bear the pain inseparable from a rupture without pangs of conscience, is only in the power of those who act from their innermost necessity. That pairs of lovers outside the law now so often commit suicide together is no proof of the overmastering power of love; it rather proves the powerlessness of their emotion to dare and win the right of direct and immediate living and thus increasing the riches of life. For it is only to a love that is throughout a will to live that circumstances become as wax in the artist's hand.

From the point of view of the religion of Life this impotence is regrettable, just as much as secret adultery. Doubtless both may possess the beauty of a great love-tragedy. Probably no one who has read the *Inferno* wished Francesca strength to reject the love of Paolo. And so strangely does a soul find the way home to itself, that there are cases where a person in adultery feels himself purified from the defilement of marriage—since he thus for the first time experiences the unity of soul and senses which was his dream of love from the beginning.

But even in these exceptional cases—so much the more, therefore, in others—the secret transgression, which the older morality found comparatively innocuous, is from the point of view of the new morality greater than the open rupture. For the personality is humiliated by the duplicity and the weakness whereby one avoids the responsibility of the consequences of one's actions. And this, moreover, decreases the life-value of love to the race. New experiments in life, which are made openly, which enhance the strength of the individual through conflict and earnestness, may possess an importance for the personality itself and for society which secret transgressions in most cases lack.

A poet or an artist, for example, has a wife, as to whose insufficiency for him all are agreed—so long as he still has her. Suddenly he finds the space, that was empty and waste, filled by a new creation; the air becomes alive with songs and visions. He not only feels his slumbering powers awake, he knows that great love has called up in him powers he had never suspected; he sees that now he will be able to accomplish what he could never have done before. He follows the life-will of his love, and he does right. Marriages kept inviolable have doubtless produced many great advantages to culture. But it is not to them that art and poetry owe their greatest debt of gratitude. Without "unhappy" or "criminal" love, the world's creations of beauty would at this moment be not only infinitely fewer, but, above all, infinitely poorer. Nay, after such an exclusion the whole spiritual world might appear as some mediæval church, decorated from floor to roof with frescoes, appeared after the white-washing of the Reformation.

But in a choice such as we have just mentioned, public opinion is always certain that the sufferings of the wife, unimportant as she is to the community, are the great thing, while those of the man, important to the community, may be disregarded.

He, however, who experiences the new spring which flowers in song, in tones, in colours, raises the life of generation after generation, centuries after the one person or the few who suffered through him have long ceased to suffer.

Who would have gained what the race would have lost through his self-sacrifice? Not the wife, if she had a heart, and not only a pride, which could suffer.

Not only from the point of view of universal, but from that of individual life-enhancement, we ought not to give all our sympathy to the one who is called "heart-broken." Why is the heart that is broken considered so much more valuable than the one or the two which must cause the pain lest they themselves perish? And why will people not see that he who is looked upon as "broken-hearted" sometimes finds a new and richer happiness? But, above all, why is it constantly forgotten that one who suffers through sorrow often becomes greater than he could ever have been in the secure possession of his "property"?

There are other ways of living on a great emotion than that of being in the usual sense made happy by it.

This must, however, be remembered above all by him who, already tied, is seized by a new feeling. If all three parties are high-minded enough, it has sometimes happened that the feeling has been transformed into an *amitié amoureuse*, which has made all of them richer and none of them unhappy—even if it has made none of them completely happy.

But even under other circumstances people ought to remember, that one does not always own what one has—and sometimes possesses most surely what one has never owned.

The sanctity and loftiness of one's own feeling is the indestructible part of happiness in love. No longer to be able to love is the greatest sorrow. But a person no more becomes less worthy of love because his own love is dead, than he becomes so through leaving love unrequited.

Therefore, he alone can feel himself really ruined who has been nothing but the means of another's pleasure or sport, development or work; a means that is cast off when it no longer affords enjoyment or profit. The person who is thus betrayed in love, either because love never existed or because its past existence is denied; who sees the personality he loved unveiled as another than he believed himself to be loving—this person must exert his whole soul to save it from being narrowed, embittered, and destroyed. All other great blows of fate may be borne in such a way that a man grows by them: but to lose faith in a human being is the greatest pain of all, since it is also the most unfruitful; since it in no respect enlarges the soul or enhances the existence.

But even from this suffering the soul may finally raise itself through the consciousness that it has too great a value of its own to allow itself to be destroyed by the baseness or pettiness of another. Only he who has fought out the battle alone in all the horrors of the desert night knows what the sunrise is. Years later it may fall to the lot of such a man, who at one blow has lost everything—the sanctity of his memories, the meaning of his experiences, the faith of his love—himself to see the truth of the great, calm thinker's exhortation: that one ought neither to laugh nor weep at, exalt nor curse a human being's actions, but only to try to understand them (Spinoza). And then there begins for him a great and difficult work, which perhaps will last as long as life lasts, the work of looking into the depths of this other soul; of again reviewing the past in the perspective of distance; of perceiving his own limitations as well as those of the other, and thus beginning to understand. This is the only forgiveness there is.

But thus a person once dead and buried in the midst of life may finally see the grass grow green and the sun shine over his grave.

.   .   .   .

If this can become true—and it has become true for many people whom others regarded as broken-hearted—how much more then is it not true to him who has once been really rich and has never been robbed of his greatest treasure, the glory of his own love?

A woman, for example, who for years of her life has possessed complete happiness and through this has become a mother—will she be robbed of it all, if this happiness comes to an end?

There is still the happiness of others to serve, the sufferings of others to alleviate, the great ends of humanity to further. To many a one who has never even had a happiness of his own this must still be sufficient consolation. But we judge of happiness as of wealth. That innumerable human beings daily perish from want makes little impression on us. But if one of our friends falls from riches into poverty, this seems to us dreadful. We forget that he may perhaps, through poverty, attain a development that riches never won for him; that he who is robbed by fortune may make a new position for himself.

Life has countless possibilities as well as countless contradictions. It is full of secret remedial powers as well as of hidden causes of death. And, finally, it is, therefore, very uncertain whether it is not the two who come together that are "torn asunder"—while the one abandoned remains whole.

For loving is a healing medicine even for the wounds love gives. Only one thing a loving person cannot bear, to see the dear ones suffer. To take one's self silently away in order to spare them pain is within the power of great love. And this does not mean a tame resignation watering the red stream of the blood. It means that love has become so great that it takes seriously the great words so lightly uttered in happiness, that torments caused by the beloved were dearer than joys given by others. When love has become the power in which a person lives and moves and has his being, the words of the *Epistle to the Corinthians* on love are fulfilled in a more beautiful way than Paul dreamed of. Great love does not only love for the sake of loving; it attains the incredible: to love the loved one more than one's own feeling. If it were a question of thus providing for the other a more perfect happiness, this love would be able to quench its own flame and with it the fulness of pain and of joy that life had gained from this feeling. Women sometimes make such a sacrifice. Here and there a man has been capable of it. But he who has

attained to this height of emotion lives so wonderful a life that the happiness the united couple
create for each other must be extraordinarily
great if these two rich ones are not in reality to
be the poorer.

When the thought has once become inherent in
mankind that no one can be happy without the
feeling that he is making others happy; that
only the highest development of one's own feeling
is imperishable happiness; that all other happiness
is charity, not justice—then there will be fewer
torn asunder, even if there be no more happy
ones.

But love is still such, men, women, and the
people around them are still such, that one would
rather wish a tied man or woman strength to
endure marriage than to break it, at least if they
have children who must share with them the
unknown fortunes of their love.   Before these, if
ever, one feels the meaning of the Breton fisher's
song:

. . . la mer est grande et ma barque est petite . . .

How often has not the little boat, fraught with
life's last riches, been lost on the wide sea?

But therefore it is that no one there seeks
his pleasure, but only his life.

.   .   .   .

That our actions in the erotic sphere—as in
every other—must call forth the criticism of

others is just as unavoidable as that our figure should be reflected in a mirror as we pass. But public opinion is a convex mirror, a globe swollen by prejudice, which distorts the image. Only a clear and calm soul gives a true picture of another's actions.

And to such a soul, it will not unfrequently be apparent that the "transgression" was right for one nature and not for the other. The latter will have felt that its innermost being would have been outraged if fidelity to the past had not been preserved to the uttermost—and will have chosen to allow its erotic powers to wither and to live only by the will of duty. Of this kind of self-immolation the same is true as of its bodily counterpart: sometimes they are great souls, sometimes great cowards. Nay, the same sacrifice may be sublime at one period of our lives and shameful at another.

Life never shows us "marriage," but countless different marriages; never "love," but countless lovers. He who sets up an ideal in these matters must, therefore, be content with possibly working for the future, but should not use his ideal as a criterion for the present. Nay, he ought not even to desire in the future the sole authority of his own ideal—since a descent from the diverse to the uniform would be a retrogressive development.

The effort of society to press into a single ideal form life's infinite multitude of different cases under the same circumstances or of the same cases under different circumstances, the same influences on different personalities or the same personalities under different influences—this has been in the field of sexual morality as violent a proceeding as would be the establishment for all figures of Polycletus's canon of beauty. The madness of the latter proceeding would be obvious. But violence to souls is not so obvious. Therefore it is always established by law.

Not until the diversity of souls becomes in our ideas a truth as real as the diversity of our bodies shall we perceive that of all dogmas monogamy has been that which has claimed most human sacrifices. It will one day be admitted that the *auto-da-fés* of marriage have been just as valueless to true morality as those of religion were to the true faith.

The Grand Inquisitors of the past probably resembled those of the present day in that, when confronted by a particular case within the circle of their own friends and relations, they found easily enough extenuating circumstances which they did not otherwise admit. But we must learn to see that every case is a separate case and that, therefore, sometimes a new rule—not only an exception to an old rule—becomes necessary. We cannot any longer maintain this double standard for known or unknown, for friends or enemies, for literature or life. It must be abolished by an earnest desire for genuine morality.

This double standard shows us, however, that even among the orthodox of monogamy the impossibility of carrying out a monogamous morality which shall apply to all is beginning to be perceived. But the effort, nevertheless, to attain in some degree the impossible now stands in the way of the possible, which is germinating here and there: the attainment of the morality of love.

Although the new life is already showing its strength—like spring flowers that push their way through last year's carpet of dead foliage—the withered leaves must yet be cleared away.[1] And only they who do not perceive the power of the

---

[1] Before 1857, no legal divorce in the usual meaning of the term existed in England. The ecclesiastical courts could grant a sort of "divorce from bed and board," whereupon the aggrieved party could get rid of his unfaithful half by a special Act of Parliament in each particular case. As a consequence, only very wealthy people could afford this luxury, for it cost immense sums to get a special motion of this kind through Parliament. The further injustice prevailed, that in practice this course was open only to men, not to women.

It was, moreover, with the greatest difficulty that Palmerston succeeded in carrying the reform of 1857. The friends of reform urged above all that the old law was unjust to poor people, and that among both rich and poor it had become increasingly common to marry again in an illegal way, so that in the eyes of the law thousands of people in England were living in bigamy.

The new law of 1857 introduced a separate secular court for divorce causes, divorce was made legal, and the possibility of taking advantage of it was placed within the reach of others than the wealthiest.

But the experience of fifty years has shown that divorce procedure is still altogether too costly for the poor, and entails

new spring are afraid that the earth will not be able to dispense with its withered protection.

---

an infinity of time and trouble. Furthermore, a number of revolting injustices remain.

Thus, for instance, a wife cannot obtain legal divorce from her husband either because he is an habitual drunkard, or an incurable lunatic, or is imprisoned for life for some grave crime, or has abandoned his home and refused to contribute to the support of his wife and children! The most she can obtain under such circumstances is a judicial separation—which makes it possible for either party to enter into any illegitimate connection they please. A husband can obtain divorce from his wife if he can prove a single case of infidelity on her part; but the wife cannot obtain divorce from her husband even if he can be proved to be living in continual adultery. In order to get rid of him she must be able to prove that he has been guilty of cruelty towards her or has deserted her for a period of two years.

The worst thing is that the greater offence is punished far more leniently than the less. A wife can get a judicial separation on account of her husband's infidelity, but loses therewith the right of proceeding against him for divorce, and neither she nor her husband may marry again. But if the husband has also been guilty of cruelty to her, she obtains a divorce, and then both she and her husband are at liberty to remarry. The man who deceives his wife is not free to marry another; but if he both deceives her and beats her, he is divorced and may marry again!

In general the opponents of the existing law declare that it contributes powerfully to the formation of illegitimate connections.

CHAPTER IX

A NEW MARRIAGE LAW

It results from the foregoing that the ideal form of marriage is considered to be the perfectly free union of a man and a woman, who through mutual love desire to promote the happiness of each other and of the race.

But as development does not proceed by leaps no one can hope that the whole of society will attain this ideal otherwise than through transitional forms. These must preserve the property of the old form: that of expressing the opinion of society on the morality of sexual relations—and thus providing a support for the undeveloped—but at the same time must be free enough to promote a continued development of the higher erotic consciousness of the present time. The modern man considers himself supreme in the sense that no divine or human authority higher than the collective power of individuals themselves can make the laws that confine his liberty. But he admits the necessity of a legal limitation of freedom, when this prepares the way for a more perfect future system for the satisfaction of the needs of the individual and a more complete freedom for the use of his powers. Insight into the present erotic needs and powers of individuals must thus be the starting-point of a modern marriage law, but not any abstract theories about the "idea of the family" or juridical considerations of the "historical origin" of marriage.

Since, as already pointed out, society is the organisation which results when human beings set themselves in motion to satisfy their needs and exercise their powers in common, it must also be in a condition of uninterrupted transformation according as new needs arise and new powers are developed. This has now taken place in the erotic sphere, especially since those emotional needs and powers of the soul, which formerly were nourished by and directed towards religion, have been nourished by and directed towards love. Love itself is thus becoming more and more a religion, and one which demands new forms for its practice.

But while the individualist can only be satisfied with the full freedom of love, he is compelled by the sense of solidarity, at least for the present, to demand a new law for marriage, since the majority is not yet ready for perfect freedom.

.   .   .   .

The sense of solidarity and individualism have equally weighty reasons for condemning the existing institution of marriage. It forces upon human beings, who are seldom ideal, a unity which only an ideal happiness renders them capable of supporting. It fulfils one of its missions—that of protecting the woman—in a way that is now humiliating to her human dignity. It performs its second function—that of protecting the children—in an extremely imperfect fashion. Its third—that of setting up an ideal of the morality of sexual relations—it performs in such a way that this ideal is now a hindrance to the further development of morality.

From a realistic point of view, what is the value of matrimony to a woman? That the present law compels the husband to provide for his wife and for the children born in wedlock, and that at the death of the husband it secures to her the widow's share in his estate and to the legitimate children their inheritance. But she pays for these economical advantages by resigning the right over her children, her property, her work, her person, which she possessed when unmarried. Even when there is a marriage settlement the husband—as guardian and administrator of his wife's property—may squander this, as well as the proceeds of her work; he can forbid her exercise of a calling or sell the implements of its exercise. In the eyes of the law, she is placed on a footing with her children who are under age: her husband has to sue and to answer for her, and there are certain functions of a citizen which she cannot perform at all, while others, which she could perform if unmarried, she can fulfil only with her husband's consent.

As concerns the children, the law leaves those born outside wedlock entirely without rights, except for an insufficient contribution to their bringing-up, if the father does not free himself from this by oath. The law provides very imperfectly for the welfare of the new generation by limiting the right of marriage to certain degrees of affinity, refusing it in the case of certain diseases, and fixing the age for lawful marriage at fifteen to seventeen for the woman and twenty-one years for the man.[1]

Finally, marriage binds the wife to the husband and him to her, by the fact that neither can obtain a divorce without the other's consent unless certain acts of ill-treatment or misconduct can be proved. Even when married people agree to a divorce, it entails a painful procedure for both of them and poor guarantees for the children's welfare. If the man refuses a divorce, the woman—owing to the above-mentioned obligation of proof, frequently impossible—is forced to remain with a man she despises, since only thus can she keep her children and receive support. If the husband is no longer capable of providing this; if, perhaps, he has squandered means belonging to her which would have provided it; nay, if the

[1] These details refer, of course, to the Swedish law.—TRANS-LATOR.

wife, by her own work, is keeping him, herself, and the children, he still retains the same authority over her and them.

The unmarried woman, on the other hand, who has given her love "freely"—that is, without legal compensation in the form of a right of maintenance—retains full authority over her children, as well as personal liberty, responsibility, and civil rights. In other words, she retains all that gives her a dignified position as a human being in society—but loses the respect of society and economic security. The married woman, on the other hand, loses all that is important to a member of society of full age, but retains the respect of society, her right of inheritance, and her support.

Truly, society has not made it easy for woman to fulfil her "natural mission"! That she nevertheless—under one or other of these two alternatives—still gladly performs it, is strong evidence that it must be the most powerful demand of her nature. If other needs become stronger—as is already the case with some women—then the conditions of either alternative will be unacceptable. And as the new women are still less likely to content themselves with the two other extremes— lifelong asceticism or prostitution—a new marriage has become for them a condition of life.

．　　．　　．　　．　　．　　．　　．

The marriage law now in force is a geological formation, with stratifications belonging to various phases of culture now concluded. Our own phase alone has left few and unimportant traces in it.

It has been perceived in our time that love ought to be the moral ground of marriage. And love rests upon equality. But the law of marriage dates from a time when the importance of love was not yet recognised. It, therefore, rests upon the inequality between a lord and his dependent.

Our time has given to the unmarried woman the opportunity of making her own living, a legal status, and civil rights. But the marriage law dates from a time when women had none of these things. The married woman, thus, under this law, now occupies a position in sharp contrast to the independence of the unmarried, which has been acquired since that time.

Our time has displaced the ancient division of labour, by which the wife cared for the children and the husband provided maintenance. But the law of marriage dates from a time when this division held full sway and when it was, therefore, almost impossible for a woman to receive protection for herself and her child otherwise than in matrimony. Now society has begun to provide such protection for unmarried mothers, and the renunciation of liberty by which the wife purchases the protection of marriage is seen to be not only more and more unworthy, but also unnecessary.

Our time has recognised more and more the

importance of every child as a new member of society and the right of every child to be born under healthy conditions. But the law of marriage was framed at a time when this aspect had not presented itself to the consciousness of mankind; when the illegitimate child was regarded as worthless, however superior in itself, and the legitimate child as valuable, whatever might be its hereditary defects.

Our time has recognised the value to morality of personal choice. It admits as really ethical only such acts as result from personal examination and take place with the approval of the individual conscience.

The marriage system came into being when this sovereignty of the individual was scarcely suspected, much less recognised; when souls were bound by the power of society, and when compulsion was society's only means of attaining its ends. Marriage was the halter with which the racial instinct was tamed, or, in other words, the instinct of nature was ennobled by being brought into unity with social purpose.

Now love has been developed, the human personality has been developed, and woman's powers have been liberated.

On account of woman's present independent activity and self-determination outside marriage, the law must provide that the married woman shall retain her freedom of action by giving her full authority over her person and property.

On account of the individual's dislike of being forced into religious forms that have no meaning for him, the legal form of marriage must be a civil one.

On account of the individual's desire of personal choice in actions that are personally important, the continuance of marriage—as well as its inception—must depend upon either of the parties and divorce be thus free; and this all the more, since the new idea of purity implies that compulsion in this direction is a humiliation.

These are the claims the people of the present day make upon the form of marriage, if it is to express their personal will and further the growth of their personality. The actual institution of marriage, on the other hand, involves forms that have become meaningless and therefore repulsive, and places the parties under the law in a position with regard to one another which, looked at ideally, is as far beneath the merits and dignity of the modern man as it actually is beneath those of the modern woman.

While thus the development of the ideas of personality and of love have resulted in these demands of increased liberty for the individual within marriage, the idea of solidarity and evolutionism, on the other hand, demand great limitations of individual freedom. The knowledge that every new being has a right to claim that its life shall be a real value—as well as knowledge of the right of society that the new life shall be a valuable one—has involved the demand of prohibiting marriages which would be dangerous to the children, and of better protecting the children where there is no marriage or where a marriage has been dissolved.

.   .   .   .

The economic factor has in modern society an importance for marriage which is felt to be more and more degrading as marriage becomes established on the basis of love.

Marriages inwardly dissolved are now often held together because both the parties would be in a worse financial position after divorce. The husband can not or will not make his wife a sufficient allowance; he is, perhaps, unable to realise her fortune, which he has invested in his business, or perhaps he has spent it; the wife at marriage has abandoned an occupation which she cannot now take up again in order to support herself—and so on to infinity.

But even happy marriages suffer through the wife's subordinate position, economically as well as judicially.

It is, therefore, of great importance both in happy and unhappy marriages that the wife should retain control over her property and her earnings; that she should be self-supporting in so far as she can combine this with her duties as a mother, and that she should be maintained by the community during the first year of each child's life. Similar proposals have been made from the socialist side, but also in other quarters.

A woman ought to be able to claim this subsidy if she can prove:

That she is of full legal age;

That she has performed her equivalent of military service by undergoing a one year's training in the care of children and in hygiene, and—if possible—in nursing the sick;

That she will, herself, care for the children or provide other efficient care;

That she is without sufficient personal means or earnings to provide for her own and half of the children's support, or that she has given up work for the sake of looking after the children.

Those who are unwilling to conform to the above conditions will not apply for the subsidy, which naturally cannot be greater than what is strictly necessary, and which will only in exceptional cases be distributed for longer than a child's *three* first and most important years.

Those who renounced the subsidy would thus be as a rule the well-to-do, or those who wished to devote themselves to self-support and thus gave up, either altogether or after the first year, this help from the community. The arrangement would fulfil its purpose in those classes of society where at present the mother's outdoor work, both in country and town, involves equally great dangers to herself and the children. The charges for this most important of defensive taxes ought, like other similar ones, to be graduated and thus to fall most heavily upon the rich, but upon the unmarried in the same degree as the married.

Inspection should be carried out by commissioners to be appointed in every commune, varying in number according to the size of the commune, but always composed of two-thirds women and one-third men. These would distribute the subsidy and supervise the care not only of young children but also of older ones. The mother who neglected her child would, after three cautions, be deprived of the subsidy and the child would be taken from her. The same would also apply to other parents who subjected their children to bodily or mental ill-treatment.

The mother's maintenance would always amount to the same sum per annum, but for every child she would receive in addition the half of its maintenance, until the number of children was reached that the community might consider desirable from its point of view. Any children born beyond that number would be the affair of the parents. Every father would have to contribute a corresponding half of the child's maintenance from its birth up to the age of eighteen. At present the community affords a man help as breadwinner for a family in the form of higher wages calculated to that end and a rising scale according to age, which, however, he receives whether he is married or single, childless or the father of a family. But by paying the subsidy to

24

the mother, all need of unequal wages for the two sexes would cease, and the subsidy would really further the purpose that is of importance to the community: the rearing of the children.

The present system, on the other hand, maintains that most crude injustice, the difference between legitimate and illegitimate children; it frees unmarried fathers from their natural responsibility; it drives unmarried mothers to infanticide, to suicide, to prostitution.

All these conditions would be altered by a law which prescribed that every mother has a right, under certain conditions, to the support of the community during the years in which she is bearing the burden most important to the community; and that every child has a right to maintenance by both its parents, to the name of both and—so far as there may be property—to the inheritance of both.

Since the mother must now, with increasing frequency, be a breadwinner as well as the husband, it is just, even from this point of view, that she should share with him authority over the children. But since, furthermore, she has suffered more for them, thus loves them more and understands them better—and thus, as a rule, not only does more for them but also means more to them—it is likewise just that, whereas the mother now has to be satisfied with what power the father allows her, the conditions should be reversed, so that the mother should receive the greatest legal authority.

When the husband is not alone in bearing the burden of breadwinner, there will be a possibility of his duty as educator being realised. He will then have time to develop his qualities in this direction and the growing value of his fatherly care and fatherly love will lighten for the mother the task of education which at present often overwhelms her, since with a growing consciousness of its responsibility this task is becoming more and more difficult to perform with her increasing need of personal freedom of movement.

The mother and child would, therefore, not have to look exclusively to the father for the necessaries of life, and they could not become entirely destitute through his incapacity or downfall. But he would, nevertheless, continue to bear his half of the responsibility and the family would still be dependent on the father and his voluntary contributions for a great part of the pleasures of life, while he would, moreover, be freed from the often unbearable burdens under which his spiritual worth as a father and his family joys now suffer to so great a degree. Far from its being the case—as one has heard certain women declare—that the majority of men are nothing but egoists, countless numbers of them have borne and still bear burdens of slavery, not only for wife and children but also for the support of other female relations. On the other hand, the prevailing system of society has prompted fathers still more to enslave themselves in order to create an advantageous position for

their children.   The existing rights and duties of a
father stand in immediate connection with the
right of inheritance, one of the greatest dangers
of our system of society.   For inheritance often
keeps inefficiency in a leading position, but
efficiency in a dependent one; it favours the possibility of the degenerate propagating the race,
above all if the parents have died early, although
—as it has been asserted—it is precisely such
children that are the least apt to have offspring.
It is unfavourable to the chances of the efficient in
this as in every other direction, where birth in
poor circumstances involves hindrances to education and the use of personal powers which wealth
permits.   On the other hand, poverty favours
natural talent, in so far as it braces the capa-
bilities, while it is often one of the misfortunes of
heirs not to experience this inciting and pleasure-
able tension.   It is only the strongest or the finest
natures that become stronger and finer through
the advantages and the sense of responsibility
that inherited wealth brings with it.   In the
main, the productive sources of society would be
multiplied upwards as well as downwards, if
wealth became personal in the fullest sense of the
word, depending on each person's contribution
of efficient force, but the goad of acquisitiveness
would be broken, through the limited possibility
of increasing one's wealth and the needlessness of
thereby securing the existence of one's children.
A new system would do away with the necessity

of applying to the state for increase of salary for the education of children as befits their class.   For if all children were placed in an equal position by the community providing everything—from school materials to travelling scholarships—for the complete education of the bodily and mental powers of individuals, an education in which a true circulation of the classes would take place by consideration being given only to ability; if each thus had the same position when all entered upon their different careers; if each had the same chances of there attaining to the right use of his special powers, since he had had every means of training them; if society gave—as a right, not as a charity—to every worker full care during sickness and full support in old age, then the desire to favour one's own children at the cost of the rest would disappear.   The father whose activity had procured him a position of power, which during his lifetime made his children's circumstances more favourable than those of a number of others, would certainly thus be able—and to the advantage of the whole community—to allow his children to enjoy that differentiation and refinement which, for instance, the richer culture of their home might give.   But when the right of inheritance disappeared—or at least was greatly limited and heavily taxed—he could not exempt them from permanently securing by the exercise of their own powers the advantages of a higher or lower kind that they had learned to value at home.

When the difference between legitimate and
illegitimate children is abolished in every respect,
the paternal home, as in classical and Scandinavian antiquity, may include more often than at
present the children of more than one living
mother; sometimes even a mother's home may
include children of more than one living father.
In either case this would be a recognition of the
children's rights which would leave present day
customs with respect to children born out of
wedlock a long way behind.

.   .   .   .

No relation shows better than marriage how
morals and emotions may be centuries in advance
of the laws within whose limits they have been
developed.

Many men now show their wives a delicacy of
feeling and allow them a freedom of action which
render these fortunate wives unconscious of the
fact that—in the eyes of the law—they possess
these only by the grace of their husbands. It is
not until relations become unhappy that the wife
discovers that all the legal power is placed in the
hands of one, who thus has judicial support if he
wishes to use his power alone, to the exclusion of
his wife, or if he wishes to misuse it, to the detriment of her and the children.

That, in spite of these circumstances, married
men so often voluntarily place themselves in a
position of equality with their wives in regard to

authority in the home and with the children is the best proof of the power of the feelings to protect essential values. And that men, in spite of these marriage laws, have become more and more considerate, redounds as much to their credit as their success in becoming human beings—in spite of all hindrances—redounds to that of royal personages. Just as the latter have more excuse than others when they abuse their position, so the same is true of the husband, who must be a very fair-minded person if an *I will* is not to be the conclusion of a difference of opinion between himself and his wife; for not even the tenderest love will hinder the sense of mastery from flaring up in the face of her obstinate resistance in one direction or another.

To the majority of men, however—and this is the more the case the lower they are in other respects —the present marriage law still forms the great hindrance in the way of their development to a higher humanity. To have wife and child in his power makes of the wicked man a torturer, of the low-minded a wretch. There is no exaggeration in Stuart Mill's words, that so long as the family is based upon laws which are at variance with the first principles of social life in other things, the law will be favouring what education and civilisation are counteracting in other spheres, namely, the right of force instead of that of personality. Everywhere—in morals as in politics—it is now held that not what a man becomes through being born in a certain sex or class, but what he is personally worth determines the respect he should enjoy; that only his conduct and merits can be the source of his power and authority. But marriage reverses the whole of this principle of modern constitutional law and, therefore, the social application of the principle of personality has not yet gone beyond the surface.

That the law continues to sanction what reality has begun to transform is, as we have said, of comparatively little weight, since the law is—in the better sense of the words—a dead letter. But the immediate danger to the individual and the indirect danger to society become greater in proportion as the possessor of uncontrolled power is worse, or the life less ideal in which this authority is decisive. And even when circumstances are favourable, the authority of the husband is the more painful to the modern woman in proportion as she is more conscious of being able to attain only through perfect equality a satisfactory co-operation with her husband in every direction. It is this profound vexation of the modern woman with her dependence which, amongst other things, makes many women, even when they do not need it, wish to remain at least self-supporting after marriage.

The labour market has hitherto favoured this desire of theirs. It can, however, only be a question of time when the unmarried women will begin to thrust out the married ones—owing to the conditions of competition being more favourable to the former—when legislation has begun to deal with the present disproportionate state of things, where the wives lower the wages of the husbands, the children those of the parents, and the result is the neglect of the homes and the physical and moral degeneration of the children.

But when married women's labour has been limited by legal "protection for mothers"—especially if this takes the form proposed above—and when, further, the married and the unmarried are protected by the fixing of a minimum wage, an eight hours' day, and prohibition of working at night and in certain industries dangerous to health, then the mothers will still be able—when their children have passed the age of infancy—to take part in several occupations. This will be still more the case if a collective system of dwellings sets them free from the work of the kitchen and renders possible a good collective superintendence of the children while their mothers are absent.

But the best thing for the children—especially if by the prohibition of home work they were rescued from earning a livelihood to the advantage of their school and home life—would be the liberation of married women from outside labour through the higher wages of their husbands, while in return *their home work would acquire the character of spiritual care.* This would be brought about in the fullest sense by the mothers being allowed the above-mentioned *subsidy from the community* for bringing up the children. In such an arrangement, approved by the community, the majority might find that agreement between their occupation and their powers which constitutes the true joy of work. For it can scarcely be doubted that even now the wife, as a rule, finds more employment in her home work, however heavy, for her special talents, and thus finds a greater satisfaction than the husband, who often slaves, not at the work he has chosen, but at that he has been able to obtain.

But what, in spite of this, now makes women more and more unwilling to undertake the duties of the home and to prefer outside work, is that they carry out their domestic work under conditions derogatory to themselves.

First and foremost, women are determined to enjoy the facilities in their domestic work which here and there are already beginning to be provided. These, however, will probably not become general until women make more use of their capacity for thinking out the most convenient and agreeable methods, both for labour-saving co-operation and for the performance of domestic duties, which will in any case always remain; and this again necessitates their educating themselves to a real knowledge of the questions of consumption and other details of modern household management. This will be the more necessary as the servant problem within a short time will have reached that point at which women of all classes will have to choose between doing the work themselves and the complete dissolution of the home. Woman's domestic work and the care of children will be facilitated for all women only in so far as the educated agree in making new and higher demands in the matter of domestic arrangements as well as in practical and ornamental appliances. They would thus not only further their own work, but also evoke a higher culture as regards beauty and appropriateness, both in architecture and industry.

But this is not enough to enable domestic work to regain its dignity.

This will not take place until society shows such appreciation of woman's domestic work as shall remove her present sense of being kept by her husband to perform a subordinate work, a work which does not receive the appreciation which at the present time has become the absolute standard of the economical value of labour, that of a money wage.

The existing institution of marriage came into being when woman had no real field of employment outside the home, since its income was for the most part received in kind, and the wife was thus indispensable for turning it to account. Her domestic activity was of great value from the point of view of national economy, and under these circumstances the joint estate was natural. Furthermore, the mistress of the house possessed at this time—as manager of the consumption of the commodities she had prepared from raw materials—a freedom of action and an authority which she now quite naturally lacks in her own eyes and those of her husband. It is of no avail that she has a legal right to be supported by her husband according to his position and circumstances; for if her task frequently consists simply in asking her husband for money and keeping an account of its expenditure through the cook and the needlewoman, she has reason to feel herself kept in a humiliating way. Neither indirectly nor directly is it through her work that the food comes to the table or the clothes are fitted to the body, since the husband alone earns the means wherewith she—efficiently or otherwise—keeps house.

For this reason wives are becoming increasingly desirous of personally earning a livelihood. They see how their husbands are developed through devotion to a profession, through the patience, the accumulation, and tension of forces which this demands. And only professional training, in the opinion of modern woman, can give her the same energy, only a direct income can give her the same certainty of her fitness for work.

But there is another expedient which would afford these advantages without, however, driving women away from home, namely, that their special training for, and their work in, the field of housekeeping and the care of children should be as serious as in any other occupation. Not until she

has a sense of the new value of her domestic
work will the wife be able to demand that it shall
be economically estimated like any other efficient
work.

When wives speak of the humiliation of being
kept by their husbands—since they have more
and more frequently been self-supporting before
marriage—their husbands always become profoundly idealistic. They use fine words about
the wife's important mission, the adapting power
of love, until one asks some particular man:
whether any love could make it pleasant *for him*,
instead of drawing his own income, to be obliged
to ask his wife for what she considered necessary
for their joint expenditure or for his own. In
spite of the consciousness of having herself brought
wealth, or in spite of the knowledge of constantly
making important contributions of work in the
home, the necessity of asking for money is the
wife's unbearable torment. For the husband in
his heart has often the same feeling as she; that
work nowadays means earning money outside,
since the management of an income—in spite of its
immense importance to the strength, health, and
comfort of the workers and thus indirectly to the
whole national economy—is more and more overlooked. In part this idea of the husband is due
to the very fact that women have not acquired
the new kind of domesticity which is necessary
for the efficient conduct of expenditure, and that
the husband is, therefore, often right in thinking

that his wife neither works nor saves, but only wastes.

However touchingly idealistic a girl may be in this question before marriage; however confidingly she allows her husband to handle her fortune, after a few years of married life experience will turn her into a complete realist. However happy she has otherwise been, she will, nevertheless, remember more than one occasion when she has bitterly regretted the absence of the freedom of action a separate income gives; when, for instance, her husband has refused to allow her to use—for some ideal purpose or other—the means which in many cases she herself brought him, and how perhaps this for the first time really made a division between them.

The dependence of woman can only be abolished through the *economic appreciation of her domestic work*. This appreciation is an easy matter when she has left a salaried employment for her domestic duties, for the performance of the latter must be regarded as worth at least as much as her occupation formerly brought her. Where there is no such measure of value, she ought to receive the same amount as a stranger in corresponding circumstances would receive in salary and cost of keep.

The wife would thus be able to meet her personal expenditure, her share in the joint housekeeping and in the maintenance of the children, when the subsidy for this purpose came to an end

but the couple were agreed that the wife's work
at home was of such value that she ought rather
to continue it than to try to earn money outside.

The carrying out of this arrangement need not
cause any dislocation of existing conditions. The
wife would continue to manage the domestic funds
to which each would contribute according to
agreement, but she would probably be better able
to solve the problem of making them suffice for
their joint expenses. She would be perfectly
free to forego her allowance, as her husband would
be to increase it according to need and ability.
The direct economical appreciation of her domestic work would transform her own and her husband's respect for it and thus give wives, on the
one hand, a sense of independence which even the
conscientious are now without, on the other, a
sense of duty which in the case of the less conscientious is doubtless in need of strengthening;
for the existing arrangement favours not only
domestic tyranny on the part of the husbands,
but also inefficiency on the part of certain wives.
But the fact that a small number of women of the
upper class now do no work at all in the home,
or that a number of others do it badly, must not
obscure the truth that innumerable women are
constantly expending in their homes great sums
of working power, without being able legally to
claim any corresponding income of their own.
This applies not only to the wives but also to the
daughters of the house, who often work from

morning till night, but are nevertheless obliged to accept as gifts from their parents all that they personally need, and thus also have to do without anything that their parents consider unnecessary. The same is true of the wife in relation to her husband. When unmarried—whether she was in private or public service, a factory hand or a clerk—she had the chance of in some measure providing for her own interests. When married, every present she gives, every contribution she makes for a public purpose, every book she buys, every amusement she allows herself, has to be taken from her husband's money. The wife who, in a farmer's home perhaps, saves thousands— both by economy and by the direct contribution of her labour—frequently has not a silver piece at her disposal.

This dependence, as we have said, now drives wives and daughters from their homes to earn a livelihood, which often does not by any means compensate economically for the loss of their work at home. But they simply cannot endure to be without the personal income, which to them has become a more and more important value, according as their general freedom of movement and their needs in other directions have increased— above all, through increase of education and social interests.

Woman's present unpaid position in domestic work is an obsolete survival from earlier conditions of housekeeping and production, as from the ecclesiastical doctrine that woman was created to be man's helpmate and he to be her head. Women have thus often received worse heads than nature gave them—and thereby man has had less valuable help than life intended for him.

Not until an incorruptible realism establishes the principle within the family as elsewhere, that each retains his own head and that every labourer is worthy of his hire, will idealism find there a full field for unforced generosity in the free will of mutual help.

While what is said above applies to all women who wish to work at home, it need not apply to those who are able through the fortune they brought with them to meet their household expenses and those of the children and who wish in return to be free from the trouble of domestic work.

Every attempt at mediation in the question of married women's property—such as an obligatory marriage settlement and similar proposals—only introduces endless complications. It will be simple and clear only when—as in Russia even from the time of Catherine II—the woman simply retains her fortune. The law ought to express the great principle, that either party owns what is his or hers, while those, on the other hand, who desire to introduce another arrangement, must decide by contract how much of the property is to be held jointly.

Only a separation of property carried out as a

25

principle will be able to form the new and clear
ideas of justice that the present time demands.
A separate estate places two individuals side by
side, co-operating with the freedom that is enjoyed
by a brother and sister or two friends. Both
parties retain full right of decision and full
responsibility. Either leaves transactions to the
other only in that degree that the other's qualities
have won his confidence. Both show each other
mutual consideration in the planning of joint
undertakings and neither can be drawn into such
without a personal examination. The rights of a
third party are, in these circumstances, equally
well protected as when brothers and sisters or
friends work or live together. For the mutual
transactions of married people must to this end
have the same publicity as all other similar transactions between business partners.

.   .   .   .

Not only as regards her property, but also in
her full civil rights and the disposition of her person, the married woman must be placed on an
equal footing with the unmarried. It is true that
the law is not so favourable as many people believe
to "conjugal rights." But this belief has sur-
vived for centuries and in turn influences morals;
moreover, it is not without a certain legal support,
in case such a question is brought into court. As
a rule, of course, this does not happen, but, on
the other hand, the idea of legality—which is

further encouraged by the Bible—influences the husband's sense of right and the wife's sense of duty. So long as the law maintains even a shadow of "rights" in that relation which ought to be the most voluntary of all, it involves a gross violation of love's freedom.

This—like all other obsolete laws—is meaningless to the erotically refined, who live above the law's standpoint. But the lower the level, the more certainly does the husband enforce his "right" under circumstances the most repulsive or most dangerous to the wife, just as—contrary to his present right—he extorts from her the earnings of her labour.

No law will be able to hinder the wife from continuing voluntarily to allow her husband to violate her person, squander her property, or ruin her children; for the law cannot seal up the sources of weakness and conflict which arise from the human being's own nature.

But what we have a right to demand of the marriage law is that it shall cease itself to extend these sources.

The law must be so contrived that it leaves to happiness the greatest possible freedom for its own formative power, while, on the other hand, it limits as far as possible the consequences of unhappiness; and this can be brought about only by each party's complete independence of the other.

It is, therefore, not sufficient that the husband's

guardianship and the wife's legal incapacity should cease. Every provision also which has for its object to bind the wife by her husband's condition and circumstances must be revoked.

The majority of men now cherish the belief that a wife who leaves her husband's house can be brought back with the aid of the law. This is, doubtless, a mistake. But even if the letter of the law in this case also is better than the popular idea of it, the whole spirit of the law, nevertheless, entails the obligation of married people to live together.

The more personality is developed, however, the more uncertain it becomes that every person's erotic needs are answered by this arrangement. There are, on the contrary, such natures as would have loved for life, if they had not, day after day, year after year, been forced to adapt their wills, their habits, and their opinions to one another. Nay, many misfortunes depend upon pure trifles, which two people with courage and foresight might easily have dealt with, if the instinct of happiness had not been silenced by consideration for convention. The more a woman has enjoyed personal liberty before marriage, the less she can endure not to have a moment or a corner in her home which she can call her own. And the more the people of the present day enlarge their individual freedom of movement, their need of solitude in other respects, the more will both man and woman enlarge them in marriage.

But even if those desiring solitude remain in the minority, they must still be granted both by the law and by public opinion full liberty to shape their married life according to their own requirements.

Conventionality and mental inertness pronounce this unheard-of, even immoral. On the other hand, it is regarded as equally natural and moral that the majority of sailors and commercial travellers should live for the greater part of the year apart from their wives; that journeys for scientific or artistic purposes should separate married people for years, or that—in exceptional cases—one of them, for instance, should spend the winters as a gymnast in England while the other is a teacher in Sweden.

All these things, it is thought, are nothing but external necessities. And to these one always submits! Ought we not, nevertheless, to find room for the thought that there may also be necessities of the soul?

Our time, for instance, tends more and more to bring together artists who work at different, or, still more often, at the same art. The nerves of both are worn in the same way; both need the same freedom of movement and the same undisturbed quiet. But in the claims of everyday life for mutual sympathy and mutual consideration, nearly all their spiritual energy is used up. They see that, if they are not to consume one another's mental resources, they must adopt a system of spiritual separation, which is possible only at a certain distance. The holiday happiness of these natures may be rapturous, the sympathetic union of their souls richer than any others. But each feels for the other what is expressed by one of Shakespeare's joyous young women, when she calls a suitor "too costly for every day's wear." Each is tempted at times to exclaim, like another young woman in a modern book: "I want to be able to say, let me now for three weeks be altogether free from loving you"—since each knows that this freedom would only renew the feeling. But now married people are bound by custom to a common life, which often ends in their separating for ever, simply because conventional considerations prevented their living apart.

Natures of other types may also feel the constraint of narrow dependence, enforced association, the daily accommodations and constant considerations. More people ought, therefore, quietly to begin reforming matrimonial customs, so that they may more nearly correspond to the need of renewal just alluded to. Let each, for instance, travel separately, if he or she feels the desire of solitude; let one visit by himself the entertainment the other does not care for, but formerly either forced herself to, or kept the other from visiting. More and more married people have separate bedrooms. And in another generation perhaps separate dwellings will have ceased to attract attention.

Companionship on week-days as on holidays, co-operation in the satisfaction of everyday claims as well as of life's highest purposes, will, nevertheless, continue to be the form of married life chosen by the majority, even when public opinion has left room for other systems of living. But full freedom for the latter will not be won till the law ceases to place any limit to the self-determination of each partner in marriage.

Another matter that ought to be left to personal decision is the degree of publicity that is to be given to a matrimonial union. An otherwise conservative father of a family once put forward the weighty reasons which might be in favour of keeping secret a marriage that was, nevertheless, intended to be fully legal. Amongst the reasons which now frequently cause the postponement of a marriage are, for instance, the necessity of completing studies, or reluctance to hasten, through sorrow, the death of parents or others. The possibility of not having to publish the union in these or similar cases would spare the lovers unnecessary waiting without in any way encroaching on the rights of others.

Further, to personal determination belong not only free divorce but also new forms of divorce. As divorce itself has been treated in the last chapter, we will speak here only of the method of it. The wife's infidelity, as well as the husband's right to refuse divorce, at present frequently affords an opportunity for blackmail on the part of the

husband from his wife, who, in the latter case, has
to buy her freedom, and in both cases often has to
buy permission to keep her children. The husband,
too, may be exposed to blackmailing by a wife
who refuses divorce or who can prove his infidelity
and tries to take from him the children, whom he
knows to be exposed to corruption in her hands.
But, since society and nature favour the man's
infidelity, while both are against that of the
woman, it is in the nature of the case that the wife
often has difficulty in proving the husband's
infidelity, while he can prove hers easily. His
repeated acts of unfaithfulness have, perhaps,
been the cause of her single one. But it is,
nevertheless, he—since there is no valid evidence
against him—who has the children assigned to
him, or, it may be, sells them to his wife.

The same applies to divorce on account of
"hatred and ill-will." Before a court which cannot test the reasons that have most spiritual
weight, but only the evidence that has most to
say, all the details of married life have to be
dragged forth, all its wounds inspected. The
evidence which, as a rule, is decisive is that of
servants! The profoundest spiritual concerns of
educated people are thus made to depend upon
the opinion of uneducated persons on all the complicated circumstances of an unhappy marriage.
And not only this: the result in most cases is
determined by the indelicacy with which the husband and wife have drawn their servants and their

acquaintances into the conflict. If husband or wife has summoned the servants to witness violent behaviour, then that party is in a much better position in an action for divorce than the one who has sought to the utmost to preserve the dignity of their marriage. There are, moreover, some sufferings of which no proof can be produced. Such, for instance, is misuse of "conjugal rights"; another is the power of either party, under forms of outward politeness, to make life entirely worthless to the other; a third, the constant opposition of two conflicting views of life.

It is only in the case of the grossest and most palpable evils that it is now possible to furnish the necessary evidence without such difficulties as—both in the granting of divorce and in the disposal of the children—may give rise to the grossest injustice. And all this is only a part of the humiliations and sufferings which now—especially for the wife—attend a divorce. Finally, an action for divorce is sufficiently expensive to render it on this account alone a matter of great difficulty for many people in poor circumstances to obtain justice.

Such a system of divorce—which makes either partner dependent on the worst qualities of the other; which calls forth all that is indelicate in the nature of both; which drags their weaknesses and sufferings before the eyes of strangers, and which, nevertheless, provides no real protection for the children—such a system ought to give no thoughtful person peace until its degrading and deteriorating influence is abolished and a new system, which shall protect both personal dignity and the children, introduced.

.   .   .   .

In looking back upon the preceding, it would seem to result clearly that nothing that has been said here contemplates the establishment of a single form—recognised as the only moral one—for sexual life.   But since only the fixity possessed by the law is capable of transforming in a profound and permanent manner the feelings and customs of the majority, there is need, for the present, of a new law to support the growth of the higher feelings which will finally render any marriage law unnecessary.

In connection with the course of development of sexual morality it was pointed out that the ecclesiastical and legal establishment of the ideal of monogamy as *the only form of sexual morality* has had for its result the unconditional acquiescence in the idea that the claims of evolution are in complete agreement with existing laws and customs; with the further result that we are now —through the want of a recognised right to manifold experience—almost in the same position of ignorance as to the form of sexual morality most favourable to the development of the race, as we were a thousand years ago, and that, therefore, the vital needs of the race as well as the individual's demands of happiness speak for a more extended right to such experiences.

No one knows whether, at the end of the new paths, we shall not again be confronted by the riddle of the sphinx: how the parents are to avoid being sacrificed for the children or the children for the parents. The one thing certain is that on the path we have hitherto followed we have arrived at the sphinx. And all those who have been torn to pieces at its feet are witnesses that on this path mankind did not arrive at the solution of the riddle.

The point of view which has here, throughout, been the leading one is, that in the same degree as life itself becomes the meaning of life human beings will also in all their sensations and all their undertakings become more and more conscious of regard for the race. It is thus only a question of time when the respect of society for a sexual union shall not depend upon the form of cohabitation that makes a couple of human beings become parents, but only upon the value of the children they thus create as new links in the chain of generations. Men and women will then dedicate to their mental and bodily fitness for the mission of the race the same religious earnestness that Christians devote to the salvation of their souls. Instead of divine codes of the morality of sexual relations, the desire of, and responsibility for, the enhancement of the race will be the support of morals. But the knowledge of the parents that the meaning of life is also in their own lives, that they thus do not exist solely for the sake of their children, may liberate them from other duties of conscience which at present bind them in respect of the children, above all that of keeping up a union in which they themselves perish. The home may then more than at present be synonymous with the mother, which—far from excluding the father—contains the germ of a new and higher "right of the family."

When every life is regarded as an end in itself from the point of view that it can never be lived again; that it must, therefore, be lived as completely and greatly as possible; when every personality is valued as an asset in life that has never existed before and will never occur again, then also the erotic happiness or unhappiness of a human being will be treated as of greater importance, and not to himself alone. No, it will be so also to the whole community—through the life and the work his happiness may give the race or his unhappiness deprive it of.

For himself, as well as for others, the individual will then examine the right of renouncing happiness as conscientiously as he now submits to the duty of bearing unhappiness. The importance to children of their parents' life together will depend upon the kind of life it is, when it has been seen that when all is said the new generation has most to gain by love being always and everywhere set up as the condition of the highest worth of cohabitation.

This is the rich promise that the new path offers; but the majority cannot see the promise on account of the possible new dangers. It is this dread that still paralyses the courage to dare the untried, in order to win the valuable.

It is astonishing that those who tremble for the future never seek consolation in the past. They would there find, for example, that when the family ceased to be the match-maker, when the guardian could no longer keep a woman in a position of legal incapacity and prevent her marrying—then there were prophecies of exactly the same "dissolution of society and of the family" as are now dreaded in freer forms of matrimony. But the same people who now laugh at the former forebodings are convinced that the latter will be realised; for man believes in nothing so reluctantly as in his own nature's power of replacing outward bonds with inner ones. And yet, long before the new forms are ready, there is an abundance of the new feelings which are to fill them. Nothing is more certain than that, if feelings were no better than laws, we should never have new laws (Mill). But human beings will never believe in the possibilities of development of their own feelings until they leave off seeking their strength from above. They will never have faith in themselves as pathfinders until they no longer believe themselves "guided." As soon as a change has taken place, it is regarded "historically," as a given consequence of "rational" causes and "divine" guidance. But to look historically at the future; to trust in regard to what has not yet happened to the given consequences—for good and evil—of the same constantly operating causes, this does not occur to the guardians of society. Their belief in God's guidance is always—retrospective.

The believers in Life, on the other hand, know that vital needs were the productive soil of the feelings that gave the pith to those laws, whereof now only the straw remains. But the earth has not exhausted its powers of fertility, any more than the feelings have lost their creative force. The believers in Life, therefore, attach small importance to the old straw, but consider the increasing of the earth's productiveness of supreme significance.

A great and healthy will to live is what our time needs in the matter of the erotic emotions and claims. It is here that there is a menace of real dangers from the woman's side; and it is, amongst other things, to avert these dangers that new forms of marriage must be created.

A human material increasing in value and in capacity for development—this is what the earth will produce. The chances of obtaining this may be decreased under fixed, but favoured under freer, forms of sexual life. It is not only because the present day demands more freedom that these claims are full of promise. They are so because the claims are coming nearer and nearer to the kernel of the question—the certainty that love is the most perfect condition for the life-enhancement of the race and of the individual—and because the present time acknowledges the necessity of temporarily limiting freedom, though only by means of laws which will form an education in love.

Such a law must, for the sake of woman's liberty, deprive man of certain of his present rights; for the sake of the children, limit the present liberty both of man and woman. But these limitations will all be to the final profit of love.

.   .   .   .

Those who believe in the perfectibility of mankind for and through love must, however, learn to reckon not in hundreds of years, and still less in tens, but in thousands.

THE END